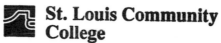

THE CHARNEY REPORT

THE *CHARNEY* **REPORT**

CONFRONTING THE ISRAELI-ARAB CONFLICT

Leon H. Charney

Barricade Books
Fort Lee, New Jersey

Published by Barricade Books Inc.
185 Bridge Plaza North
Suite 308-A
Fort Lee, NJ 07024

Design and typesetting by Sam Sheng, CompuDesign

Library of Congress Cataloging-in-Publication Data

First Printing

Manufactured in the United States of America

To Mickey and Nati

My Twins

May they see a peaceful resolution to the conflict.

TABLE OF CONTENTS

Acknowledgments

• x •

Publisher's Foreword

• xi •

Author's Note

• xii •

A Brief Chronology of Middle East History

• xiii •

The Background

• 1 •

The Political Scene

• 19 •

January, 1989
Yitzhak Rabin
• 23 •

November, 1990
Ephraim Katzir
• 37 •

March, 1991
Mordechai Gur
• 51 •

September, 1991
Yael Dayan
• 65 •

April, 1992
Ezer Weizman
• 77 •

June, 1992
Teddy Kollek
• 91 •

December, 1993
Gad Yacobi
• *101* •

June, 1994
Ori Orr
• *111* •

September, 1994
Benny Begin
• *123* •

September, 1994
Professor Dov Schifrin
• *129* •

October, 1995
Avigdor Kahalani
• *137* •

October, 1995
Yitzhak Shamir
• *147* •

October, 1996
Shimon Peres
• *155* •

November, 1997
Dr. Joseph Burg
• *169* •

November, 1997
Ruby Rivlin
• *176* •

January, 1998
Rabbi Avraham Ravitz
• *185* •

January, 1998
Ehud Barak
• *195* •

March, 1999
Dore Gold
• *205* •

May, 1999
Lally Weymouth
• *219* •

May, 1999
Tommy Lapid
• *229* •

August, 1999
Naomi Blumenthal
• *235* •

June, 2000
Yehuda Lancry
• *243* •

June, 2000
Raghida Dergham
• *251* •

July, 2000
Nasser Al Kidwa
• *261* •

July, 2000
Colette Avital
• *273* •

July, 2000
Eric Fettman
• *285* •

Afterword
• *293* •

Index
• *297* •

ACKNOWLEDGMENTS

Writing about Arab and Jewish relationships is a contentious venture. During the past eleven years I have moderated a weekly current affairs television program. It covers facets ranging from finance, politics and health to art and the entertainment world.

I have long been involved in the Middle East, both as diplomat and lawyer and the program has been watched for its expertise and insights on the area. From the inception I have conducted more than 600 interviews with individuals ranging from heads of state to entertainers, from journalists to philosophers to authors.

My publisher, Lyle Stuart of Barricade Books, conceived the idea of focusing this book on Middle East personalities, both Arabs and Jews. The interviews, edited for readability but not for content, were solely selected by the editorial staff. I made no recommendation as to which interviews should be included.

I wish to thank publisher Lyle Stuart for his vision in narrowing the topics to Israeli-Arab conflict. I am also grateful to the following: Bob Berkel, who contributed his knowledge of the Israeli situation, to my peripatetic and energetic editor Allan J. Wilson, and to Jeff Nordstedt (of Barricade Books) who worked diligently to make these pages as readable as possible.

I also offer thanks to Regina Runes Najar who made the marriage between the publisher and myself, to Bob Weil, who was my first friend in publishing, and to Nati Laor, who inspired publication. And, lastly but not least, I thank my office staff, headed by Sharon Hart-Wagner, which spent many days and nights in researching and digging for material.

I bear sole responsibility for my personal reflections and apologize aforehand in the event I have made errors in judgement or analysis. I hope this book will enhance the knowledge of every reader and that the conflicts discussed will not be eternal.

PUBLISHER'S FOREWORD

This book represents an edited version of a series of television interviews with the Middle East's premier political figures and journalists from 1989 through 2000.

Leon H. Charney figured prominently when President Jimmy Carter hosted the Camp David meeting between Egyptian leader Anwar Sadat and Israeli Prime Minister Menachem Begin, which resulted in the first recognition and peace treaty between an Arab nation and Israel.

To quote former President Carter: "Leon Charney is one of the unsung heroes of the peace process. Very few people played as significant a role."

The weekly interviews continue. But, as we go to press with this book, the Israeli–Arab situation remains in flux.

AUTHOR'S NOTE

It is virtually impossible to give a background history of the Middle East without error in interpretation.

The region has so many historical facts that are constantly challenged by historians of every faith. The Middle East is a cradle of religion and civilization. Far be it for me to have the hubris to say that my interpretations of which or what events are of major historical importance.

I therefore ask the reader to understand that what I have compiled is a subjective brief summary of Middle East events so as to introduce the reader to the historical complexity of the region.

In no way is this to be taken as the only thorough historical account of that region. I ask that my words be read with the above caveat.

A Brief Chronology of Middle East History

1882   • Persecution of East European Jews leads to mass immigration to Palestine

1891   • Arabs petition the Ottoman Empire to prohibit Jewish immigration and Jewish ourchase of land

1892-97 • Theodore Herzl publishes the "Jewish State". Zionist organization is founded in Basle, Switzerland

1916   • The Sykes-Picot Agreement awards Britain control of Palestine, ending Ottoman rule

1917   • Balfour Declaration is issued by Britain favoring establishment of a Jewish homeland

1922   • The League of Nations establishes a British mandate for Palestine

1936-39 • Arabs attack Jewish settlements and the British army in an effort to stop creation of a Jewish homeland

1939-45 • World War 11: 6 million Jews are murdered by Nazi Germany

1947   • The United Nations Resolution 181 calls for partition of Palestine into two states, Jewish and Arab

1948   • David Ben-Gurion declares the State of Israel

1948-49 • The Israel War of Independence. Outnumbered by nearly 40-1, Israel achieves victory over 5 Arab states

1949   • Jerusalem is declared capital of Israel. Syria, Egypt, Jordan and Lebanon are forced to sign an armistice agreement with Israel

1951   • King Abdullah of Jordan is assasinated at the Aqsa mosque in Jerusalem

1953   • Gam Al-Nasser becomes leader of Egyptian Republic

1956   • Israel, Britain and France take control of Sinai Peninsula from Egypt

1957   • The United States and the Soviet Union pressure Israel to withdraw from Sinai

1958   • The United Arab Republic (a union of Egypt and Syria) is formed

1964   • Backed by Arab heads of state the Palestinian Liberation Organization is created

1967   • Israel defeats Egypt, Syria and Jordan in six days. Jerusalem is reunited under Israeli control. The U.N. passes Resolution 242

1968-70 • Egypt continues to attack Israel in a the War of Attrition

1968   • The Palestinian National Council passes a resulution calling for the destruction of Israel

1969   • Yasser Arafat is elected chairman of the PLO Executive Council

1970   • King Hussein's military puts down Arafat's guerrillas when they try to take control of Jordan. This revolt is called Black September

1972   • Arab terrorists murder Israeli athletes at the Munich Olympics

1973   • Egypt and Syria launch attacks on Israel (the Yom Kippur War)

1974   • Arab Summit conference declares the PLO the sole legitimate representative of the Palestinian people

1977   • Egyptian president Anwar Sadat visits Israel, offers peace in exchange for Sinai

1979   • The Camp David Peace Treaty between Israel and Egypt is signed in Washington with President Jimmy Carter

1981 • Egyptian president Anwar Sadt is assasinated. Vice president Hosni Mubarak takes over leadership

1982 • Israel completes withdrawal from Sinai

1982 • Operation Peace for Galilee expels the PLO from Lebanon

1985 • Israel withdraws from most of Lebanon

1987 • Palestinians commence widespread violence against Israel in West bank and Gaza referred to as Intifada

1988 • The U.S. recognizes the PLO after Arafat recognizes Israel's right to exist

1991 • The United States attacks Iraq in a war to liberate Kuwait. The PLO and Jordan side with Iraq
      • The U.S. convenes a Peace Conference in Madrid, bringing most Arab countries for a first time meeting with Israelis

1993 • Israel and the PLO sign a Declaration of Principles on Interim Self-Government. Prime Minister Yitzak Rabin and Yasser Arafat shake hands on the White House lawn

1994 • Palestinians implement self government in Gaza and Jericho
      • Israel and Jordan sign a Peace Treaty in the presence of President Clinton
      • Yitzak Rabin, Shimon Peres and Yasser Arafat receive the Nobel Peace Prize

1995 • Palestinian Self-Government is broadened in West bank and Gaza
      • Prime Minister Yitzak Rabin is assasinated on 4th November by an Jewish fanatic angered by perceived concessions to the PLO

1996 • Israel responds to Hizbollah attacks on northern Israel under Operation Grapes of Wrath
      • Yasser Arafat becomes President of the Palestinian Council at its first election
      • Benjamin Netanyahu becomes Prime Minister of Israel, the first direct election of that office

1999 • Ehud Barak, a protege of Yitzak Rabin, is elected prime minister. He promises to pursue a peace treaty with Syria

2000 • Barak and Syrian Foreign Minister Farouk al-Shara meet in Shepardstown, West Virginia to attempt the negotiation of a peace treaty. They fail. Barak unilaterally withdraws from Lebanon under domestic pressure.
      • Ariel Sharon makes controversial visit to Temple Mount
      • Syrian President Assad dies. Bashar Assad, Western educated doctor, replaces him
      • President Clinton hosts the Camp David Summit #2 for 14 days of meetings with Arafat and Prime Minister Ehud Barak. The talks fail. Barak resigns as Prime Minister

2001 • Ariel Sharon, chairman of the Likud party, is overwhelmingly elected prime minister of Israel. He forms a unity government with Shimon Peres as foreign minister. The law involving direct election of the prime minister is rescinded

THE BACKGROUND

Modern Israel lies on the western tip of the ancient Fertile Crescent. The northern and coastal parts of the country have been from ancient times agriculturally productive areas while the southern part of the country is mostly desert interspersed with pastureland. Archeological evidence for Hebrew occupation of the country is manifold but Biblical tradition places the reign of King David as the establishment of an Israelite state around 1000 BCE. Subsequent conquest and enslavement by the Assyrians, Babylonians, Persians, and Macedonian Greeks had scattered the Hebrew community over large parts of the Middle East. A revolt against the Greek suppression of the Israelite worship of Yahweh resulted in an independent Hebrew kingdom circa 168 BCE. This kingdom was politically weak and allied itself with the rising Roman Empire against the Greeks.

Subsequently, the Romans abolished the independent kingdom and made it part of their empire. The Israelites again rose in revolt, which resulted in the destruction of their Holy Temple and capital, Jerusalem and their permanent banishment from the city. The area had previously been called Judea but Romans renamed the area Palestine, after the Philistines, to signify that the Hebrew Judeans no longer had a claim upon it. Widespread emigration resulted. Hebrew enclaves abroad, already established, enlarged and later spread all around the Mediterranean basin, in addition to those already in the Persian Empire.

This was known as the Diaspora. The Pharisaic interpretation of Hebraic law predominated in Diaspora communities and evolved into rabbinical Judaism.

The rise of Islam saw the Roman Empire lose the province of Palestine to Arab conquerors in 636 CE. The pagan inhabitants converted to Islam, while tiny Jewish and Christian minorities were tolerated but not accepted into mainstream Islamic society. Immediately after gaining control of Jerusalem the Muslims built a mosque on the Temple Mount, Judiaism's holiest place. Upheavals in the Islamic world saw the country fall to a succession of Turkish conquerors the last of whom were the Ottoman Turks. Muslims dominated Palestine for nearly thirteen hundred years until the defeat of Turkey in World War I by British-led forces. In 1920, the League of Nations awarded Great Britain the Palestine Mandate, i.e., Palestine was ruled by Great Britain in trust under the mandate of the League of Nations.

In the late nineteenth century, there arose a movement in Jewish communities known as Zionism[*], which advocated a Jewish state as a home for Diaspora Jews. Very few Jews had remained in Palestine. In 1800 it was estimated that there were still 5,000 Jews out of a population of about 350,000. By 1882 the Jewish population of Palestine had increased to approximately 24,000, many of whom were very religious. Later, the pogroms of Czarist Russia made Eastern European Jews more attentive to Zionism. At first, Arabs ignored Jewish emigration, since Arabs and Jews had lived side by side in the area for over a thousand years. The first anti-Zionist riots by Palestinians occured in 1901. By 1907, Jews responded by organizing paramilitary groups called Hashomer or Guardians. In 1909, a secret military organization and an official Jewish armed guard were formed. These were the forerunners of the Irgun and the Haganah. In 1910, more anti-Zionist riots followed.

By 1914 the community numbered some 85,000 Jews but due to World War I, it had decreased to about 56,000 in 1918. Jews, at that time, owned about 2 percent of the land. During the war, the British had promised the

---

[*] Zionism is both the political and spiritual renewal of the Jewish people in their ancestral homeland.

Arabs independence for their help in fighting the Turks. Simultaneously, the British government issued the Balfour Declaration in 1917 in which it declared that it was in favor of a homeland in Palestine for the Jewish people. This was reiterated in a Mandate of the League of Nations for Palestine in 1920 and called for the establishment of the Jewish Agency, which was to be a liaison between the Jewish community and the British Mandate government. The membership of the Agency was composed of Jewish Community Council members and Zionist Organization members but soon the Zionists dominated the Agency. The Jewish Agency swiftly became a government within a government. British pro-Zionist policy and the continual denial of Arab independence sparked riots in 1920. The British suppressed the riots. A Jewish militia was formed to defend the settlement.

Increasing Jewish immigration to Palestine created friction and resentment from the Arab population which complained about economic losses to Jewish immigrants. However, their complaints were unfounded, since the technology and production brought by new immigrants actually improved the Arab standard of living.

The major focus of Arab hostility was the British Mandate government. They felt that it had refused them their promised independence, it failed to allow them to develop self-governing institutions and it excluded them from higher administration posts. The British sent more troops to Palestine in order to crush the Arab revolt. In 1939 the British trained and equipped the Zionists, who later became the Jewish Brigade of the British Army and fought in World War II against the Nazis. Thereafter these trainees became the foundation of the Israeli Defense Force (IDF) upon the declaration of the State.

With World War II approaching the British could no longer afford to maintain troops in Palestine. To placate the Arabs, a Royal Commission studying the political situation in Palestine issued, in 1939, what became known as the MacDonald White Paper. It stated that an earlier commission's report to partition Palestine into Arab and Jewish states was impractical and that it was not part of British policy that Palestine become a Jewish state. The Jewish Agency angrily responded that it would defend Jewish immigration, the Jewish homeland and Jewish freedom. Shortly afterward a campaign of terror against British and Arab targets began. David Ben-Gurion, Chairman of the Jewish Agency, called these acts, "The beginning of Jewish resistance to the disastrous policy now proposed by His Majesty's Government. The Jews will not be intimidated into surrender even if their blood be shed." On August 25, 1939, Ben Gurion went on to say, "For us the White Paper neither exists nor can exist. We must believe as if we were the State in Palestine until we actually become the State in Palestine."

World War II intervened and most of the Zionists* sided with the Allies. While the Jewish Brigade was fighting with the British, the political and religious leader of the Arabs—Haj Amin Al Husseini—was cooperating with the Nazis. After World War II in late 1945, the Zionists demanded Palestine as a Jewish state but the British were not ready to yield. So the Zionists started a program of terrorism and armed insurrection against the British Mandate.

There were three main Jewish military organizations: the Haganah, the Irgun Zvai Leumi, and the Lehi (the Stern Group). The Haganah were regular British-trained militia, which would later become the Israeli army. The Irgun, numbering about 5,000, were irregulars and Revisionist Zionists who engaged in sabotage and other underground activities. The Lehi were a splinter group of the Irgun, numbering very few, who were more extreme than the Irgun and, in 1944, assassinated Lord Moyne, British High Commissioner to Egypt.

With their empire disintegrating around them, the British could no longer afford to suppress nationalist independence movements and, therefore, asked the United Nations to take responsibility for Palestine. On November 29, 1947, the UN passed Resolution 181, which partitioned the Palestine Mandate into Jewish and Arab states. The Jewish Agency accepted the resolution but the Arabs rejected it. Five Arab countries immediately amassed their armies to attack the proposed new Jewish state.

As British troops vacated areas they created a power vacuum in which Arabs and Zionists fought for control. On the night of April 9, 1948, Irgun and Stern Group members launched an attack on the 400 Arab vil-

---

* The Stern Group, right wing Jewish militants, venting their anger against the British, discussed the possibility of aligning themselves with the Axis. This plan never materialized and is still debated among historians.

lagers of Dier Yassin[*] on the outskirts of Jerusalem. Two hundred and fifty Arabs were killed. The Irgun and Stern Group held a press conference publicizing Deir Yassin as a "victory" and described it as, "the beginning of the conquest of Palestine and Transjordan [i.e., modern Jordan]." The Jewish Agency and the Haganah publicly denounced the incident. It was a central viewpoint of the Jewish Agency that Arab and Jew could live peacefully together. Despite their overtures to the Arabs many fled and became refugees, which has today become one of the central issues of the Oslo Agreement and the Israeli-Arab conflict.

On May 14, 1948, one day prior to the end of the Mandate, the State of Israel was declared. Both the Soviet Union and the United States immediately recogonized the state. (President Harry Truman overruled his State Department and General George Marshall who were fearful of Arab hostility and the availability of oil.) This precipitated a full-scale war in lieu of the sporadic fighting of the previous months, as the troops of Jordan, Egypt, Syria, Lebanon, and Iraq invaded Palestine to establish Arab sovereignty. It was essentially the whole Arab world, 40 million strong, against slightly more than half a million Jews.

The fledgling Israeli army had serious supply problems and looked like it couldn't hold out. On June 11, 1948, the UN negotiated a truce between Israelis and Arabs. Despite UN protestations, both the Arabs and the Israelis used the breathing space to resupply their beleaguered troops and call up reserves. By July 9, 1948, open warfare had resumed. On July 15, 1948, the UN passed a cease-fire resolution that was reluctantly accepted by both sides. This second truce was violated repeatedly by both sides with sporadic attacks. By September 8, the Israelis managed to gain footholds in the Negev Desert.

The UN desperately tried to negotiate a settlement but the Arabs refused to negotiate until the refugee situation was alleviated. The Israelis used this time to prepare for an offensive they launched in the Negev on December 22, 1948. Six days later, the Israelis had pushed into the Sinai and the Egyptians sued for peace. On February 24, 1949, an armistice was signed between Israel and Egypt.

---

* Deir Yaisin was a strategic vantage point on the road to Jerusalem, allowing Arabs to fire on convoys en route to the city which was under seige and starving.

With the withdrawal of Egypt from the fray, the other Arab states also began armistice negotiations. On March 10, 1949, Israeli forces reached the Gulf of Aqaba and occupied a Jordanian police outpost that was later to become the port city of Elat. Only after the capture of this outpost did the Jordanians accept a cease-fire with Israel. On March 23, 1949, the Lebanese signed an armistice with Israel. In the interim, Israel had taken the territory of southeastern Palestine and obtained a Jordanian withdrawal from a strategic strip of land in Central Palestine. Israel signed an armistice with Transjordan on April 3, 1949. In March of 1949, there was a military coup in Syria. Later, in April, a cease-fire was negotiated with Syria and in July an armistice was signed. During this periosd Israelis were precluded from visiting Jewish holy places, including the Temple Mount.

None of the Arab countries signed a peace treaty with Israel and were still technically in a state of war, although the fighting had ended. The Arabs refused to recognize the State of Israel and would only negotiate through the UN as mediator. Refugees created unstable political situations in their host countries, particularly Lebanon and Jordan. The Arab rejection of UN Resolution 181 created an opportunity for Jordan to seize the Westbank of the Jordan River while at the same time Egypt took control of the Gaza Strip.

The political situation in the Middle East remained chaotic as various Arab states vied for supremacy. A pan-Arab movement sprang up but was ultimately defeated by factionalism and nationalist aspirations. Severe acts of terrorism against Israel allowed tensions to remain high in the region. In 1955, Egyptian leader Gam Al-Nasser, under the guise of protecting the Gaza Strip, armed the Palestinians in Gaza to launch guerrilla attacks against Israel. Against this high-tension backdrop, Nasser nationalized the Suez Canal, declaring Egyptian sovereignty over the East-West trade lifeline. Britain and France immediately responded by assembling a huge invasion force in Cyprus. When Nasser moved his troops from his northeastern border, the Israelis invaded on October 29, 1956, and took the entire Sinai Peninsula up to the Suez Canal. The United States was outraged by the tripartite act of aggression and, with UN backing, forced

Britain, France, and Israel to withdraw their forces from Egypt. UN forces then monitored the Egyptian-Israeli border.

In 1967 Syria was preparing to go to war against Israel. Egypt had a mutual assistance pact with Syria. Nasser asked the UN to remove peace-keeping forces from the Sinai so he could move his troops up to the Israeli border in case of attack. Tensions mounted as Anti-Israeli rhetoric became more strident and Nasser blockaded the Gulf of Aqaba, cut off Israel's out-let to the Red Sea, its Asian and African markets and announced to his people that he would destroy the State of Israel.

On June 5, 1967, the Israeli Army launched a fierce multi-pronged pre-emptive attack against Egypt. On June 9, 1967, Israel attacked Syria. Despite warnings from the Israeli high command not to join the war, Jordan ignored the warnings and entered the fray. After six days of fight-ing, the UN negotiated a cease-fire. It was a stunning victory for the Israelis. In less than a week they managed to capture the West Bank and East Jerusalem from Jordan, the Gaza Strip and the Sinai Peninsula up to the Suez Canal from Egypt, and the Golan Heights from Syria. These were all strategic areas for Israel. The West Bank and the Golan Heights gave Israel control of the majority of the water in the region all the way from the Sea of Galilee (Lake Tiberius) along the entire length of the Jordan River to the Dead Sea. The Suez Canal was a defensible barrier in the southwest and the Golan Heights was a bulwark that commanded the entire southern portion of Syria. East Jerusalem contained the most holy shrine of Judaism, the Wailing Wall, and it was now in Israeli hands for the first time in nearly two thousand years.

The UN responded to the Six-Day War and demanded that Israel withdraw from the occupied territories. On November 22, 1967, through its security council, the UN drew up Resolution 242, emphasizing the inadmissibility of acquisition of territory by war and the need to work for a just and lasting peace for every state in the area. They demanded the freedom of navigation in the area, a settlement of the refugee problem, and guarantees for the territorial integrity, sovereignty, and security of all states in the area. This resolution has been the basis of all subsequent peace talks.

The Arabs who fled Israel in 1948 saw their people fragmenting in many Arab countries. The Arabs formed various organizations to fight a fedayeen (guerilla or commando) war against Israel. The best known of these organizations, although by no means the only one of its kind, was the Palestinian Liberation Organization or PLO, founded in 1964. In 1968, Yasser Arafat was established as its leader. This and other radical organizations such as the Popular Front for the Liberation of Palestine (PFLP), resorted to airplane hijackings, terrorist activities, and guerilla warfare against Israeli and Jews worldwide,[*] including brutal actions against civilians to try to receive world recognition. This backfired severely and these organizations were deemed terrorist by most of the world community.

In 1970, growing unrest among Arab refugees in Jordan led to open warfare with the Jordanian army and the expulsion of the PLO from the country. Arafat sought refuge in Lebanon. Recent documentation indicates that Israeli intelligence informed the King of Jordan about the PLO's intention to overthrow him. This is known in middle east history as Black September. Documents reveal that King Hussein, ever grateful, had a multitude of secret meetings with Israeli leaders at various destinations including at times in Tel-Aviv.

In 1972, Palestinian extremists kidnapped and murdered athletes in the Israeli contingent to the Munich Olympic Games. This heinous, draconian act against civilian athletes exemplified to the world the terrorist and guerilla tactics of the PLO. The organization was universally condemned and was branded as terrorist.

In the aftermath of the 1967 Six Day War, the situation was not improved. After six years of diplomatic efforts, the Arab nations decided that they would use force to drive the Israelis from the conquered territories. On October 6, 1973, the 1,350th anniversary of the Battle of Badr, commemorating Mohammed's victory over the city of Mecca, combined Syrian and Egyptian forces launched an attack on Israeli positions in the occupied territories. Coincidentally, this date was also Yum Kippur, the Jewish Day of Atonement and the holiest day of the year for Jews. The

---

[*] In one such instance, Leon Klinghofer, an American Jew confined to a wheelchair, was killed in cold blood by Palestinian terrorist hijackers and then thrown overboard from the Achille Lauro, an Italian ship.

resulting war has been called the Yom Kippur War. The Israelis had ignored warnings that the Egyptians and Syrians were massing for an attack, so the onslaught took them initially by surprise. They sustained great losses and were temporarily driven back and were in peril. The United States slowly supplied Israel with massive amounts of armaments, while the Soviet Union did the same for the Arab countries, stretching the détente between the superpowers virtually to the breaking point. The Israelis counterattacked and drove back the Syrians and then the Egyptians and crossed the Suez Canal.

On October 21, the UN adopted Security Council Resolution 338, which called for a cease-fire within twelve hours, for the belligerents to hold in their present positions, to implement Security Council Resolution 242 immediately after the cease-fire, and to start peace negotiations forth-with. The cease-fire did not hold until the UN authorized sending in a police contingent and U.S. and Soviet forces were deployed in the area. Only then was the UN able to negotiate the cease-fire on October 24th. Peacekeeping forces were sent into the area to enforce the truce. The following year Israeli forces withdrew to the eastern bank of the Suez Canal.

While victorious, the Israelis suffered more than 2,500 dead and 7,500 wounded which, viewed in terms of its population, was staggeringly high; also huge amounts of military equipment needed for defense were destroyed. The Yom Kippur War cost Israel $9 billion, gravely harmed its economy, and made it seek military aid from the United States. For the United States' help to Israel, the Arab countries cut oil shipments to the U.S., nationalized some U.S. companies' oil wells, and raised oil prices 17 percent.

In 1974, in Rabat, Morocco, an Arab summit recognized the PLO as the sole representative of the West Bank Palestinian Arabs. The PLO is comprised of three parts: (1) the Executive Committee, a decision-making body; (2) the Central Committee, an advisory body; and (3) the Palestine National Council which is an assembly of the Palestinian people. While Arab nations regard the PLO as the sole representative of the Palestinian people, there were factional groups who did not join the PLO umbrella. By 1975, the PLO and other Palestinian groups had terrorized

the Christian population in South Lebanon and destabilized the government of Lebanon resulting in a protracted civil war.

In 1977, the first breakthrough for real peace in the Mid-East occurred
when Egyptian President Anwar Sadat visited Israel. In 1978, President
Jimmy Carter helped facilitate a peace accord between Egypt and Israel
at Camp David, Maryland.* The United States gave economic aid to assist
a settlement. On March 26, 1979, a historic peace treaty was signed
between the two countries by Sadat and Israeli Prime Minister Menachem
Begin, ending thirty years of hostilities and gave diplomatic recognition
to Israel for the first time from any Arab country.

Three years after the Egyptian–Israeli peace accord Anwar Sadat was
assassinated in 1981 by Islamic fundamentalists. Also in 1981, Israel
annexed the Golan Heights that had been conquered from Syria in the
1967 War. In 1982, Israel withdrew its troops from the Sinai Peninsula in
accordance with the Camp David Peace Treaty.

On June 6, 1982, Israel launched a full-scale invasion of Lebanon in
order to curtail continuous attacks from that country. The PLO had amassed
a large force in Lebanon with Syria's blessing and subjected Israel to in
excess of 250 terrorist attacks. This was known as Operation Peace for
Galilee which besieged the PLO in West Beirut. The main armed contingent of the PLO evacuated Beirut and most left Lebanon to scatter to other
Arab countries. Arafat and his loyalists made their headquarters in Tunis.
Israeli troops then entered West Beirut. Later Israeli forces withdrew from
most of Lebanon; they remained in the southern part of the country. During
this period Christian Falangist militia were accused of mass killings in two
refugee camps, Sabra and Shatilla. Ariel Sharon, now Prime Minister of
Israel – then Defense Minister – was sanctioned by an Israeli commission
for his negligence in allowing the Christian killings to take place in the
refugee camps. The commission's findings led to his being barred for life
from becoming a defense minister and resigning his post. This war also
caused Menachem Begin to resign as Prime Minister and retire from all
political life. He remained in isolation until his death.

In 1982, widespread violence erupted by the Arabs in the West Bank
with attacks against Jewish settlements. Jerusalem was a particular stick-

* The author worked behind the scenes to bring about this accord.

ing point since the Israeli government announced in 1980 that Jerusalem would be its undivided capital.* Several radical groups sprang up whose aim was to destroy Israel. One of these groups, founded in 1984, is called Hamas, which is an acronym for the Islamic Resistance Movement. All of these groups are small but extremely violent, even up to the point of committing suicide if it means destroying the Israeli enemy. As violence escalated against Israel, the Israeli Air Force bombed Arafat's headquarters in Tunis in 1985 but Arafat escaped unharmed.

In June of 1985, Israel evacuated most of Lebanon but still occupied a twelve-mile zone just north of the Israeli border. In September, Prime Minister Shimon Peres of the Labor Party, proposed a peace initiative with Jordan and asked for an international conference. The U.S. tried to facilitate talks among Israel, Egypt and Jordan. Yitzhak Shamir, leader of the right-wing Likud Party, whose policy was against the formation of a Palestinian state, opposed the talks. This was the beginning of a seesaw peace process with generally left-wing Israelis trying to negotiate a peace and right-wing Israelis opposing the process. However, if some Israelis were willing to talk about peace, the Palestinian Arabs were not. The PLO had never accepted any of the UN resolutions and continued to assert that Palestine was their territory. This intransigence led to a break in early 1986 between Jordan's King Hussein and the PLO.

Later in 1986, Yitzhak Shamir was elected prime minister of Israel and new peace talks were initiated. Jewish settlements in Judea and Samaria continued to flourish and, by the end of 1987, the situation in Israel was so tense that a Palestinian uprising called the Intifada broke out in the West Bank and Gaza Strip. This Intifada, although sporadic, was to last nearly five years. Jordan, beset by its own problems, cut its ties to the Palestinians in the West Bank in July of 1988. By the end of the year the PLO realized that there was no longer any Arab unity over the Palestinian question and announced that they would accept UN Resolution 181 (the 1948 borders). Had the Arabs accepted this resolution 40 years earlier untold bloodshed and five major wars could have been avoided. They acknowledged Israel's right to exist and abandoned terrorism as a tactic.

---

* The policy of every Israeli government, whether Labor or Likud, stands for Jerusalem being the undivided eternal capital of the Jewish state.

However they never changed their charter which called for the destruction of the State of Israel. Unfortunately, terrorism as a tactic was never abandoned and exists as of this writing.

With signs that the PLO was now willing to negotiate and with rising pressure to end the Intifada, Shamir outlined a plan in 1989 to allow elections and a certain amount of self-rule for the Palestinians in the West Bank and Gaza. Meanwhile the United States continued to try to establish peace talks with Israel and its Arab neighbors as well as the Palestinians. U.S. Secretary of State James Baker offered a peace plan but was rebuffed by Shamir. This rejection of the peace proposal led to the dissolution of Shamir's National Unity coalition with the Labor Party and he had to form a right-wing Likud-based coalition.

In August of 1990, Iraq invaded Kuwait setting off a series of events that were to have far-reaching repercussions. Yasser Arafat's support for Iraqi leader Saddam Hussein alienated the United States and the Persian Gulf states. The U.S. government ceased peace talks with the PLO. Palestinian immigrants who had been working in Persian Gulf countries were now deported and funding for the PLO began to disappear as countries that formerly supported them now stopped. Arab countries formed a UN coalition along with the United States, Great Britain, and other countries to drive Iraqi troops out of Kuwait. The UN coalition spent months bombing Iraqi positions in Kuwait and Iraq. Iraq retaliated by firing Scud missiles into Israel; the missiles did relatively little damage but reminded the Israelis of their vulnerability. By March of 1991, Iraqi forces had been driven out of Kuwait and Saddam Hussein's army had been soundly defeated.

With the Gulf War at a close, President George Bush announced that the time was ripe for a new round of Middle East peace talks. On October 18, 1991, in conjunction with the Soviet Union, the United States announced a peace conference to be held in Madrid at the end of that month. This *Madrid Conference* was the first direct bilateral negotiation between Israel, a joint Jordanian–Palestinian delegation, Syria, and Lebanon. After a couple of false starts and much squabbling, the talks continued through December. This was a monumental step forward for countries that had been at war for forty-three years.

On December 26, 1991, to the surprise of most of the world, the Soviet Union collapsed. This left the United States as the world's only superpower. The Arab governments and Palestinian factions that had been supported by the Soviet Union were now on a totally different political footing as economic and military aid evaporated.

During 1992 the Madrid peace process continued in various places around the world, including Lisbon, London, Moscow, and Washington. In early March, Israel rejected a Palestinian proposal for elections in the West Bank and Gaza. Despite this setback talks continued. In June of 1992, Yitzhak Rabin of the Labor Party became prime minister and gave impetus to the peace process. By the late summer, Israel began talking about a partial pullout from the Golan Heights and later in the year the Palestinians asked for a similar withdrawal from the West Bank and Gaza. Extremists on both sides tried to disrupt the peace process and in December, 1992 six Israeli soldiers were killed, resulting in heightened Israeli security measures and increased tension. All during this time the Intifada was still in progress as the growth of Jewish settlements continued.

In January 1993, the Knesset, the Israeli parliament, lifted a 1986 ban on communicating with the PLO. In addition to talks sponsored by Washington that continued the Madrid peace process, secret talks ensued between the PLO and the Israelis at the invitation of the Norwegian government in Oslo. This led to a Palestinian–Israeli formal mutual recognition and, a month later, the signing of a Declaration of Principles (DOP) on September 13, 1993, in Washington on the same desk where fifteen years earlier the Camp David accords were signed. This later became known as the *Oslo I Agreement*. The Declaration of Principles outlined negotiations between the PLO and Israel to lay the groundwork for Palestinian autonomy in the West Bank and Gaza for a transitional period of five years, after which UN Resolutions 242 and 338 would be implemented. The questions of Jerusalem, Palestinian refugees, Jewish settlements in Palestinian territory, the make up of the Palestinian entity, borders, security arrangements, etc., were all to be mutually negotiated.

The first step in the Oslo I Agreement was the Gaza–Jericho Autonomy Agreement signed in Cairo on May 4, 1994. This is also known as the *Cairo*

Agreement. In this agreement, the Palestinians would set up a self-governing body called the Palestinian Authority, and Israeli troops would withdraw from Gaza and Jericho to allow Palestinian police control of the areas. Israel would still have military jurisdiction and control of Jewish settlements in the areas. This was to last for an interim period until May 1999.

Progress was being made in other areas as well. In late 1993 and throughout 1994 various declarations by Jordan and Israel paved the way on October 26, 1994, for a formal peace treaty between the two countries, ending forty-six years of war. Symbolically, the peace treaty was signed at the White House, the place where all other Mid-East peace agreements had been signed. By May of 1995, Israel and Syria reached an arrangement over mutual security concerns.

On September 26, 1995, in Taba, Egypt, the Interim Agreement on the West Bank and Gaza Strip was concluded and signed on September 28 in Washington. This agreement is also known as the *Oslo II Agreement.* It gave specific geographical designations that were to be given autonomy. It divided the West Bank and Gaza into three areas: A, B, and C. Area A included territory already under the Palestinian Authority and the six major population centers of the West Bank (Bethlehem, Jenin, Nablus, Qualquilaya, Ramallah, and Tulkaram), all of which would come under Palestinian civil and police jurisdiction. Area B included other Arab areas of the West Bank, including smaller population centers and refugee camps, all of which would come under Palestinian civil jurisdiction but police and security would be handled jointly by Israelis and Palestinians. Area C included military posts, government land and roads, and Jewish settlements, all of which would remain under Israeli control except for certain Palestinian civil matters not related to land. Areas A and B contained about 90 percent of the Palestinian population but only about 29 percent of the land. Area C, which contained the vast majority of Palestinian land, was to undergo partial Israeli military withdrawals every six months for the following year and a half. The Palestinian Authority would be autonomous but Israel was to retain control of external security.

In October 1995, Israeli troops began to withdraw from Area A and redeployment from this area was completed by the end of the year with the exception of Hebron.* Extremists on both sides were unhappy with the Oslo II Agreement. Some Arabs felt that they weren't getting enough, and some Israelis felt that they were giving up too much. Unfortunately, a right-wing religious fanatic, Yigal Amir, assassinated Prime Minister Yitzhak Rabin on November 4, 1995, ostensibly over his unhappiness over the Oslo II peace agreement. Rabin's successor, Shimon Peres, delayed negotiations over Hebron until after the May 29, 1996 elections. In the meantime, Palestinian extremists triggered a series of bombings to halt the negotiations. This played right into the hands of the right-wing who were swept into power under Prime Minister Benjamin Netanyahu. Although Netanyahu was generally against the Oslo II Agreement he, nevertheless, concluded an agreement with the Palestinian Authority on Hebron in January of 1997. The Hebron Agreement ceded 80 percent of the city to the Palestinians but kept control over the rest of the city, which had a small number of Jewish settlers.

However, in February 1997, the Netanyahu government decided to go ahead with another Jewish settlement in East Jerusalem. Palestinian protests over this tactic fell on deaf ears and the negotiations over further Israeli withdrawals came to a standstill. After a year-long deadlock and unfruitful visits to the Middle East by Secretary of State Madeline Albright, President Bill Clinton invited Netanyahu and Arafat to a conference on the Wye River in Maryland. This resulted in the *Wye River Memorandum*, which was signed on October 23, 1998 at the White House. The memorandum called for a withdrawal of Israeli troops from 13 percent of the West Bank, but after only 2 percent of the area had been vacated, on December 21, 1998, the Knesset voted for new elections and stopped the process. Just a week prior on December 14, 1998, Yasser Arafat and the Palestinian National Council voted to abolish the clause in the Palestinian charter that called for the destruction of the State of Israel, even though they claimed they had already agreed to this in principle long beforehand (though some extremeist within the PLO still reject this abolishment). However, to this day, there is a split in Israel as to whether the covenant has been truly revoked. Supporters of the peace

---

* Hebron has been a cause of great strife and conflict for a century. It is considered a holy burial place for Arab and Jew.

process are satisfied. Right wing parties believed that the covenant was not properly revoked.

The following May, Netanyahu, after a short term in office, was succeeded by the Labor Party's Ehud Barak as prime minister. In September 1999, at the behest of the Egyptian government, a conference took place at Sharm-El Sheikh. On September 5, Israel and the Palestinian Authority signed a revised Wye agreement, known as *Wye Two*. This delayed the complete Israeli withdrawal from the West Bank until January 20, 2000, and set a new timetable for partial withdrawals and further talks on the final status of the Palestinian Authority. On November 8, 1999, the first redeployment of Israeli troops from the West Bank began, but was halted a week later when the two sides couldn't agree on which areas to be vacated. Talks reached a total impasse on December 5, 1999 when the Palestinians withdrew from talks after the Israeli government refused to halt more Jewish settlements.

Bill Clinton invited the two sides to Camp David for another summit. In late May 2000, Israel unilaterally withdrew all its troops from Lebanon in a surprise move. As the Camp David talks loomed on the horizon, Ehud Barak had to scramble to keep his coalition together as a couple of parties threatened to leave over further concessions to the Palestinians. The peace talks started in August 2000 and continued sporadically until January 2001.

These talks were known as Camp David Two. The issue of the status of Jerusalem, and the Palestinian insistence on the right of the refugees to return to Israel, were two of the major stumbling blocks in these talks. The issue of the right of return has had a very strong influence on the Jewish population of Israel. It has caused even the left wing parties to unite in its objection to implementation of this concept. It is thought to be self-defeating since the refugees could conceivably occupy all of Israel's major cities. This could eventually mean that the State of Israel would lose its Jewish majority and identity. The initiative was heightened by a controversial visit to the Temple Mount by Ariel Sharon, the leader of the Likud party. At the time of his visit he was a known opponent of the Oslo II agreements. Violence erupted when Palestinians and Israeli Arabs vented their anger in rock throwing demonstrations. Israeli troops tried to contain the demonstrators. The violence escalated until it reached the proportion of a second Intifada. Sharon's allies state that this visit was pre-arranged well in advance with all necessary permission required for such a visit, including the knowledge and acceptance of the Muslim authority having jurisdiction over the Muslim holy sites. Sharon was always on Israeli territory and never entered Muslim holy places. Sharon's followers vehemently discount his visit as the cause of the second Intifada.

In late October, Barak officially announced the suspension of the peace process previously agreed upon. In late November, more than ten thousand people demonstrated in Jerusalem in a right-wing protest against Barak's handling of the situation. As the violence continued, the Israeli public lost confidence in Ehud Barak's government. Barak, in a move designed to keep the Knesset intact and also his ruling coalition, resigned as prime minister on December 10, 2000, and called for a new election. This allowed him to run against only standing Knesset members and eliminated his former rival Benjamin Netanyahu. The ploy, however, backfired as Ariel Sharon was elected prime minister in February 2001. Nevertheless, Sharon inherited Barak's Knesset and was forced to invite the Labor Party to join the Likud in a National Unity government. Barak's Labor Party would receive the powerful defense and foreign ministries' portfolios. By the time the Labor Party and Sharon had reached an agreement, more than 680 people had been killed in the newest Intifada.

As of August 2001, barbaric terrorist attacks against Israeli civilians persist. The Sharon government continues to retaliate against PLO military targets for these attacks. Paradoxically, talks between the parties continue from time to time.

THE POLITICAL SCENE

Israel does not have a constitution. Disputes over whether a constitution should be based on secular law or Jewish religious law have defeated every attempt to draw one up. Up until 1996, Israel worked on the parliamentary system (much like Great Britain's) where people voted for a political party. A certain percentage (which could be as low as one and a half percent) of the vote was needed to gain a seat in the Knesset, the Israeli parliament. The Knesset is the legislative branch and is considered the representative of the Israeli people and not the government (despite the fact that it is a branch of the government). The number of seats a party is apportioned in an election depends on the percentage of the votes it receives. There has *never* been a majority party in Israeli elections. All governments, i.e., the executive branch, are formed by coalitions of parties put together to form a majority. The Knesset elects a president whose functions are largely ceremonial, like the Queen of England or other constitutional monarch. The president used to ask the leader of the party with the most seats to be prime minister. In 1996, Israelis changed this system to directly elect the prime minister much like the direct election of the President of the United States. This process has recently been revoked.

Since there are so many parties, the inherent nature of Israeli politics is unstable. If a party or two withdraws from a coalition it can cause the collapse of a government and force new elections. Prime ministers are forced to give cabinet positions and other governmental posts to small-party officials in order to get them into their coalition. The two biggest parties are the left-wing Labor Party, which dominated until 1977, and the right-wing Likud Party, which has alternated with Labor as the dominant party since then. Left-wing and right-wing are relative descriptions since both parties tend toward socialist policies, perhaps liberal and nationalistic are more apt terms for Labor and Likud respectively.

There are several religious parties, the largest of which, Shas, has been gaining seats and is the third largest party in Israel. Shas is a Jewish ultra-orthodox party that caters to the Sephardic (descendants of Spanish–Portuguese Jews) minority, many of whom feel that they are discriminated against by the Ashkenazi (descendants of Eastern European Jews) majority. Mafdal, the National Religious Party, is a coalition of ultra-orthodox parties who banded together for more political clout. United Torah Judaism is a coalition of two ultra-Orthodox parties. Agudat Israel and Degel HaTorah. The religious parties tend to be ultra-nationalistic as well as theocratic.

There are several Russian immigrant parties, Yisrael Baaliya, a moderate right-wing party headed by Natan Sharansky, Yisrael Beitenu (New Russian Immigrant Party) headed by Avigdor Lieberman and Democratic Choice, a liberal splinter group formed from Yisrael Baaliya. They all cater to the special needs of the former Soviet peoples.

Moledet, an ultra-right nationalist party, is generally viewed as extreme and the successor to Meir Kahane's Kach Party, which was outlawed. Herut is a far right-wing party led by Benny Begin, Menachem Begin's son. Other small far right-wing parties have come and gone. In the latest election these parties were united under Benny Begin's National Union Party flag.

Meretz is the far left-wing party. It tends to be more sympathetic to the peace process and wants to separate synagogue and state to form a socialist secular society. Shinui is a liberal-center party that often aligned with Meretz in the past. There are also several Arab parties who generally vote left-wing.

The Center Party led by Yitzhak Mordechai and Dan Meridor and the Third Way Party led by Avigdor Kalahani are two center-right parties that broke off from the Likud and Labor parties respectively.* This splintering of parties into new parties is a frequent phenomenon in Israeli politics, especially when a charismatic leader cannot rise in the ranks of the larger parties and decides to strike out on his own.

Israeli politics resembles nineteenth century American politics where opponents were often shouted down or debates erupted in fisticuffs. All extremes of the political spectrum are represented in the Knesset, and while every voice is heard, political will and farsighted planning are often lost due to factionalism.

The law of direct election of the prime minister was recently vetoed by the Knesset. The former election laws have been re-established, allowing the leader with the majority of a coalition to form a government, given a period of time by the president.

---

* As this book goes to press, both parties are in the process of being dissolved.

THEINTERVIEWS

YITZHAK**RABIN**

Yitzhak Rabin, at the time Defense Minister, former Chief of Staff, Israeli Defense Force, former Israeli Ambassador to the United States, and future Prime Minister of Israel. He was assassinated by an Israeli fanatic on November 4, 1995.

LHC: Yitzhak, last Thursday the United States government changed its policy in that it said that it would initiate some direct talks with the PLO. What's your feeling about this situation?

YR: Well, I must admit that I didn't expect such a dramatic change immediately after his speech at the General Assembly, that took place at Geneva. The American reaction was along the traditional lines of its policy for the last fifteen years. Twenty-four hours later, after the press conference of Mr. Arafat, there was a dramatic change in the position that was made publicly by the U.S. administration.

What worries me, and carries the potentialities of changing of U.S. policy is as follows: since the end of the war of 1973, there was some basic understandings between the United States and Israel in regard to the peace policy toward the region, to solve the Arab-Israeli conflict. One, to work together. Second, to try to cope, first

with Egypt; and not to try to
achieve comprehensive peace by
one act, realizing that the problems
have to be dealt with one by one.
Therefore, peace between Egypt
and Israel was achieved, and no
doubt, it was a dramatic achievement for Egypt, Israel, and the
United States. We were the three
partners for the achievement of this
peace.

Yitzhak Rabin

In approaching the complex of
issues eastward of Israel, with the
purpose to achieve peace on Israel's
eastern border, first and foremost, with Jordan. Second, to solve
the Palestinian problem. You cannot achieve peace on our eastern border without tackling and solving the Jordanian and the
Palestinian problems.

The essence that was laid down in the Camp David Accords
that was the solid basis for our common policy—the United States,
Israel, and Egypt—was to tackle it gradually. First, to autonomy,
as a transitional period, and later on, Jordan: the Palestinian representation of the residents in the territories; Israel and Egypt will
solve it, permanently.

The essence was linking the solution of the Palestinian problem to Jordan. Therefore, even in 1975, before the peace between
Egypt and Israel was achieved, Dr. [Henry] Kissinger, as secretary
of state, and I, in signing the first step towards peace with Egypt—
I was then the Prime Minister—worked a memorandum of agreement signed by Dr. Kissinger and submitted it to the Congress of
the United States, in which the United States committed itself
not to have a dialogue with the PLO before: first, the PLO will
recognize the right of Israel to exist; and second, we accept resolution 242 and 338 of the United Nations Security Council as

the sole basis for the solution of the Arab–Israeli conflict and all its powers.

Later on, and rightly so, Secretary [of State George] Schultz added a third condition renouncing terror and violence. I don't believe that Mr. Arafat, in his press conference, has taken upon himself anything that really changes, or must change, the U.S. position.

Let's take only the terrorism. One of the closest assistants to Mr. Arafat came on one of your networks and said very clearly, they would attack military targets in Israel, on Israel sovereign soil, attacking Israeli targets in the territories, and for them, a settlement along the Lebanese border is a military target. A bus is a military target. Second, he said, we will continue to cooperate with the Lebanese forces fighting Israelis along the Lebanese–Israeli border. Three, he said, the uprising in the territories, what they call the Intifada, we will support and we are not committed, practically, not to stop it. Therefore, all practical terror and violent activities against Israel, in accordance to their official spokesman, are going to be continued.

Maybe an incident like that will not take place, even though we are aware that a group that belonged to Mr. Arafat's PLO intends to continue with their terror activities. Therefore, I'm afraid that the United States, by its dialogue with the PLO, practically, did not keep its commitments in accordance to the '75 agreement. Second, by trying to move towards the PLO, the U.S. severed itself from the essential and the vital principle of linking the solution of the Palestinian problem to Jordan. If this is the change, we are facing something entirely new in the efforts to bring about peace. I am afraid it will not enhance the prospects of peace, but might reduce them.

LHC: Why do you think the United States did this, at this point? I mean, you had a Reagan administration that was very favorable towards Israel, you had Secretary of State Schultz, who was considered a really good friend of Israel. He did not allow a visa for Arafat to visit, and twenty-four hours later, the whole policy reversed. Do you have any idea why this happened?

YR: I can't give you an answer that I'm sure about. I believe that certain disappointments of the administration emerged. First, the lack of positive response to Secretary Schultz's initiative of March–April '88. The secretary of state came with his own initiative to bring the parties around the negotiation table, and it was not received in a positive way by Israel and Jordan. Second, the decision of King Hussein to cut the legal and the administrative ties between Jordan and the population of the West Bank, and to a lesser extent, with Gaza. Three, the need to appear, on the part of the United States, of trying to do something that might look at bringing closer the capability to talk with the Palestinians. And four, might be, since it's not a very popular move, to do it in the last months of the Reagan administration, rather than to put it on the new administration in the United States. I'm sure it was done in coordination between President Reagan and Secretary Schultz and President-elect Bush and future Secretary of State James Baker.

LHC: Many of your friends in Congress, are calling for you to talk with the PLO. Do you think this will push Israel into an isolation that will be hard to come out of?

YR: Well, first allow me to say, that I would answer such talk in the United States with what I said to the Speaker of the House in 1977. The Speaker said to me, "Mr. Prime Minister, the United States is a superpower. And we were ready, in the context of the war of Vietnam, to talk not only to North Vietnam, but also to the Viet Cong, which we considered to be a guerrilla terror organization. If we could speak to a terror organization like the Viet Cong, why can't you, Israel, speak to the PLO?" My answer was simple. The basic difference, I said to him, is that the Viet Cong did not demand Washington to be their capital. The PLO demands it. Would you negotiate with a terror group that demand your capital to become their capital? This is the basic difference.

        But at the same time, allow me to say, I believe that on the part of Israel, we have to do the following things: one, to continue our intimate dialogue with the U.S. administration, Congress, the American public—and to explain: Look, wait and see to what extent Mr. Arafat implements what he says.

So far, Mr. Arafat did not say in Arabic to the Palestinians to stop terrorism. So far, practically, they put all violent terror activities against Israel, from within, from Lebanon, toward the borders, from the sea, as part of what they consider not to be terror, and therefore it doesn't come under what they have committed to the United States. Second, Israel has to come with some fresh new ideas. How to move under the present circumstances towards peace, sticking to the basic principles of the strategy that has been agreed between the United States and Israel in the last fifteen years, especially as part of the Camp David Accord and the peace treaty between Egypt and Israel.

What I would say, first, let's try to allow the one and a half million Palestinians that reside in the territories of the West Bank and the Gaza Strip to participate in deciding their own fate and future. They must be a party, a partner of Israel, and Jordan, for peace. They alone can be a partner to Israel for negotiating some interim arrangement that will serve as a transitional period. I believe that the time has arrived that we will come up and offer free democratic elections of the Palestinians in the territories to elect from themselves political representation. Whoever will be elected from themselves will be elected from our point of view, from the international point of view. Second, to sit with them with Jordan, with the participation of the United States, if the United States and others say "The Soviets do," alright, the Soviets do. Egypt of course. And let's try to work along the principles of expanded autonomy, which will, for a transition period of five, seven, ten years, allow them to run by self-governing authority, their own affairs with the exception of foreign policy and security. That will be in the hands of Israel.

Why should we run their affairs? Let them have an elected body that will run their affairs. Second, to offer them, if they want it for the transitional period, to link this entity, which its borders have to be negotiated, in a context of permanent solution, to be part of a federation with Jordan, or even a part of a federation with Israel.

LHC: A canton?

YR: In a form of canton, one or two might be there, parts of the West Bank will be there, canton, the Gaza will be another canton. Many ideas can come up once we find a partner that will represent the one and a half million Palestinians, their fate and future. These are the people that suffer today from the uprising in the territories. These are the people that reside in the territories. To deal with the solution of their problem, I believe that once we come with such an idea, and maybe develop it in talks with the Palestinians, Jordanians, Egyptians, and Americans, it can create more incentive to those who are daily affected by the unsolved present situation, and bring them around to a negotiation table.

LHC: Do you think that a policy like this is feasible and viable and acceptable with the United States today?

YR: I can't say, because unfortunately I can't speak now in the name of the whole government of Israel. I hope that in the coming days a new government will be formed that in its center will be the Likud and the Labor Party with some other small parties, and no doubt one of the first jobs will be to try to formulate a new policy.

We have seen that in 1980 practically no one agreement was reached between another country and Israel. In the '70s we had the disengagement agreement between Egypt and Israel. The disengagement agreement between Syria and Israel. The Sinai too, or what we call the interim agreement of '75. And no doubt later on, the Camp David Accords and the Peace Treaty.

The '70s, unfortunately, had one major war, but at the same time, it was a decade of real efforts that bore fruit, and led to the historic achievement of the peace between Egypt and Israel. The '80s were one war in Lebanon, that was a miserable war, and without any meaningful move towards peace. It's time, that at the end of this decade, we resume our combined activities to move, not through the PLO, but through the Palestinians relevant to the problem, towards negotiation and political process.

LHC: Yitzhak, the way I hear you, is in a sense, there were eight years that were lost where we didn't move towards a Palestinian resolution. And the second thing, is that perhaps maybe the Israeli government should have used this Jordanian option which I think you and Shimon Peres put together. I'm not sure the American public understands that. If you could explain a little of that to us, I think it would be helpful.

YR: 'Til a few months ago, all the Palestinians who reside in the West Bank, and even today, saw themselves, to a certain extent, as Jordanians. Everyone here, in the West Bank, every Palestinian, is a Jordanian citizen, and carries a Jordanian passport, and there is not a word that, even today, they are ready to give it up. Therefore, we cannot achieve peace on our eastern border, that by the way, is the longest line between Israel and any one of our other three neighboring Arab countries, without bringing together to the negotiation table Jordan and Palestinian representation.

The United States and Israel, in the past, talked about a joint delegation, a Jordanian–Palestinian delegation. Therefore, we called it the Jordanian Option, linking the solution of the Palestinian who resides in the West Bank and the Gaza Strip, to Jordan. And finding through territorial compromises, giving parts of the West Bank and the Gaza Strip, which are populated densely by the Palestinians, to be a Jordanian–Palestinian State, under one sovereignty, one government, one capital. This was the essence of the Jordanian Option.

Basically, today we don't call it the Jordanian Option. But we need to solve it, either by the Jordanian Option, by linking as a federation of cantons considerable parts of the West Bank and the Gaza Strip to Jordan, or by federation with us, bringing in the Palestinian cantons in the West Bank and the Gaza Strip, to be within the framework of Israel in a modified way to what it is today.

Therefore, the Jordanian Option was a terminology here in Israel in contradiction to the idea of the whole land of Israel, it is to say, of annexing the whole West Bank and the Gaza Strip, to be part of the sovereign soil of Israel. It showed readiness to compromise on population and territory if the solution will be linked to Jordan under one sovereign entity.

LHC: Why did it fail?

YR: I believe the straw that broke the camel's back, at least for a while, was the failure of Secretary Schultz's initiative in March–April this year. When Jordan realized that as the uprising in the territories goes on, there was no hope for any political move that would lead to negotiating a political solution.

And a realization that with a new administration in the United States, who knows what would be its policy? Jordan decided about three and a half, or four months ago, to sever its administrative and legal ties with the population of the West Bank and Gaza. It created a vacuum that forced the PLO to take the steps that were taken first in the meeting of the Palestinian National Council in Algeria, that later on led to their appearance in the General Assembly, that later on brought about the U.S. acceptance of Mr. Arafat, and as a legitimization of having a dialogue with the PLO.

LHC: Do you think ten years from now it's possible that you'll see Palestinians having their own flag, their own post office, their own civil rights, their own human rights, everything except a foreign ministry and a defense ministry and they'll have full entitlement as citizens? Is that what you project?

YR: I believe that the ultimate solution must be, in the context of the triangle: Israel, Jordan, Palestinians. It can be linked to Jordan. It can be linked to Israel. As you know, even the Israeli Arab citizens carry with them Israeli citizenship, but we have never denied it. We assist them, to maintain their national heritage, their own identity, as Muslims, as Arabs, as Palestinians. We don't try to make them Jews.

They are Palestinian Arab-Israelis. We have never tried to make the Palestinians anything other than Palestinians. We opposed the creation of an independent Palestinian state between Israel and Jordan. We believe that there must be a solution linked either to Israel or to Jordan, in which they will be able to express their own identity, their own heritage, their own self-rule.

LHC: What do you think the effect of the new excellent relationship, so to speak, between the Soviet Union and the United States will have on the Middle East?

YR: If the relationship between the two superpowers will continue to develop the way that it has developed, especially lately, as a result of the speech of President Gorbachev in the United Nations, in which he spoke about cutting the size of the armed forces, that no doubt, is very vital to both the Soviet Union and to the United States, and will allow a reduction in the price tag of the defense for both the superpowers. They'll make sure that regional tensions will not interfere with their movement along the road of improved relations, and they'll reduce the potential for outburst of hostilities even in remote places in the world that might drag them into them.

Therefore, I will not be surprised if we will see a continuation of cooperation between the two superpowers to find a solution or at least to reduce the danger of explosion of hostilities everywhere, all over the globe. We saw it in their combined efforts to end the war between Iraq and Iran. We saw it in the efforts to end the Soviet involvement in Afghanistan. We saw it in the efforts to reduce the U.S. involvement in Nicaragua, under the Contra Affair. We see it in their efforts to find a solution to Angola, Namibia, problems in Africa. And I wouldn't be surprised if we see cooperation between the two in trying to find ways to solve the Arab–Israeli conflict, or at least parts of it.

LHC: Two Fridays ago, in Israel, you did a brilliant job in returning a hijacked plane from the Soviet Union. Do you think that this is going to have a precipitous effect on good relationship between Israel and the Soviet Union, possibly lead to a new diplomatic relationship?

YR: Well, as a matter of fact I was surprised when I got the information in my office in the Defense Ministry that a Soviet plane was given to some hijackers, and they decided to go to Israel. A few hours later we got an official request from the U.S. government, in which they supplied us the information. How many people there were. What kind of crime they carried out. What kind of weapons they carried. And sent an official request, first to let them land.

Normally we are careful to not allow people to land in our airports. Second, once it was over—they know we are experts in coping with hijacked planes—to send back the plane and the crew. And three, to behave in accordance to international law and to give them those criminals that were on board the plane.

We took all the precautions, we prepared all our elite forces, though there was no need to use them. The people gave up, and we returned them safely to the Soviet Union without any problem.

Since then, unfortunately, we have sent two teams to the Soviet Union, in Armenia [for earthquake rescue]. They're waiting there in a hospital for children to rescue people. We sent five planes, full of medical assistance, engineering equipment, and about fifty people who are still there. They work with other teams that come from all over the world, in addition to those of the Soviet Union. And I believe that these two events bring closer, on a humanitarian basis, the Soviets to Israel, and Israel to the Soviet Union.

LHC: Yitzhak, one of the problems you've been grappling with, or at least your party has been grappling with, is the "Who is a Jew" problem. Do you have any specific feelings about this, especially as it pertains to the American community?

YR: I believe that many in Israel realize now that it was wrong, for both parties, the Likud and the Labor. That as a result of the last election, none of us could form a government to run after the religious parties, to form a narrow based coalition government. In the efforts to try to buy them, let's put it in a brutal way, both parties made too many commitments. I can't blame the Likud alone, that they did it. We were in competition with them and we didn't succeed.

And now I believe that we all realize that we cannot afford to do what both parties intended to do. To give in on the amendment of the law of return, which is the question of who is a Jew, the way that it was planned. I believe that if there is a wide based coalition government of the Likud and Labor together, there is a very good chance that this law will not pass, and will not bring about a rift between Israel and some of the Jewish communities all over the world. I will not give in to many demands without the results of the election, and without the readiness of the two major parties to form a government, based on them. I hope that in the next wide-based coalition government, we also change the election system.

LHC: Skipping to another subject, Yitzhak, you were in the Labor Party, the minority, when the Camp David Agreements were signed, but I know you supported them very strongly. What do you feel today are the relationships between Egypt and Israel? Are they okay, are they flawed, are they cold? What's your feeling?

YR: Well, to many people, especially in the United States, it's very difficult to understand what it means to an Arab country, a key Arab country, to cross the Rubicon of suspicion, hatred, and to make peace with Israel. Let's not forget that for almost ten years, there have been daily flights between Israel and Cairo, and Cairo to Israel. Every day, one day Egyptian, the next day Israeli airlines go, the borders are open. It's something that was a dream fifteen years ago. A dream that many of us did not believe that we would see in our own life. It has materialized. It was proved that it was not a dream.

That the peace between Egypt and Israel, regardless of the fact that the wars, practically, were a freeze of all political efforts to expand the peace process to at least another Arab country, that for ten years, the peace has, in essence, remained. I would not deny it. We expected and hoped that the normalization of relations between human beings would develop better than they have developed. But the absence of war, the existence of embassies, the fact that the Egyptian flag is in Tel-Aviv, the Israeli flag is in Cairo, by itself, is a revolution.

LHC: Also that they didn't come into the Lebanese war.

YR: And this peace has passed quite a number of tries. Therefore, it gives me hope that peace is not anymore a dream. If peace could be achieved with Egypt, could be maintained, regardless of whatever in the Middle East in the last ten years, has stood firm, there is a chance for peace if it is done wisely from a standpoint of strength, country by country, not an attempt to achieve the unattainable, to work with all the Arab countries at the same time.

LHC: Yitzhak, I remember December 9th was the first anniversary of the Intifada and I think that you were in the United States when the Intifada commenced. Did you believe that this thing would prolong itself to the extent that it has, and do you think it's put together basically by the PLO ruling group or do you think it's self-perpetuating by the population itself?

YR: Well, let's face it. What has taken place in the territories, the uprising, the so-called civilian violence, is a new phenomenon to us. For thirty-nine years, Israel experienced wars between the armed forces of the Arab countries against Israel, we experienced terror all through the thirty-nine years and we continue to experience it. We did not experience this kind of violence for years for the achievement of political goals. No one can really explain why it happened on December 9, 1987. Many people believed that the status quo would not have been maintained for a long time.

Therefore, basically, we have to deliver a message that Israel will not give in politically, will not turn away, because of the use of storms. We have not run away from tanks, artillery, planes, we will not run away from storms. Therefore we are determined, even if it will take longer, to deliver the message: "You want a solution around the negotiation table? Not by the use of force."

LHC: Yitzhak, you have been Mr. Israel: The chief of the Defense Forces, the ambassador of Israel to the United States, the prime minister of Israel, the defense minister of Israel. I don't think anybody's held as many offices of public government as you have. What has been your greatest challenge?

YR: I hope that the greatest challenge is still ahead of me. Even though
        I'm quite old, I belong to the generation of '48, the young gener-
        ation the military forces called "mortal '48." The greatest day of
        my life was during the Six Day War, when Jerusalem was liber-
        ated and united. I was born in Jerusalem, I fought in '48 in
        Jerusalem; you know, the siege, Jerusalem, along the road to
        Jerusalem, and I was the youngest brigade commander of the IDF
        [Israeli Defense Forces]. And as the chief of staff, I finished what
        I felt to achieve as a brigade commander in '48. For a Jewish boy
        or a Jewish man, who was born in Jerusalem and fought the two
        wars that decided the fate of the city, to be united under Israel
        sovereignty, and the capital of the independent Jewish state—
        what can be better than that? The greatest challenge is to see Israel
        growing in peace, and at least having six to seven million Jews
        who live here.

LHC: So peace is the answer?

YR: Peace is part of the answer. To be strong, to achieve peace, and
        to make sure that more Jews will come to Israel.

*Some four or five months after this interview I met again with Mr. Rabin. He confided
that he had reservations about Mr. Arafat's eagerness in negotiating a permanent peace.
Basically he felt Arafat's roots were similar to those of the terrorist groups. Some years
later, while sitting on the White House lawn, I witnessed President Clinton (with Shimon
Peres at his side) cajoling Rabin to shake Arafat's hand which he reluctantly did. Years
later, after the assassination of Rabin, Arafat paid a Shiva (condolence) call on Mrs.
Rabin in Tel Aviv.*

EPHRAIM**KATZIR**

Ephraim Katzir, fourth Israeli president. He discusses the lack of a constitution in Israel as well as the pros-and-cons of direct election of the prime minister. He explains Zionism as he sees it and its current meaning.

LHC: A lot of people in the United States don't understand how the presidency of Israel operates. Technically, you are the most senior official of the Israeli people, is that correct?

EK: We don't have a constitution, but we have a special law concerning the president, which has been passed by the Knesset, by our parliament. The president is supposed to represent the people of the country. So the country is, at least legally, not represented by the prime minister, but by the president.

The president has many official kinds of functions, which are not executive functions, so his impact on everyday life is not very great. I would compare him with the status of the queen of England. He's highly respected, people will come to him to talk about their dreams, about their activities, achievements, and failures. People see in the house of the president the place where every event that has occurred during the time of the presidency should be reflected.

Sometimes people in the country feel that if the president said, "You have done something good," this means that that person's action will be recorded in the diary of the Jewish history of the State of Israel! Writers would send me their books! If I wouldn't respond within a week, they would call me every day, "What do you think about the book? What do you think about the book?" I had to read it and give my opinion. But it stems from this feeling that the best that the coun-

Ephraim Katzir, former President of Israel

try can offer, that this is reflected in the house of the president.

It's really an outstanding position, I feel, where you really share with the people, not only an understanding of their achievements, but of their dreams. Their dreams they'll discuss with the president, but not with the ministers. They are busy! Not with the prime minister, he's terribly busy. So in this respect, it's really a remarkable position. The president has a couple of official duties. After elections, he has to appoint from the newly elected members of the parliament, the person whom he wants to form a government. That person will come back, if he succeeds in forming a government. He will report to the president; he'll then present the government to the Knesset; if he gets a vote of confidence, then we have a government. If not, the President is allowed to ask any other member.

I became an expert in the field, because during my term, from '73 to '78, of course I had Golda Meir, who was at the time the prime minister, and she was a wonderful woman. I admired her. I knew her as a child, and we were very great friends. She was, for me, a kind of mother image. I had to listen to what she said, but she resigned. I nominated her again. Then she resigned. Then I nominated Rabin. Then, after elections, I nominated Begin. So I really became an expert in this part of the activities.

LHC: Recently, President Herzog has gone through a lot of activity concerning the formulation of the last government. So the presidency *does* have a very strong impact on the people of Israel.

EK: At this stage, very much so. When we don't have a party with a marked majority, then it's more technical. If one of the parties has a majority, a very significant majority, then the President will ask the representatives of this party to form a government, because they'll get the vote of confidence of the Knesset. But this has not happened for years in Israel. So we always have a coalition government, and then the President has a very important function in selecting the right man who will be able to form a government that will be able to function and get the confidence of the people and of the Knesset.

LHC: There are two questions I have. Number one, I know that you respect Mr. [Yitzhak] Navon very much, your successor as president. But what are your feelings about a president entering politics once he has assumed the role of president of Israel?

EK: As a matter of fact, not only do I respect Navon, I know him very well, I was his officer in the underground! So I have known him for many years, and I have the highest regard for him. But frankly, I was not very happy that, after serving as president of the country, Navon decided to enter politics and became minister of education. My feeling was that once he becomes a leader of a party, somehow, the concept of a party man does not fit exactly with the concept that the people have of a president. The president is the father of the country, but the party man has to fight for the program of his party. He should criticize others, and the president should encourage everyone! So I thought that if you have chosen to become president, or have been chosen, after completing your term you should do something else. You can have many intellectual activities, Navon is a writer, but not to go back to politics. Even if you came to the presidency from politics.

39

LHC: So in your opinion, the presidency is a special office, and once you've attained it, it should be retained at that stature and status.

EK: I don't think that we have this custom that the Mexicans have. After completing your term as president, you're out! Nobody wants to talk to you anymore! It's the other way around. People respect you and like you, and you know a lot about what's going on. But you shouldn't be involved in an active way in politics. That's my opinion.

LHC: Ephraim, there's a feeling in this country that some people would appreciate having direct election of prime minister. What's your feeling on that?

EK: It has its advantages, and it has its disadvantages, because our constitution [sic] is not the constitution of the United States, nor are our customs towards the constitution the same.

LHC: There is, by the way, no country in the world, that has direct election of the prime minister. This would be the first.

EK: It would give very strong powers to the prime minister. Whereas in our case, if the parliament votes against the government, the government falls. It also has advantages, if suddenly the majority of the people find out that the government is not fulfilling the function that should be fulfilled. Whereas if the prime minister is elected by direct election, you can't fire him in the middle of a term. You can't fire a government. The criticism will not be as strong as it is now. And citizens of Israel, they are experts in criticizing the prime minister, they hesitate to criticize the president! It has its advantages.

LHC: I get a feeling from you that when you were president, although you had this wonderful job, you really missed your science. Is this correct?

EK: Yes, I missed it, it's true. And science is a creative kind of activity. The president, he encourages people, he's involved in the life of the country, but his impact on each day, on politics, on economics, on security, on defense, is really marginal.

The prime minister has to report every second week or every week, or one of the ministers, to the president. They will discuss openly what's going on. They will listen to the president, but it's an indirect impact. So in this respect, I missed science, no doubt about that. I could read, but I couldn't work in the laboratory.

LHC: I understand that after five years, you really wanted to get back to your science. You thought that five years was enough, you had served your nation, and more importantly, you wanted to contribute to science.

EK: Yes, and moreover, I felt that to be a president of the State of Israel was a distinction. It's not another job, or an administrative office. People look up to you. You should know about the lives of the people. You should really serve as an example in your life, in your way of thinking, in your respect for intellectual, moral values. By building up defense, building up agriculture, and building up industry people saw how from nothing places were built, institutions, the country. The Weizmann Institute was built in '48—I came here in '48! This is unbelievably satisfying. And when you talk to people, you are encouraged. You must become an optimist. To see what people can do if they are determined, capable, and have the right qualities to do it.

LHC: We're at the Weizmann Institute. I think the two greatest institutions in Israel are the Israeli Defense Force, and the Weizmann Institute. In a sense they're paradoxical—one is a military force, the other is a scientific force to create a better, more useful society. Tell me about Chaim Weizmann.

EK: Of course. I knew about Chaim Weizmann as a child—studying in school. But I became quite close to Chaim Weizmann when I came to the Weizmann Institute in 1948, when it just started. While he was here, he worried about the future development of the Weizmann Institute, and used to come practically every day to his laboratory, which is here. It's a small institute, which started around 1936, and was really functioning mainly in chemistry, and a little in biology. Areas that Weizmann was interested in. In '48, Weizmann started a bigger institute, and an institute that was really donated to him as a gift for his seventieth birthday. I came in '48, and there were about ten scientists: five Israelis and five scientists from abroad. We decided to build an institute for basic research.

Almost every week Weizmann would ask me and my late brother, Aaron, to come to his laboratory and tell him what was new. Within a half an hour, I had to tell him what was new in science, which is not the easiest task in the world! But it was wonderful. He was such a clever man. Witty, knowledgeable; he knew a lot of chemistry! So we became great friends, and thereafter, since his home was not far from the Institute, we used to go to his home. One day, while I was sitting opposite him—he was already the first president of the State of Israel—and he didn't like this position too much, as you know! But then he looks at me, and he knows about my activities, and he says, "Look, young man. I know that you are a chemist, a biophysicist. I think you'll become a good scientist. But I warn you: don't mix in politics! If you do it, your end will be like mine! And look, I'm not very happy about it!"

As a young man, I didn't listen. So finally, I had the job as the fourth president. But at least I had a little bit of revenge on Weizmann by the fact that I was the fourth president. I was a chemist, he was the first president, he was a chemist. So out of four presidents, 50 percent were chemists. And I used to tell my students, "Look, if you study chemistry, you'll have a 50 percent chance to become president of the State of Israel!"

But it was always a remarkable occasion to sit with him, to listen to him, and when I tried to understand why we were all so enchanted by his personality, it was not only because he was a great Zionist leader; he understood, at an early stage, that if you are going to build a new state, a modern state, you must develop science and technology. Because they will be an enormous help in building the country, in building a modern society. But then he had this wonderful combination. He had an excellent traditional Jewish training and education. He had Russian training. He knew Russian literature! Then he went to Switzerland, and he had Swiss training. Then he worked in England for many years. And all this together—he would tell you a joke in Yiddish, and after three minutes he would discuss with you a formula of a complicated organic compound! Thereafter he would tell you about Churchill! It was just unbelievable. So this was Weizmann. And I must say, till this day, when I talk about him, I'm always excited because these were wonderful times to be with him.

LHC: It's sad that without his intervention with President Truman, one doesn't know whether you would have had a state in 1948.

EK: This is what Truman says in his memoirs. That finally he came in and this man who worked with Truman, who had some business—

LHC: Harry Jacobson. A Jewish haberdasher.

EK: That's it. I understand that Jacobson used to come to Truman— they were still great friends, in spite of the fact that Truman was already president—but he would come and tell him about his family, and start to cry! Truman would ask, "Why are you crying?" He said, "Chaim Weizmann is here, he wants to see you! Why won't you accept?" Truman, he was so fed up with Jews and pressure, didn't want to see him, but finally he yielded. Of course, once you faced Weizmann, you had to yield!

You know the story that Weizmann tells? About his meeting with Ehrlich, the man who discovered the magic bullet, the drug salvarsan, against syphilis. He wanted Ehrlich to be involved in the establishment of the Hebrew University. He came to Ehrlich, and before he entered, the nurse told Weizmann, "Look, Ehrlich is so busy! Here are people who have syphilis! They are executives and distinguished members of the administration! You have ten minutes!" So Weizmann goes in and he starts to talk to Ehrlich about the Hebrew University, about Zionism, and then Ehrlich tells him, "Look, they are waiting for me, I have no time!" So Weizmann told Ehrlich, "Look, all these people waiting for you, they came to get an injection from you. But I came to *give* you an injection! You'd better sit down and listen!" And they became very great friends. He was an irresistable man.

LHC: Charismatic.

EK: Charismatic. In a remarkable way.

LHC: Ben Gurion.

EK: Ben Gurion. Let me admit something that I found out only during the last couple of years. As a young man, we would always go to him for help in science, when he was prime minister. He was always interested in science, and he was always very friendly toward my late brother and me. After listening to us, he would always ask us, "Alright, so now tell me what are you doing in science?" So we would tell him. I was interested in protein, my late brother in studying polymers. He would listen and say to us, "Yes, but why don't you do something interesting?" He would always come back and say, "Why don't you study the brain?" I suspected that he thought about his brain, and that we should study his brain! Nevertheless, in spite of the fact that he was very friendly and he contributed to science in a remarkable way, we were very close. When we were interested in building up research and development for defense, he helped us unbelievably.

He was interested in so many things, always curious to know what was going on, the genetic code—he wanted to understand the genetic code. And we sat with him to explain the genetic code! He wanted to understand what was the difference between living and non-living! I suspected that he was very absorbed in many things, but basically he had the character of a journalist. He knew a very little about many things, but nothing very very seriously!

LHC: I'm going to change my profession, I'm getting nervous!

EK: But, I must say during the last couple of years, I read many of his writings in the most critical way. I was completely wrong! Those areas, those topics that he was really interested in, he carried out an analysis and a study that the best scientists would do. He was interested in water in Israel, in energy in Israel, in agriculture. He wrote in scientific terms! Amounts! He knew every detail—how to purify, desalinate water, every technique that was around in his time, critically analyzing them. So I was completely wrong! As a result of this, my admiration for Ben Gurion has increased with the years, not decreased.

LHC: Have you ever met Einstein?

EK: I was in his home, and I met him once. In Princeton.

LHC: A remarkable man.

EK: Unbelievable. But very naïve. He was the greatest scientist that we had in the last generation. But when you read what he said about man, about his behavior, about countries; well, he was wonderful in his decency, but also in his naiveté. He couldn't act as a politician, I can assure you.

LHC: They had offered him the presidency of Israel, and he declined it. Is that true?

EK: I think he was very wise in declining. He wouldn't have been very happy as a president of the State of Israel. Because life is so complicated in Israel, and the people are so complicated here. I was raised here, from the age of six, and it was complicated enough for me! It would have been extremely complicated for him!

LHC: The Weizmann Institute is very revered. What makes it so?

EK: You have here a group of scientists who are dedicated to science, to increase the amount of knowledge of mankind in the natural sciences—the amount of information. The fact that there is hardship around, this helps us, I think. Because those young scientists who have the privilege to dedicate their lives, or many years, to science, they understand that it is a remarkable privilege. In comparison to their friends, who serve in the army, who have to fight to build up a modern industry, who still have to fight to build up a modern country, and a modern government, and a modern administration.

And then there is something else. We don't feel it sitting here in our garden—we have here several hundred scientists and their families living on the grounds. They live in little houses or apartments that belong to the Institute. But they have formed a big family, sharing interests, sharing responsibility, trying to be of help to one another. So in this respect, it's a remarkable place.

LHC: Ephraim, any problem between religion and science in Israel?

EK: I would say very little. You know, we have this joke that when a non-religious scientist carries out an experiment in the lab, he addresses the Almighty, and he says, "Look Almighty, I'm going to carry out an experiment. I don't want you to help me, but for God's sake, don't interfere with my experiment! Allow me to carry it out as I want to!"

The religious people, they say, "Look, the Almighty has created everything that we have around. He has given us this benefit of having the possibility to learn what he has created! We have the scientific method, which is a powerful method. Let's use it to understand the wonders of the Almighty!"

I'm not a religious man, but the more I learn about life—the complexity, the wisdom—I wonder, can one have a very simple explanation? Maybe not! Because it's unbelievable, complex, beautiful, and interesting. So in this respect, no I don't think there is a conflict.

LHC: The Israeli people are currently getting a tremendous influx of Russian immigration, and especially scientific personnel. Do you think they bode a great future for Israel?

EK: I hope so, indeed. We hope that in several years, if this will continue, we will have almost a million Jews coming from Russia! First of all, their quality and standing—it's rather high. Some of them have had an excellent education in good mathematics, in physics, in chemistry, even in the life sciences. They excel in music and art. They love poetry. It's a wonderful element in many ways. You have among them engineers, doctors, professionals. Some of them are really of interest, there is no doubt.

And when they come to us, they feel, "Now, we can really use our talent." So it's a remarkable opportunity. And it's a challenge. We have now, about four million people and if we add another million people, it will be a remarkable achievement. But it's a very serious obligation. We have to absorb them. We have to provide these families with housing, to allow them to have positions and to work and to have a salary. And as you have among them people who deserve high standing and quality of life, it's an enormous responsibility.

If we will be able to do it, and I hope we'll be able to do it with the support of the Jewish people from all over the world, on the one hand, with the help of the United States and perhaps other countries who are interested, and who see the problem. For me personally, it's of enormous satisfaction. Because when I and many of my friends, we fought for the establishment of the State of Israel, quite a number of those boys and friends of mine, they were killed and wounded, and when I ask myself, "Why did they do it?" My feeling is, because they wanted to have one place in this world that would be a real home for the Jewish people.

The Jews, if they want to go home, they'll have a home. At least one place. And we dreamt of a State and a country which will distinguish itself by its highest qualities—morals, ethics, social life. The utilization of modern science and technology in the best possible way. They can help us to do it.

You know I am often asked by our good friends, "What do you want? Zionism is dead. We already have a State. What do you want?" But if you look at the dream of the leaders of Zionism, it's not true that they wanted only a state. They wanted a state that would be an example state, an outstanding state. And this is what we are doing.

As a chemist with all my love for Israel, I look at Israel as a pilot plant—a state pilot plant. We make experiments. Will we be successful in showing the world what one can do with this element of people? With ability, dedication, and love for a country? I hope we'll be successful.

LHC: I went to a meeting with Ezer Weizman in Atlanta, Georgia, and he got up and he addressed the group and he said, "You people are not Zionists, you're pro-Zionists. A Zionist is a person who lives in Israel. Is that correct?"

EK: Well, I understand this desire that every Zionist should come and live in Israel. But we understand that it's not practical. And many people who feel very warmly towards Israel, who have relatives who have undertaken various activities, helping the Institution, in many ways they identify themselves with Israel, nevertheless, they don't live in Israel, physically. Quite a number of such people have apartments, houses. Most of the year they live outside. I wouldn't make such a sharp distinction, that a Zionist is only a man who wants to live, or lives already in Israel. I would say now that the broader kind of definition is the one which appeals to me: people who identify themselves with Israel, who support the development of Israel, who participate in many activities. I would include them, really, within this category of Zionism.

I feel that one of the main aims of modern Zionism is to continue to help Israel to be a home for Jewish people from all over the world. Now for the new immigrants from Russia, but also to build the right state, that the Jewish people will be proud of. This is where Jews who live in many countries all over the world, can be of enormous help. So I wouldn't exclude them from this group of Zionists.

LHC: World events in the last two weeks have put Israel unfortunately, on the map again in terms of the press and the United Nations, etc., you've been through this since 1948. You've seen a lot of response, with respect to this. What do you feel is really going on now? What's happening?

EK: Of course I'm very very sad about what has happened. I grieve with every family who has lost its beloved son, or a father, or a child. We want to have the possibility of praying at the Temple Mount without any disturbances. We don't want Palestinian Arabs to throw stones at anybody, and certainly not at people who are praying. But I was very sad that the police force, the military forces that were there, took the step that they took without really knowing the details. It's now under investigation. Were they threatened, as far as their lives go, did they have no choice? It was certainly a very sad occasion, there is no doubt.

What is perhaps most unpleasant and serious, that as a result of all these activities, hatred between Palestinian Arabs and Jews in Jerusalem is being built up. Whereas the hope of the Mayor of our Jerusalem is that it will be a united city. That not only will people be able to move from one place to another, but people will cooperate, will help one another, in trade, in education. Unfortunately, such events don't help to build this up. I hope that finally the Palestinian Arabs will be able to build a leadership that is more advanced and more liberal, and more moderate, and that they will understand you cannot wipe out Israel.

In my opinion, Palestinian Arabs in the West Bank and in Gaza are entitled to autonomy. They should build up their economic life, their own education, and their own cultural life. They should not threaten the existence of the State of Israel, but they are entitled to have independence. I feel that the time is right, that the Arab leaders and the Arab countries around will understand our problem.

If you are weak, people will exploit you, but not if you come to negotiate in a sensible, intelligent way. This is why we had to build up our strength, our economic strength, our social strength, our agriculture, and our defense. I was involved in helping to build up research in defense, and I used to tell my friends, "Look, as a scientist, for me biophysics is the most important thing. But I realized that if you want to carry out research in biophysics, you'd better stay alive! This is why I spent many years helping in the defense of Israel. I was the chief scientist of the Ministry of Defense during the Six Day War. And I don't regret it. It helps us now to carry out biophysics and biochemistry!

So I hope that the Palestinian Arabs, and I hope also the neighboring Arab countries, will understand that the time for really modern wars has passed. Let's negotiate and talk in a sensible way. We should have our leaders also talk sense.

LHC: We're going to close the program on a hopeful note, that science can bring the world together, and I'm going to give you some encouraging words. I just returned from Bahrain and people who are very high in the government there, with the Emir, told me that they would like to trade scientific help and data with the State of

Israel. I've said it publicly on television. So maybe it's the beginning of a new beginning.

EK: Of course we'd be delighted to cooperate, to help with our knowledge, to exchange ideas, and to work together. It will be one of the most wonderful achievements that one can have!

LHC: Everything is possible.

Katzir was prophetic at the time of the interview. He said he was against direct election of the prime minister. The country paid no heed and passed such a law. Rabin, Netanyahu, and Barak were elected but not one lasted more than two years in office. Direct elections were reverted in March, 2001.

MORDECHAI**GUR**

Mordechai Gur, former chief of the Israeli Defense Force and Labor Party member of the Knesset. The interview took place on the 18th day of the Gulf War. He discussed Saddam's military policy and Israel's reaction to scud missile attacks. He talked about his work as a children's book author as well as his policy of restraint with the Palestinians.

LHC: Motta, militarily, was it the right move to restrain the government?

MG: I believe so. At least, that's what I recommended to the government. I thought that that should be the policy of the government, because we had to prove that this was not our war at all. We should go to the maximum to stay out of it, and as a matter of fact, the first week of our restraint brought a lot of advantages to Israel, both on the political side and for security. So for about ten days it was okay.

LHC: The Israelis are known to have terrific intelligence. Did the Army expect that Saddam Hussein was this strong?

MG: We knew quite well, not only that he was relatively strong, but objectively, he has great military power. That does not mean that it's a very effective power. So we knew, especially when we followed him in the war with Iran. He created more and more divisions and he got more and more weapons of all kinds. The fact that we bombed his nuclear reactor in 1981 proved that we were very much concerned with what he might do. Yes, we were ready for that.

Mordechai Gur,
former chief of staff

LHC: Did you agree with that bombing in '81? I know that Shimon Peres opposed it. At that time he was leader of the Labor party.

MG: We were not sure that the government had really done the maximum in order to prevent that by political moves. We thought that any military action connected with nuclear power is relatively dangerous, and we did not want to be the first to do something of that kind.

But in retrospect, we know that first of all, political efforts were made, and unfortunately were not effective. So I believe that the government decision was very right, was very good. Anyhow, we proved that we were very concerned with the Iraqi armed forces.

We believed, when I was still Chief of Staff, that they might send a body of about five to seven divisions [approximately 60,000 to 100,000 combat troops] to future fights in Israel to combine forces with the Syrians and Jordanians. And we have built very specific means in order to face them. So, yes, I believe that we knew that the Iraqis were powerful.

I think that what surprised most of us was that after the war with Iran, he would dare to contradict the world and do something like the invasion of Kuwait, and up to the last moment, when he still had the chance to move back, to face a war of that kind. I believe that he made a big mistake.

LHC: The United States counts sorties. Every time an airplane goes up they consider it a sortie. In the Israeli Defense Forces, I believe you count hits. Am I correct or incorrect?

MG: It's in between. You know, Air Force people all over the world count sorties. When they see the bomb explode, they believe that they've done it. I remember these discussions when we were young paratroopers and they were young Air Force people. The discussion still goes on.

That's why the general philosophy of the Israeli Armed Forces is that for our conditions, especially when we have a very short political time in every war—because as you know, whenever we start succeeding, somebody will stop us—so we have to achieve a decisive victory very fast. That can be achieved only by a combination of air activity and ground activity. But, the United States is a big power. They think, and maybe they're right, that they have all the time in the world, and they can hit again and again with the air force.

LHC: There are people in the world who think that Israel has this magnificent, invincible army and that had Israel been attacked by Iraq, and not Iraq going into Kuwait, Israel might have been able to take care of Iraq more rapidly than the United States. Do you think that's a fallacious argument?

MG: No, I believe it's true. First of all, I don't believe that we would have gone to fight in Iraq.

LHC: But if Iraq attacked you—

MG: Assuming that they would have sent a substantial military power against us, no doubt that our strategy would have been entirely different, to smash them as fast as possible. And in the days before the war started in Kuwait, it was my proposal, and I made it known, and I still think that in a certain way, Americans will be able to prove that, that the big Iraqi force in Kuwait is a big bluff.

I mean, they have a lot of forces. They have a lot of infantry and a lot of tanks and so on. That does not mean, as I said before that these forces are very effective. I believe that once powerful highly motivated ground forces attack them, and stabilize them, then the American Air Force will be able to smash them, really, as we did in 1956 and 1967 and in the second part of 1973, which proves that this is a working strategy. I'm talking about the Middle East.

No doubt, that if we had to do the job against Iraqi forces, we would have done it in an entirely different strategy. An airstrike, but an immediate attack on the ground in order to smash them, as I said to stabilize them, and force them to move. Once they move, the Air Force is very capable.

LHC: Henry Kissinger predicted the war in the Middle East would last fourteen days. It's now in the eighteenth day, so obviously he's not a prophet. Your prediction: how long can this war last?

MG: That depends mainly on the appreciation of the political development, mainly among the Arabs. There is no sign of any break in the Arab countries that are members of the Coalition. There are demonstrations in far away countries, like Morocco and others. This is the main constraint for the President—to what extent will the Arabs continue to fight with him. As long as he believes that the coalition can hold, I believe that they will continue with the air bombardment.

They find it working, they find it successful, and if they believe that it might save casualties, they think it's a good strategy. By the way, it's not only a lesson from Vietnam, the wish to save casualties. Whenever you fight a war that is not a war of survival, you have to be very careful. When we have to fight terrorists, for example, this was always one of the major calculations because whenever you have to compare strategies, saving lives becomes a major element in your calculations. So I believe that as an American, as a human being, as a President, his calculation is very correct. So he will have to examine almost daily the reaction of the Arab world and the success of the air bombardment. If he can combine these two elements for quite a long time, I believe that they will continue bombardment and maybe they are doing the right thing.

LHC: The Scud attacks on Israel. Are they having any real effect on the population psychologically?

MG: Until now, no real effect. Psychologically, very much. First of all, the damage has been done. It just comes out of the black skies—

nobody knows when. And people are concerned. But I would say that people mainly are concerned because of the prospect of chemical warfare. This has become something very terrifying. Because people don't know what it really is. Nobody knows. And when you don't know, you're afraid. So, no doubt, the Scuds have initiated in Israel a certain new kind of fear and concern, which was never there before, and only when the war is over, maybe we will be able to analyze what effect it will have on our future strategy and national stability.

I believe that the effect will not be very substantial, but there will be certain effects. I can judge it from the people I know, and the effect it has on political decisions. So it is a new dimension, and a very negative one, no doubt about it.

LHC: How does it feel to have American soldiers on Israeli soil, in a sense, defending Israel?

MG: To see American soldiers here is not so bad. We have seen a lot of British, Australians, during the years. But the fact that they have to participate in our defense, this is something we don't like very much. It was always against our basic doctrine, and I hope it will be over very soon and our troops will be able to replace them. Still, I believe that because of the sudden changes in the war and some of the surprises by Saddam Hussein, nobody takes it seriously as a real participation of America in the defense of Israel. Everybody understands that it became a necessity, but not a strategy.

So talking to Israelis, they don't feel that suddenly we became dependent on the United States. The reactions from the world are not such that they feel that we became dependent. I think that the major importance of the question you have presented is that if we come back with a policy of restraint. The fact that we did not react, and the Arabs are used to it that we do, and the fact that some so-called experts all over the world started to analyze whether we can do something or we cannot. The fact that there was a question of whether we can do better than the Americans, that had a very bad effect.

That's why I thought that after the seventh missile attack on Israel, we should initiate our activity and we should try to pre-empt and strike the missile sites before they start shooting, if they have chemical warheads. Because you know, if we are talking about the deterrents, the importance of Israeli Defense Forces, you never know when you lose it and how much you are going to pay for it. So this is something that you have to make sure exists all the time on a permanent basis. I still believe that we have the right, and the government has to choose the right moment—of course, the right strategy—to hit the Iraqis directly by Israel.

LHC: The war ends; Palestinian issues still remain. How do you solve it?

MG: That's a very good question, because this is a question that nobody has an answer to. We know that we have to solve this problem. We know that we have both people and we have to establish a basis for co-existence. I was born in Jerusalem. I've known the problem since birth. That's why I say that it is very difficult to find a solution because somehow every few years, war comes up and prevents a logical solution to the problem.

There is a difference in approach by the two cultures. We came, most of us, from a world, from a civilization of logic. Most of the Arab countries base their attitudes on emotion. Always, when a certain deep question comes up, we would try to solve it in a logical way, and they become very emotional, like now. All the Palestinians supported Saddam Hussein. Not because Saddam Hussein did anything for the Palestinians, just that they were really hoping that a certain Moslem messiah would come; he would solve everything, and Israel would just disappear. That is the basic hope they have.

Now you imagine the Israelis, when we see them expressing themselves in that way, we say, "What the hell? How can you negotiate? How can you make any deal with people that openly and explicitly wish our disappearance?" This is a continuous process, and this is why it's so difficult to solve.

Because it's easy for me to say, "No more PLO. No more of

these leaders that supported Saddam Hussein." So who will be the representative of these Palestinians? This is their problem. To choose once and for all leadership that will be able to negotiate openly and willingly, understanding that there should be a compromise and concessions on both sides; a certain mutual approach, but honest. If I tell you that right now I see how this is going to happen, I would be lying to you. I know that the PLO is a factor. Their support of Saddam Hussein was just impossible for us. Whether they will be able to choose new leadership, I hope so. Because otherwise it will be an ongoing problem and we have suffered a lot, both sides, from that.

LHC: Well we know one thing for sure. The funding that they got out of Saudi Arabia, Bahrain, and the Emirate States will stop.

MG: That's why I differentiate. The PLO is over. I grew up in Jerusalem in the same quarter with Arabs. So it doesn't really depend on the leadership. It depends on the fact that we live together. We have to find a way to co-exist.

So leadership comes and leadership goes. Unfortunately until now, most of their leaders became very extreme in times of crisis. Then emotionally, it's impossible for both sides to sit together and negotiate. So we'll have to wait sometime after the dust has settled when the war is over, to see to what extent the Palestinians— mostly those who live with us in Judea, Samaria, and Gaza—can really finally create a sentiment, a basis for mutual understanding and co-existence.

I believe, knowing most of the Israelis, that once we feel that this is possible, it's an ongoing process among the Arabs, the approach in Israel would be very positive. Because people are very tired of the conflict and would like very much, and they understand logically, that it has to be established on a basis of compromise and concession. But they want to be sure that we will be safe. That's a very complicated issue.

LHC: One of your ex-Generals, Mr. Ghandi, who heads the Moledet Party, whose Party stands for the eviction, transfer, of all Arabs from the state of Israel was voted into the government as a Minister. What's your reaction?

MG: Big mistake. First of all, of course I don't like the idea of this transfer. Not that it hasn't happened in the world. The last few years, a lot of Bulgarians, for example, were chased from Bulgaria to go to other places, nobody moved. I believe this is the latest example of it happening in the world. But it cannot happen here.

When we are talking about the Jewish State, when we are talking about the Jewish State that will be based on the Jewish tradition, approach, attitude to human beings, and so on, it's just impossible for us to accept such a policy.

So this is a basic approach to that movement and to the people who represent it. So this is a big mistake. But I believe that the Prime Minister made a big political mistake right now. Because as a result of our policy, this war, we have gained a lot, both in Europe and the United States.

LHC: Public relations.

MG: Public relations, yes. I call it political gain. I believe, for example, that no president of the United States, knowing that the PLO supported Saddam Hussein, would try to force us to talk to the PLO. By the way, the French admit that openly right now. So I'm talking about real political gains for the future.

So how come that exactly at this point, he has to introduce a movement like that to the government that will have very negative reactions all over, and unfortunately justified reaction, so he made a basic mistake, a moral mistake, and a political mistake. We'll just have to minimize that damage.

LHC: A senior Likud official told me yesterday that all the gains that were made by the policy of restraint and all the goodwill that was established and the political gains that were established could go a hundred and eighty degrees from where they were because of this. Yet we know that Prime Minister Shamir is a very clever man. There must be something underneath this all. The timing was either very clever politically internally or very foolish politically externally. Does anybody understand why he did this? Is there any opinion as to why he did it politically now?

MG: You know, I've done many military and political assessments in my life, and sometimes you look too deep into the problem and the answer is very clear and superficial. If you ask me, I believe it was just a big mistake in judgement.

Shamir is very good at patience and waiting, and not doing anything. It so happened that the policy of restraint fit him very well. You wait and see. He has this problem of domestic politics, and one of his ministers proposes to do that right now, because domestically it might happen. And Shamir, like in many other cases in the past, he said okay, let's do it. Without really understanding all the implications of what he did.

If you ask me, this is a simple answer to that very stupid decision because otherwise it couldn't be so difficult to tell the religious parties of Israel to wait two weeks, wait three weeks, until the whole war is over, and then we can do it easily. What will happen? So in my view, it's only misjudgment and misunderstanding of all the implications. I just hope that it will be understood that way and not give any political implication to the influence that Ghandi, that that movement of transfer, will have on the government. But it was a mistake.

LHC: The future of Israel—we saw your grandchildren here, and everybody looks exuberant and happy and fifteen or twenty years from now, they might be people who don't live in this country. How would you feel about that?

MG: Very bad. If that would be the situation, that would be very bad. I hope this will not be the case. Until now, I have to thank God and, my wife and myself, that all the four kids not only live around us, very close, but are willing to live here and are working very hard here. So basically, I believe that there is a very good chance that they will stay.

You know, we are now in a time of war, but the really very important issue that we face today is immigration from the Soviet

Union, hoping that it will continue. This is the major issue. As long as people who live here realize that we have also a mission to accomplish as Jews, as Zionists. I don't believe that, at least in my family, that we will have problems of that kind and knowing most of the Israelis, I believe that this will become the major effect in their behavior.

Concerning the war, I have to tell you that after all, the Iraqi forces are being destroyed and smashed and we are not fighting. For people who have fought so much, this is a very big advantage. So we are concerned, as you see, because we are all going when there is an alarm, but after all, nobody of ours is fighting.

So I believe that if we put everything together and if the Americans really become victorious in that war, the fact that Jews are still coming, pouring, in huge numbers, and we have to absorb them and we have to think about how to deal with them, and to deal with the other present problems, I believe that Israel with six million Jews would be a much better place to live in.

LHC: Politically speaking, and lets look at the world map which I'm sure you do all the time, did you think a year ago that Russia would be where it is today? I should not say Russia, I should say Soviet Union—there's a big difference between Russia and the Soviet Union. Very few people understand that. Boris Yeltsin is running Russia, Gorbachev, hopefully, is running the Soviet Union. But it has changed, the concept of East vs. West. We now have Lech Walesa as the president of Poland, which a year ago none of us would have believed. Czechoslovakia is free. Yugoslavia is free. What's going on, in your opinion?

MG: First of all, it's a fact, I believe, that most people did not, maybe even could not, foresee such a development. The problem with countries like dictatorships—and the Soviet Union is a dictatorship and was a dictatorship—you deal with one man. And it's very difficult to follow what he is really going to do. Mainly, I'm not so sure that he knew right from the beginning what might be the outcome of what he started to do. But no doubt there is a basic change. You can see that I am not very open in my expression about this, because I don't know yet—I don't think anybody knows—what we still have in the future of the Soviet Union, of Russia, and Eastern Europe at large. We have had the revolution. Now it's over.

I believe that unfortunately some of the very old struggles between the different countries there and the people there will come up again. Some relatives of ours who lived there and came here only lately, have the feeling that Gorbachev is finished. Gorbachev's revolution is over, and that there will be—as a matter of fact, it's already going on—a counterrevolution by the KGB and the military power. So I believe it's too early yet to decide what really will be the outcome of, let's say, the Gorbachev revolution.

In the Middle East, unfortunately, this is not going to have any immediate effect, because in the Middle East we have a very strong Islamic movement, that frightened Gorbachev very much, when it appeared in his southern republics. So for us in Israel, we would like very much to participate in the beginning of the anti-Soviet revolution, let's say the democratic revolution.

But we have our handicap here in the Middle East, because the Arabs are not going to follow that path and the Islamic people are very much against it. So we are caught in the middle. We would like, as part of Western civilization, to take part in it, to feel as if we can behave as part of it. But our neighbors, and their reactions are exactly the opposite. So I have to tell you that many Israelis feel very ambivalent about it, because emotionally we are there, logically we know that we have to be very careful.

In that respect, the Jewish immigration brought a huge relief. Because here is something we are fighting for, something we would like very much. It presents a lot of difficulties, but it gives some chance and meaning to our life. So for a while you forget what happens in Europe and the Arab world, you deal really with what you have to deal with.

LHC: General Paz told me that Mordechai Gur is a children's story writer. You are a military tactician, a brilliant military soldier—how do the two jive?

MG: First of all, you have to have kids. We have four kids, and I started to write the stories as a matter of fact, as a result of the Israeli-Palestinian conflict. Because immediately after the Six Day War I was governor of the Gaza Strip, extremely busy chasing terrorists, and one evening I came home, I told my wife Rita about a certain operation mentioning helicopters and mines. The next morning she calls me and she said that the first words of our youngest daughter at the time, fourteen months old, were "Father, helicopters, mines." So that evening we were sitting and discussing how we could bring up normal children that at the age of fourteen months already speak about helicopters and mines. So I thought that the best combination would be if I, when I put them to bed, tell them stories combined from real life and moral lessons and imagination. Instead of reading them stories, I started telling them stories, in which I put my own experiences. I don't like James Bond, so, my James Bond I decided to make a dog. Because kids don't identify with a dog, where they might be willing to identify with a James Bond, and I don't believe in it. So the dog is the hero, and I put together my experiences, as I said, and a lot of imagination and human behavior. And then some of our friends heard this and suggested that we publish them, and that's what we did. The fact is that it immediately became a bestseller because it hit right to the target.

I once had a discussion in one of the kibbutzim in the north with a few kids because I started to write another series of stories with more imagination, and the kids said to me, "Stop it. Your first stories were very good because you treated us very seriously, and we felt that you told the truth and we can trust whatever you describe." So the message was to the point, and made me realize that in human behavior, Jews and Arabs, there has to be a way of coexistence, without one's superiority over the other.

Of course, I explained that our cause was very just, but the Arabs are human beings and they have to be treated that way. So I can tell you right now that one of those kids is now twenty-five years old, and she's a very nice lady. So that's how I started to write the stories and went on writing them.

LHC: Mordechai, that proves that you have an eclectic personality. The thing that I most remember about you, Mordechai, is that you said to me, "Leon, there's the possibility that I might be the prime minister of Israel one day." Do you still feel that way?

MG: I believe so. You know, when you serve in the military, they say that every soldier has the martial stick in his hand. When you get into politics, you have either the president or the prime minister stick in your hand. There's no doubt that what I have realized since then is that politics is much more complicated than the military. In the military, I knew that if I excelled on the battlefield, and if I didn't die on the way I'd have a good chance. In politics, this is not the issue at all. It depends on so many other elements that you do not control. Like changes of moods in public opinion, national feelings, changes in the world that are opposed to your basic beliefs.

For example, I am a Socialist. I was brought up as a Socialist. It's a fact that in the last ten or fifteen years Socialism is in crisis, all over the world. Right now, with Gorbachev's revolution, Communism is totally out, and Socialism is in big trouble. In the United States, Reagan, in the United Kingdom, Thatcher—so in Israel this has had a huge effect. If you put together all these changes, it's very difficult to say today to what extent my Labor party will be able to come back to power. Add to that the fact that religious notions are being strengthened all over the world and in Israel, too. A Socialist Party like my Party, to a certain extent, was anti-religious, which was a big mistake, because it was never really anti-religious. Some people behaved that way, and the feeling now in Israel is that more people identify to a certain extent with a need of a certain touch of religion.

When we liberated Jerusalem in '67, I got first to the Temple Mount. And for me, that was the top achievement of my life. The Temple Mount, and not the Wailing Wall. Because there, on this hill, was the temple. When Eli Wiezel interviewed me, the first question he asked me, "What was your religious feeling when you got there to the Temple Mount?" And I said to him, "Listen, I was never religious. For me, the Temple Mount is the combination of practically everything: of religion, of tradition, of kingdom, of sovereignty, of freedom. But unfortunately, some people translated my Socialist approach as anti-religious. This is another difficulty that my party has today. So dealing with politics, it's much more complicated to foresee what might happen. But I still believe that first of all, we should come back to power, and if this happens, I might try.

Mordechai Gur was Chief of Staff during the Camp David meetings. He was originally opposed to the Egyptian peace treaty but eventually endorsed it. He believed that he would become the popular choice to be future prime minister but his career faulted dramatically. He believed that coexistence with the Arabs was the only answer for Israel.

YAEL**DAYAN**

Yael Dayan is the daughter of Moishe Dayan and the niece of Ezer Weizman. Post Gulf War, she favors a "land for peace" settlement with the PLO.

LHC: I shared some time with your father, Moishe Dayan, and with your uncle, Ezer Weizman, during the Camp David period when I was working with President Carter, and all of us worked arduously to put this thing together. Was it worth it?

YD: What a question. It was the greatest breakthrough in the history of the Israeli–Arab conflict, and the only one so far. I think the Camp David Accords offered guidelines, unfortunately not to Israel, but to the Arab countries. They know that they cannot beat Israel in a war, they know that there isn't a military option, and that the only way to get anything out of Israel is by negotiations. Only while before, we were willing and they were refuseniks, it's the contrary now. We have a refusenik government, but we have a peace-wanting public on the whole. And the thing is to translate this desire for peace into ballots.

LHC: Do you think that the polls here show that most people want peace?

YD: Not only that they want peace. Everybody wants peace. The question is what price to pay for peace. Most of the people understand that the only way to acquire peace is by giving up territories. People are not stupid.

LHC: Most people?

YD: Most people. Seventy percent, 75 percent.

LHC: Really?

YD: Recent polls. Post-Gulf War polls.

LHC: So how does Shamir stay in power?

YD: People have the illusion that because it is so clear that no other peace is possible, they are sure that he, too, will come around to doing it, or that the Likud will come around to doing it. And then they think, well, that he will drive a harder bargain, he will make it difficult, he will not sell out beforehand. But when you tell people that the Likud truly will not budge an inch, they don't believe you. They say, in this case, how come they say they want peace?

LHC: If you go down memory lane, Menachem Begin chose a man called Moshe Dayan as his Foreign Minster, and people at that time thought that Begin was not a peace-loving person, either. Yet, he transformed the whole country.

YD: He transformed it, but I think it's a big mistake to compare the Israeli–Egyptian scene to the West Bank and Gaza situation. Because Begin was not enthusiastic about giving up Sinai, and he didn't have the majority for it in his own party even then. But it was very clear that he was not going to carry it one step further. That was it. That is his contribution to the history of peace-making in the world. He got half a Nobel for it, and he rests over it. The same goes for Shamir. It's not tactics. He really and deeply believes in a greater Israel. Someone else in the Likud may do it, but Shamir himself will not for one minute agree to any Arab or any sovereignty other than Israeli between the Mediterranean and the [Jordan] River.

LHC: Your uncle, Ezer Weizman, espouses the idea that there should be direct talks with the PLO. Do you feel the same?

YD: I would talk to anybody. You know, by now, if this is an obstacle, that is, if the government would talk to somebody else and not the PLO, I would go ahead with it. They don't want to talk to [U.S. Secretary of State James] Baker. I mean, it's a long way for the Likud government to agree to talk. They don't want to talk to [Egyptian President Hosni] Mubarak about things that have to do with concessions. So I don't think it's whom you speak to, it's what you speak about. Because they've got nothing to say to Arafat. It's not, let's say, okay, they'll agree to speak to the PLO. They've got absolutely nothing that's even remotely acceptable to offer.

LHC: So what's going to happen? War?

YD: It's either war or it's impose the peace process. The very initial beginning of it will make the biggest difference. The thing is to really make whatever government just do the first step without promising anything further. The Arabs have to understand that they cannot extract from Shamir, or from any Likud government, the bottom line: a Palestine.

        They shouldn't opt for it and they should have guarantees for it from anybody else but the Israeli government. The minute it begins, this government is not going to hold. The minute people see that it's a reality, that it can happen, that it's something that is possible, that we're not doomed to war after war, people will just get rid of this government.

LHC: Are you hopeful that this will happen rather quickly or do you think it's a really long process?

YD: We thought that the last war accelerated the process, but it did not.

LHC: You mean the Gulf War?

YD: Yes, the Gulf War. It did not, unfortunately. Because things were not done speedily. Baker was too gentle with everybody, gave everybody a long rope and a lot of time, and there wasn't this post-war momentum that could have happened. I still think that within a year we'll either see the beginning of a peace process or we'll see another war. We have the problem with the U.S. elections, of course.

LHC: You see war with Syria?

YD: We see war with Syria, we see war with some kind of cut-off from
       the Egyptians, we see some kind of combination, either from
       Lebanon.... If the peace option disappears, the military option will
       become evident. It may not be a total war in the Iraqi sense. It
       may be just more terrorism, more Intifada, less security, complete
       restlessness in the area. That's war, in basic terms.

LHC: When you were growing up, did you believe that forty-three years
       after the independence of Israel it would be in such a state?

YD: No, but I didn't believe that there would be a '67, either. When I
       was growing up, and when I was in the army, I thought of the pre-
       vious borders as set, and that the day would come when the Arabs
       would understand that it would be to their advantage to live in
       peace with us. I didn't foresee '67, and '67 really caused this rather
       hopeless deadlock. But I'm not a pessimist. I don't think another
       forty-three years will go by and we'll be in the same situation,
       because this is really an impossibility.

LHC: The world knows that your father was a great soldier and later on
       a great statesman. If he were living today, what do you think he'd
       be saying?

YD: I don't know. I think he was such an original and such a noncon-
       formist that it's impossible to predict what Dayan would have said.
       I know one thing: he had a constant and very positive dialogue
       with the Palestinians, with the terrorists, with the PLO. And it
       was nonstop. He didn't really need mediators. He had a language
       with them. Whether it was in battle or in peacemaking, he could
       reach an understanding with them.

       I know another thing. He had great respect for the Arabs. For
       the Palestinians, mostly. He had respect for them as human beings,
       as a culture deeply rooted in the area. He did not for one minute
       think of them as deprived of the basic human rights or rights of
       determination. And he was a believer in peace. I think Camp David
       showed it. He was not tied to any dogmas. He was flexible. He
       was absolutely pragmatic. And I think he would have seized the
       opportunity we have now with both hands.

LHC: Yael, did you make a run for the Knesset, or are you trying?

YD: I'm going to next time we have elections. Unless it's advanced, we have elections in November of '92. If my Labor party chooses to put me on its list, which is a battle of its own, I will run for the Knesset.

LHC: What about this business of direct election in primaries? I know Rabin, the former prime minister, is pushing for, in a sense, primaries like in the United States. Can it happen?

YD: We all do. We are pushing for primaries in the whole country for the elections of the prime minister and we are pushing stronger for primaries inside the party. It's absolutely impossible to conceive that twelve hundred people who are on the payroll of the government in one way or another are going to elect the list of representatives of the Knesset. We want every member and more, for more open primaries, every party member, and people who even vaguely identify with the party, to come and elect our list. That's more or less my only chance to win a seat.

LHC: Let's talk about old Turks and Young Turks. The old Turks today have to be Rabin and Peres. I saw in the newspaper, and I spoke with Rabin, that he's going to challenge Peres for the leadership of the party. Is this destructive again? Don't you splinter your party? It seems to be so splintered as it is.

YD: The party is splintered ideologically, which is fine, because it's a legitimate fight between hopes and doubts. The splintered leadership is terrible. As far as I'm concerned, they both have to go. They've done their bit, they'll go down in history in a very nice way. They're great contributors to Israel but it's time to give room to at least two generations, who are waiting.

LHC: Who are the Young Turks of the Labor Party?

YD: We have a good group. We have Chaim Ramon, Uzi Baram, Yossi Beislin, myself, although I'm not in the Knesset now. I think we've got some good people from kibbutzim. I think we can form a good group of seven or eight people my age and younger who can really put up a good fight and give a good show.

LHC: How would you go about the peace process?

YD: I would go for a very careful peace process. Careful in that I really

don't believe that you can do things overnight. There should be
an interim arrangement. There should be a period of autonomy.
There should be confidence building. But we should get the hell
out of there as quickly as we can, with the army.

Settlements, of course, should stop, and many of them will
have to be dismantled anyway. I would go into all the advantages
that peace gives you: original development, the correct uses of
water and land, and just go into the positive. This area can be fan-
tastic. What's more, we cannot do the national things we have to,
like the absorption of immigrants, unless we have peace and unless
we have the advantages of peace.

LHC: Let's talk about the immigrants. Russians are coming in by the
planeload. How is that going to change the country? You've got
an electorate here of about half a million people, am I correct?

YD: Not half a million voters. Probably they would represent ten seats
at the most. If they all go to vote.

LHC: That's enough to move a government.

YD: Yes, but the Arabs who don't vote heavily, Israeli Arabs, also represent even more, and they don't switch this number. They divide
themselves among existing parties, mostly, and I don't believe that
they will run as a Russian or Soviet Jewish Party.

The tendency to think that they will all vote right wing is
wrong, too. Because absorption is not a great success story, and
it's not voting for the hand that feeds you. This hand, this Likud
hand, has fed them very poorly, has housed them very poorly.

They're not interested in the territories. You tell the Russians
that they are going to war in order to regain full dominance of
Jericho and Nablus, they don't want to hear these names at all.
They're not Zionists and they're not Revisionists. They're hardly
Jews. They want peace and quiet and they want to lead a rather
bourgeois comfortable life, which they will not get unless we have
a peace process and eventually peace.

LHC: So you don't believe that they're really going to shake up the political system?

YD: Not really.

LHC: They're too small to really form a group.

YD: They're too small. The one thing that may matter and be good for us is that the Russians will not vote for the ultra-orthodox. They will not add to the religious parties' power. So this will reduce the proportion in power of the religious parties, and this is very important for everybody. For the system, it's important.

LHC: There is no country in the world that has direct election of the prime minister. Are you aware of it?

YD: I am aware of it. Inside the Labor Party I was against it, because originally, it went together with other changes. There were three items: direct elections of the prime minister, changes of the electoral system altogether, and a constitution. Now, the direct election of the prime minister is the worst of the three things, and to do it alone, I'm afraid of it.

LHC: You are somebody who says, let's talk to anybody as long as we can get peace. Yael, what do you see for your children?

YD: Well, I hope that they will continue being enthusiastic Israelis by choice, and not because it's the only country they've got. That is, this country has offered my grandparents, my parents, and myself mere survival. We've got a place, we've got a country, we've got a flag, we've got a passport, we've got war from time to time, but we've got a homeland. We owe to our children something, a bonus over it, because they take for granted, all this, and we owe them equality. We owe them a quality of life, not life per se. We owe them a good country, we owe them a happy country, we owe them not only a peaceful country, but we owe them excellence. We owe them all the good potential that this country has. They would like to participate in implementing and fulfilling, but we have to make it possible for them.

LHC: Did the Scuds hitting Israel change the psychological feelings that exist amongst Israelis today? Did it change the macho image of the Israeli Defense Forces?

YD: I don't think so. Just where we are sitting now, I was sitting during alarms when I was not in the army, and this is not a sealed room, and I did not have a gas mask on. From my window I could see the Patriot battery. And if I saw them take off, I knew it was coming more or less our way.

So I told everybody to put their masks on. If they didn't come off during sirens, then we all sat and watched television. I think the trauma was limited to the time. I think it was highly exaggerated to think in terms of traumatizing the whole country, in terms of the Holocaust repeating, and so on.

I think it put a very clear red light in our system saying that excessive power will not be tolerated, occupation will not be tolerated, and there is a way to integrate into something that is larger than us, that is a new world order, and have the benefit of it. Be on the winning side. I think that the nature of the army was by consensus.

Of course, we could take off and be very proud of our pilots who were bombing the Scud sites. And then what? There will be another few funerals, and another few graves of the best and the youngest of us, and we wouldn't have changed the balance of this war. We would have gone down as someone who had spoiled a new kind of coalition that emerged in the Middle East.

LHC: Do you think the United States owes Israel a lot for taking these first hits?

YD: I don't know, owes. It owes Israel something that Israel doesn't want. It owes Israel some kind of speeding up of the peace process. This should be the thinking. "We again got you into a kind of war situation, and now we're going to pull you out of it and really reassure and guarantee a peace process." But that's one thing that the Israeli government doesn't seem to be enthusiastic about as a payoff for our tolerance and patience.

LHC: President Bush has implied that settlements should be frozen and not continued and although he says there is no quid pro quo for a guarantee of ten million dollars to aid Soviet immigrants, by implication, it seems to be there. Is that policy a positive step for

Israel or not? Many times when the United States rejects aid, it's positive for Israel.

YD: Yes, but I think Israelis cannot be the ones to encourage the rejection of aid. I really think here that the innocent will be hurt. I think we should fight the settlements tooth and nail. I think there should be political sanctions. I think it should be brought to the United Nations and to the Security Council. I think there should be every political pressure, not economic, every political pressure to stop the settlements and bring about some kind of move on the part of the government. I think the immigrants and the absorption process should get all the guarantees they want.

I really think the linkage—I respect and I understand why the U.S. is linking it. I think that it's losing the point. I think that the Congress, at the end, will probably give the guarantees. So we'll lose on both ends. They won't fight the settlements strongly enough and they'll give the guarantees. Shamir will come out as a winner.

LHC: Should American Jews be involved in Israeli foreign policy?

YD: They should be heard. They should sound, loud and clear, their opinions. I don't know what "involved" means. We involve them anyway.

LHC: I've seen times, when I was with President Carter, when American Jews would really try to get involved in cabinet decisions. I personally am against it, because if I don't spill my blood and pay your taxes and fight your wars, I think that if you call me and ask me for advice I should give it, but to go public and denounce and start to attack, I think that unless you're living here, that you shouldn't do it.

YD: But then it should work both ways. We cannot ask AIPAC [American Israel Public Affairs Committee] and we cannot ask the American Jewish community to be involved in Israeli politics, basically, when it sorts the government, but then when they have a different view, suddenly we say, "Don't get involved." We don't say to them, don't get involved when it comes to decisions which the government is interested in promoting. So they're not kept out of it. And then it becomes "Israel: right or wrong." I'm supportive of it, and I will go to the President and put on pressure, I, the American Jew. Then when there's something that really disturbs me about it, they tell me to shut up because you're not doing our fighting, so it's really a double standard kind of thing.

LHC: We've interviewed a few major military figures in this country, and they're all for peace. It's fascinating for me to see this, and yet it doesn't seem to get out to the public enough.

YD: Because the public was frightened on purpose. It's very difficult to uproot fear. The problem is fear. People are afraid. People are led to believe that the territories offer them security. From Rabin to Weizman, to everybody on the security map, they've been told that the territories are a burden to security and not an asset to security.

But it's very difficult to deal with human fears, especially Jewish human fears, with all the collective memories that go with it, and this is really the job that peace campaign activists are doing. To sort of deflate this terrible fear that most of the people have.

LHC: What's going on in the Soviet Union? What do you think?

YD: I think we'll see some worse periods before we see better, but it will never go back to where it was. I really think they'll still suffer a lot. The rest of the world will have to pump a lot of money in there. I think Japan, the United States, and Europe will have to take it seriously. If they want a different Russia, it's going to cost millions of millions. And it's worth it.

LHC: Yugoslavia? Romania? What's going on?

YD: They'll settle into some kind of federation. People are now drunk with this kind of self-determination. Latvia, Azerbaijan, Uzbekistan—it's endless. Every community that was formed in the nineteenth century, you can redivide into some kind of tribal components, and it's not going to work. Economically, it's not going to work. So I think it's going to settle on something in-between. Not five little nations put together, but three and two. They'll become federations, because survival today is a way you can feed your people, feed and educate your people. Nothing else matters.

LHC: Last question: united Germany. Any affect on Israel?

YD: Not really, but it's going to have a strong effect on Germany, and we're going, economically, to see the bad end of it. Germany, which was a leader of western Europe economically, is going to be exhausted by Eastern Germany. For a decade or twenty years, they're not going to be the leader that they were, and as such, we're not going to get the support we used to get.

But this is true about the European community altogether. They will have to take care of Eastern Europe, of the new countries in Eastern Europe, and they will not have any fringe benefits to distribute to other areas of the world. That's why the Middle East should start thinking in terms of the Middle East common market and original development.

Yael is currently a Labor Party member of the Knesset, left leaning. In 1991 she strongly believed that Rabin and Peres were finished. She also believed that despite the influx of Russian émigrés, they would not form their own party. She was wrong and their strength brought Benyamin Netanyahu to power. She thought Arafat might be reasonable but, despite Barak's allegedly giving in to 95% of the PLO terms, he was rebuffed.

EZER**WEIZMAN**

Ezer Weizman, nephew of Chaim Weizmann, Israel's first President. He is a former defense minister, former Labor Party Knesset member. He is considered the founder of the modern Israeli Air Force and became Israel's seventh president

LHC: Why did you resign, Ezer?

EW: If you come to the conclusion, and I did, that your contribution to what you put up as a task for yourself is not good enough, that you are not achieving a certain percentage of what you want, then you don't sit on your chair and warm your chair, you say good-bye and go, and then decide what to do. I got up last Monday—it was planned before—I said goodbye to the House of Representatives.

LHC: How do you feel?

EW: I feel fine. I wouldn't say that I like the situation where I don't have my fingers in the public pie. But I haven't had it for some time because of various currents, various reasons and various unreasons in the state of Israel.

LHC: It's paradoxical that you can feel fine and know that your country's in sad shape.

EW: Some people feel that the country's not in sad shape. But again, I came to a conclusion, and to a very difficult decision that just to sit on my backside and do nothing and not be able to influence is not good enough for me. All my life, in the fifty years of my adult life, I've reached for certain things and achieved part of it. Sometimes more, sometimes less.

Ezer Weizman,
former President of Israel

LHC: Something interesting happened. You had a conversation with Menachem Begin a couple weeks before you resigned—why?

EW: We've had the beginning of diplomatic relations with China. This began due to a certain decision, fourteen years ago, through the Ministry of Defense, when I was defense minister. And when everything was concluded over diplomatic relations, and everybody was taking credit, I thought despite the differences in opinion that I had with Menachem Begin, which was unfortunate, because after all he was instrumental in opening the talks with the Egyptians and signing the peace treaty. Then it deteriorated, to my point of view. But I think it was only fair to the old man, who has been sitting at home for the last nine years, to remind him and remind the people that due to certain very positive and difficult action as prime minister, the first shot was fired in that direction.

LHC: How did he react when you called him?

EW: He was very happy. I think he liked the idea that I reminded the people that he did something in that respect.

LHC: Ezer, there's rumors in the presidency is seeking you, or you're seeking the presidency—any truth to it?

EW: First of all, some people are seeking the presidency for me. I'm not seeking anything, and I don't know who seeks that. I know certain people and certain voices in the media who came up with this idea. I cannot be negative, because this is the top job, the top duty in Israel. It has no teeth to it, as a political *functionnaire*. I am going to wait until we see what happens in the elections in June and the formation of the government, etc.

I'll tell you one thing that my late uncle, who was the first president of the state of Israel used to say. He used to say that thank god he had a handkerchief, because it's the only place he's allowed to stick his nose into.

LHC: I don't think that the American people understand what the presidency is.

EW: It's ceremonial to a high degree. I think that you could add more teeth to it, but I wouldn't like to elaborate on that because I'm not actually in a position to describe the duties of the presidency. I knew the first president very well and I told you what his reaction to his duties were.

LHC: So for Chaim Weizmann, the first president of Israel, I guess it was tough to sit there in that position, after being an activist.

EW: Of course. People like us, that have been in action all our lives, my generation, in the army, in the Air Force, military action, and then in politics, for them to sit back in an official capacity. But sometimes you do certain things that you don't like.

LHC: Did you resign from the Labor Party?

EW: No. Not yet.

LHC: Why?

EW: Because I didn't want to link my public duty as a member of the Knesset and as a former minister and a former general in the armed services, and at the same time link it with my political party. I'll consider when and how and if to do that. And I don't think it's fair on the eve of elections to do that.

LHC: Any possibilities of coming back?

EW: I know the old saying of "Never say never in politics," but it's going to be very, very difficult for me to come back. I'll only say one thing that sounds very high-falluting: if the country ever needs me, I'm there.

LHC: Last week, when you resigned every major newspaper in Israel was carrying a great swan song for Ezer Weizman. The country loves Ezer Weizman. Again, it's a paradox: everybody loves you, and yet why doesn't the country vote for you?

EW: It is an interesting question that I ask myself. There are reasons. Everything has a reason, like in science. Everything can be analyzed and solutions found. The country is torn into various political parties. The country now, more than ever, is torn in the political solution necessary for the future of Israel. In other words, peace or war, and I say peace or war because if there is no peace there will be trouble: a big war, a small war, a two day war, a two month war, it's irrelevant. When the Intifada started five years ago, people said, "Pooh, it'll be over in no time." And it has it's ups and downs, but it's still there. You can't drive to the Western Bank like you did in the past.

But the actual solution, how to live with the Arabs, 150 million of them—we've been there a hundred and twenty years as new Zionism, new immigration. We have our roots going back thousands of years, the Arabs have claims to the country, and this has been a conflict for the last hundred years. An active conflict, wars, battles, skirmishes—we've lost about 17,000 Israelis killed in forty-two, forty-three years in direct battles with Arabs, be it Arab armies or Palestinians. I represent a solution, which I don't want to go into too much, territories, can you trust the Arabs, can you not trust the Arabs, is a peace with Egypt a real peace, a warm peace, a cold peace, a lukewarm peace—a hundred and one questions the Israelis ask. Basically because security and trust of the Arabs, and I can say trust of the *goyim*—people who are not Jews— one of the basic problems of Jews for hundreds of years is the distrust and the insecurities, and Israel was supposed to, and I hope to a certain degree it did, give them that security. The feeling now is that if we do certain things, and the way I think is that I'm willing to leave territories, part of the territories, I'm willing to trust the Arabs a little bit more than some people, with an army and an Air Force behind me.

This causes quite a lot of argument. I think, on the other hand, since I've been open about my view in the last ten or fifteen years, especially that there are new views to the way I was pictured—I was pictured as a hawk, an Air Force commander, a general, eating enemies for breakfast, raw. And I changed my point of view because the world had changed. Because Sadat changed a few things, because Begin changed a few things, because the world is changing.

Look at South Africa, look at Russia. The only one who hasn't changed yet is Castro. The rest of the world is changing. Cuba is the only one stuck out there, poor little thing, not changing. They'll change, too. They'll erupt. But look at what goes on in Europe, what goes on all over the world. So people respect the fact that I stand by my views and am constant in them and I don't shift and I don't dilly-dally, and I'm going in my direction, right or wrong. So on one hand they like it, and the way I say it and what I stand for and stood for. Not all of them like my solutions.

LHC: What's happening to the world, Ezer? Communism's going down. I sat with the Hungarian Ambassador last night, he told me that Austria, Hungary; everything's changing.

EW: There is one good thing about what is happening in the world. It's a world revolution. One of the most fundamental ones in the last hundred years.

LHC: Did you see it coming?

EW: Unfortunately, I saw the coming of the recession in the United States. And I talked to you, too, that we in Israel depend too much on the wealth of the United States and I'm taking it from an economic point of view, not from a political point of view. Because the United States will end up in big economic trouble—and I said it in '84, '85, '86—because the only thing you have to do is pick up the *New York Times* this morning and look at the business columns, and see that the three big ones, car manufacturers, lost seven billion dollars in the last few years. I don't think the Japanese lost that much. The fact is that the United States is going through one hell of a recession, but in a different world than the recessions of the '20s and the '30s that this country had.

What is happening now, you're quite right: Communism has collapsed, but capitalism is in a hell of a crisis, from an economic point of view. The world is going through a complete change now. It'll never be the same again. What we see now and what we saw two years ago will not be the same at the end of the century. The world will most likely have to find a different economic solution of balancing between private enterprise, basic capitalism, and wealth states. America will not be able to go forever with nine or ten million unemployed. Certain things federal governments and local governments will have to decide what they do as the basic benefits and welfare for the citizens of their country.

I see that the President—I think quite rightly—is talking about a new health system for a hundred billion dollars. I think he's right. Because a country that is as affluent as the United States cannot afford homelessness in the streets. Cannot afford so many unemployed. The federal government now is looking into the problem of what will happen with the $50 billion cut in defense. What will happen to the people who will be fired? There will be a federal scheme. This is already a little bit of a planned economy. The world will also have to balance the economy between countries. Mr. Bush went to Japan. He didn't just go there to visit Fujiyama. He went to talk business with them; not defense, but business. You buy cars, I buy cars. You buy radios, I buy radios. You television, I television. And this is the new conflict in the world.

The world has always been a world with conflicts on economic reasoning. But here we have something extremely interesting and a little bit frightening. Had it not been for atomic threats, an atomic umbrella—people talk about fifty or sixty thousand megatons, people don't realize what they're talking about. It's not a hand grenade. It's not a 155 millimeter shell. It's not even a missile. This is one hell of a disaster—and look back forty-six years ago, come August, at Hiroshima and Nagasaki. But since we've had an umbrella, an atomic umbrella, over the world, we haven't had any serious wars.

Because what is happening in the world today—economic recessions, Gulf problems, Europe changing—I would say, forty or fifty reasons for which, in the past, countries went to war with each other. I'm not talking about civil war locally. I think we will not have a war, but the battles will be economic, the battles will be how to live together, the battles will be how to cope with a world that today is 5.2 billion [people]. By the end of the century it will be six. In, I think twenty or twenty-five years it will be eight billion. What are we going to do about water resources, what are we doing about food, what are we going to do about unemployment—all these will have to be taken up by the states. I think that here, probably, the United Nations will have more to say than what they have up to now. Since the United States and Russia are not the superpowers anymore, they were—America sticks out more, because it has an army and Air Force and weapons, but it has a four trillion dollar debt, which is increasing at forty billion dollars a year in the balance of trade—this is just like bombs, this is just like shells, this can knock countries out without war. Since Russia is as she is, and Europe is as she is, it could be, and I think it will be, that people will come to the United Nations as an agency to take part in foreign problems.

For instance, Mr. Baker [the U.S. Secretary of State], quite rightly, and I don't know the man but I admire the way he did it, got the whole world through the United Nations to form the forces to fight, and the okay to fight, in the Gulf War. Regardless of how the people look on the Gulf War now, but from the point of view that the whole of the United Nations, practically 90 percent of it, was for what has been done, I think the writing is on the wall. Various other agencies and various other problems, it could be that the United Nations will have far more to say. To sum up what you asked me, the world is going through a quiet revolution, from a military point of view, but great, great changes, socially and from an economic point of view.

LHC: A year ago, Israel was being Scudded, and Desert Storm was in high throttle. What was the effect of that war on Israel and on the world?

EW: The war or the Scuds in Tel Aviv?

LHC: Scuds, first of all.

EW: If you made very good moves and you merged great companies, that is the bottom line. But I say again, and this is very important for the future: the organizing of such a force by the United States with the backing of the United Nations is the writing on the wall of the future. I'll come to that in a minute, because I have another idea about that for future forces like this to be used on world problems.

Scuds on us, I thought, and I said so openly in the Knesset, I said I'm willing to compromise on territories, and I'm willing to compromise on a solution with the Palestinians. But I think we should hit the Iraqis. Because a country that is hit by thirty-nine Scuds and depends on another country, be it the great United States, for it's defense, I think is a mistake. And we should have gone, and I think we could have coordinated with America, and struck at the core where we thought the Scuds came from. Even if the results were not 100 percent, and it's very seldom that you get 100 percent results in war—we got it in the Six Day War, but it's a one-time shot.

It had negative effects. I think for the Israelis in general, the scudding of Tel Aviv was writing on the wall that if we don't have peace, what a future war will most likely look like. And we got away with murder with thirty-nine Scuds, because you saw what happened when unfortunately the Scuds did hit, and U.S. military—twenty-eight boys were killed.

LHC: The problem with Soviet Jewry: is it a big problem?

EW: Yes.

LHC: Do you need a ten billion dollar guarantee from the United States?

EW: Look, the problem is a problem. First, we have four hundred thousand new immigrants, including Ethiopians. We have some fifty or sixty thousand Ethiopians. Both immigrant groups are completely different. You don't have musicians or you don't have engineers among the Ethiopians, because there were no universities in the bush where they came from. Eventually you will see, and you see already in Ben Gurion University and other universities, Ethiopian students. We have a few officers already serving in the army. It's a very interesting immigration. In a way, more interesting than the Russians, because the Russians are graduates of universities. They come from a culture very similar to ours. There is an affinity between our roots. Ethiopians are completely different. They're interesting, and in a way I think they have more difficulties in being absorbed than the Russians and in general.

Four hundred thousand immigrants added to a population of four million Israeli Jews and some 750,000 Arabs in Israel, which is the economic structure of Israel. Let's say five million. It's as if the United States would absorb in two years something like twenty million. Imagine this country having an influx of twenty million: Europeans, non-Europeans, Mexicans, Puerto Ricans, but twenty million into this country. Could you imagine what would happen here? We have managed in the past two years to construct buildings, not withstanding the controversy about the West Bank. Most of them don't live in the West Bank. Quite a few. For my political life, too many. But you don't see a homeless person in Israel. You don't see an immigrant family without an apartment. It could be that sometimes you see two families to an apartment. Sometimes you see a family in a very small apartment. But everyone has a roof over his head. The problem is employment.

Employment—you can't blow up an economy in a year, because an economy has to find markets. Who wants to buy shoes, who wants to buy high tech, who wants to buy textiles from Israel, who wants to buy agriculture? Then you work back and see whether you can construct the industry or the establishment to cater to this market. You can't just say, "We have to improve the economy." So it is a problem.

I believe that Israeli entrepreneurs and scientists and government officials—I'm critical of this government but you cannot cut it to pieces completely, because nobody predicted that we'd have 200,000 immigrants a year. The prediction was more like 20,000 a year. I was in Moscow two years ago, and our people said, 1,000 or 1,500 a month. Let's say 20,000 a year. If this was the prediction two years ago, it's now 10 times more than that. So could there be a few who will leave? I hope not. Basically this immigration is a great contribution for the citizens of Israel, in knowledge, in scientists, in musicians, and physicians, and general knowledgeable people. And also it will put some zip into the economy. The ten billion guarantee—I would say that Israel could tighten the belt and find a solution without it. I'm speaking for myself, I'm not criticizing governments—I personally would like to have as few loans and as little assistance from the outside in the next few years, which will force us to do more than we have done up until now. We have some Israeli industries on the stock market in New York, and they're doing well, in high tech. I don't think that if the guarantees aren't exactly what the government of Israel wants that it will be a disaster or a catastrophe to Israel.

LHC: A new election is coming in Israel on June 23. How is the Russian population going to affect the election?

EW: The two factors that can affect the election—the Arab and Russian populations—are the same force. Both will have something like 200,000 eligible for election, or even more. I saw in the papers today that a new Russian party was formed. *Da*, it's called. *Nyet* and *Da*. It's a good thing they call it *Da* and not *Nyet*. So I'm glad that at least they put a positive name to the party. I have my doubts as to how positive the forming of an ethnic party is. I hope that they will merge into the Israeli community and will not need their own party. They are still an unknown entity—to me, at least. I don't know if people have studied it more, whether they will go left, right, or center.

LHC: There are two theories on this, Ezer. Number one, there are either those who came because they were Jewish or Zionist, and there were others who were escaping what they think was going to be an outbreak of anti-Semitism. They know very little about Judaism and Israel. The theory held by some people is that if they're well settled, the Likud will gain. If they're not well settled, the Labor Party will gain.

EW: The same applies for old-time Israelis.

LHC: Which is another point, by the way. Young Israelis are complaining that obviously these new immigrants are getting more benefits than young couples are, which is the perennial complaint of immigrations.

EW: Personally, I think the coming elections will make no difference. What I believe will happen is that the right-wing small parties will nibble from the Likud, which is the right-wing center, and the extreme left will nibble from the Labor Party, which is the left center, and therefore both big parties will lose four or five seats each. Likud has 40, Labor has 38 or 39. So one will be 33 or 34, the other will be 34 or 35, I don't know who will be on top, and they'll form a unity government, which, theoretically is not too bad.

LHC: But practically...?

EW: The question is the practical solution. Theoretically if they find the common denominator they can be a big force to move forward. But they haven't got the common denominator now, unfortunately. I still maintain that the main problem in Israel is not to find new economic solutions and not to persuade money to come into the country, which is important, but how do we find a way to live with our Arab neighbors.

LHC: How are you going to live with the Arabs? Your solution?

EW: It's not a recipe, like if you have the flu and the doctor gives you something and you're okay.

LHC: Let's go piece by piece.

EW: The problem of rebuilding the state of the Jews, in the last hundred years, on the roots of ancestral Palestine is a unique process in world events. I always claim that when our forefathers—my late mother was born in Palestine—in Israel ninety-seven years ago, and my father arrived in 1914. Come July, if he were alive, he would be a hundred years old. And all that generation who came quite a lot out of eastern Europe and quite a lot from North Africa—Morocco, Algiers, a few from Yemen—had the idea of rebuilding the state. They encountered climate, they encountered disease, they encountered difficulties—and we're talking about a hundred years ago when you had to go in a buggy, from what was then Jaffa to Jerusalem, etc. But the main thing that they encountered was the Arab population, who at first didn't realize what was going on.

We didn't realize who we were dealing with. Both peoples had a wrong outlook on each other. Then, when it was obvious that we were there to settle—the term settlements is not a new one—settlements were created a hundred years ago. As I said, my late mother was born in Palestine in a settlement that was started a hundred years ago. She was probably one of the first girls to be born there. This brought conflict, like many times in the world—differences of interest, buying land. We never took land, we bought it.

Then trouble started, in the '20s: '21, '29; and in the '30s: '36, '38. Then, after the war, we had the big war with all the Arab countries invading Israel in '47, '48. But all the forefathers of Zionism wanted to build, wanted to culturally consolidate. We had two universities eighty or ninety years ago—one in Haifa and Jerusalem University in 1925—so there was culture, creation, consolidation, and defending ourselves from the Arabs.

But parallel to this, there was always an attempt to talk to each other. All leaders. And it didn't always work. Now that weaponry has become what it is, and the world is changing to be what it is, and the two great leaders, Sadat and Begin, fourteen, fifteen years ago—come November it will be fifteen years that Sadat arrived. Next year it will be thirteen years since we signed the peace treaty. First of all there are certain documents that we signed that we have to stand by them.

I believe that the solution is to talk to President Assad of Syria.

He is not Sadat, and I don't think we can compare him to President Sadat—different years, different countries, different problems. But I do believe that we can sit down and talk to him on territorial compromises, and political solutions; similar to those we had with Sadat.

Once this is open, and we have the leader of Syria, the leader of Egypt, and the King of Jordan, the four of us, the five of us—Israelis and Palestinians can sit down and solve the Palestinian problem, which will have to be a territorial solution.

I don't want to say how much we'll leave and how much we don't leave, but Gaza and the West Bank will have to be put on the table for discussion. And the relation between these territories and the new entity that will grow from the solution, what will be the relation between them and us defense-wise, security, economics, resources, water, land, etc. Where there's a will there's a way. Unfortunately, sometimes there's not enough will on their side and our side. I cannot change the will on their side. I've been doing my best to change the will on our side.

LHC: Ezer, when you were in the Air Force, you were pretty hawkish.

EW: I was hawkish when you had to be a hawk. I don't like this terminology, hawks and doves, but just for the public's sake—I became dovish when it was necessary to become dovish. Look, two great gentlemen before me did it: Sadat and Begin. Sadat was the man behind the October War. Sadat was a military man himself in the past. Begin was a right-wing top leader. He gave back Sinai, he dismantled settlements, he signed the Camp David Accord, which basically opens the way to the solution with the Palestinians. It's a process that we are now discussing.

And they were quite right, because certain things have changed. For instance, I'm sure that Sadat saw—I don't think he saw the collapse of Russia—but he asked the Russians to leave Egypt a year before the October War in '72, and he was very proud of it. I think that anyone who has a set idea and doesn't change with a situation that changes is square. I'll say it in very simple English: He's an idiot. Since I don't think I'm a square, I change with a changing situation.

Ezer Weizman was twice elected to the country's presidency. He changed the office of the presidency by involving himself—by virtue of his pulpit and through public opinion—in the vital issues of the country. These were life and death political issues which previously had never been addressed by a sitting president, as that post was generally regarded as a ceremonial one. Weizman resigned his office midway during his second term. He is the only living Israeli survivor of the Camp David team. He continues to maintain close contacts with Egyptian President Mubarrak, whom he considers a key to Middle Eastern peace.

TEDDY**KOLLEK**

Teddy Kollek, recently retired as the popular longtime Mayor of Jerusalem. He has argued to keep the city a uniquely Jewish capital. Believes it an impossibility for Israel to absorb more than 1.7 million Arabs.

LHC: Should people be afraid to come to Jerusalem?

TK: Fear is never justified. You know, I'll speak about something very gruesome, about the rate of crime in Jerusalem. We have an average of one person killed a month. In a city of 570,000 people, with all the problems of tension, of difference, not only Jews alone, of a hundred and four different cultural backgrounds who are still quarreling with each other and it will take another generation or two until they gel, although you can measure the progress very visibly; forty different Christian denominations, who are not always on good terms with each other, and sometimes you have it within the various denominations; let's say within the Armenians, you have them on the left and those on the right, and they are fighting with each other. And with all this, you have of course, a hundred and thirty thousand Muslim Arabs, also not all of one origin, and all this together, and it's a quiet and pleasant city.

Multicultural cities today are the rule of the day. There are no more homogenous cities. Maybe in some corners of France or in some distant corners of Scotland; London isn't, Manchester isn't, and Paris isn't and Marseilles isn't. In all these cities you have tension. In the United States certainly, and you are at it already for two hundred years or more. We are at it only for forty years, and in the united Jerusalem, exactly twenty five years. It's a long-winded process to get people to learn to live together. And we have to know that and not make too many demands.

But as it goes, Jerusalem is a pleasant and quiet city with parks and gardens and schools and museums and synagogues and churches and mosques. You had two hundred thousand people praying on the Temple Mount in the Ramadan holy Muslim month, and you had Easter for the Western Christians and for the Eastern Christians one week after the other, and it went all beautifully well, and then you had Passover that is always a time when it goes well. But here all this at the same time and no particular difficulties. I don't want to paint too rosy a picture, we had a stone thrown, and sometimes a window pane of a car is broken and somebody is slightly hurt, and the police make a great fuss over it, and the people say, "Well, he has been hospitalized for about twenty minutes until he got a bandage, but he was hospitalized."

LHC: I saw something very interesting the last time I was in Jerusalem. By accident I was there; Menachem Begin died and I went to cover his funeral for our television show.

TK: It was a very big thing.

LHC: A tremendous outpouring, and I even saw a lot of Arabs out there. We interviewed some people. There was enormous respect for Menachem Begin. It was something I had never seen in my life, the most spontaneous feeling for a man who brought peace and started on the other side of the coin.

TK: Well, it shows you how strong the longing for peace is. I think people are on the whole quite critical of Begin. He created some tensions within the community, he played on the tension between

Sephardim and Ashkenazim and there were other things that people criticized. It all vanished against this importance of having made peace with Egypt. And even that, of course, a great many people don't know about this, but he gave it his strength. The real ideas came from Moshe Dayan to a certain extent, from Ezer, from others. Without them this would have never come about. And when he came to it he had the strength to grasp the situation and take on the responsibility. And peace is the one thing we most need and most desire.

LHC: Do you have any feelings about the United States establishing its embassy in Jerusalem?

TK: I think the embassy should be established in Jerusalem. I am all against propagandizing for it. Whenever the Senate took a decision and it didn't come about, it only proved how strong the blackmailing power of the Arabs was. So every time our best friend [Senator Daniel P.] Moynihan comes and suggests it should move to Jerusalem, and the whole Senate and the whole House of Representatives vote for it and it doesn't happen, it only shows the strength of the Arabs and it only weakens us. So I think one should not particularly demand it because it won't happen at this time.

LHC: I'm fairly friendly with President Carter. He told me that the most fascinating city he had ever visited in his life was Jerusalem, and the sense of religious serenity he had there he couldn't get any other place. What is it that brings this feeling out in Jerusalem?

TK: It's a combination of many things. It's the clarity of the sky. And we take care of that. We don't have a single industrial chimney permitted in Jerusalem. The architecture is all stone, and we have taken care of good architecture. We have taken care of the holy places. They are today in much better shape, the Christian holy places, the Moslem holy places than they were ever in before. And there is a serenity.

You know, if you take Jewish holidays—the most famous holy day is Yom Kippur. Not a car is moving, everything is quiet, and it's done without a law. All these ideas that you have to have laws to preserve the sabbath, and you have laws to preserve Yom Kippur, and you have laws that you cannot eat bread on Pesach [Passover], is silly. I think religion is a moral force, and it should not be enforced by legal means. That is only counter-productive.

You have that feeling in Jerusalem on a Friday afternoon. The traffic practically stops. So all right, so a car is driving here or there—but you feel the difference between the morning and the afternoon on that day, and the next seven, and you see that even people who are not religious at all, and I'm not particularly religious myself, but the sabbath is the sabbath and you honor it and you take it into consideration.

The fight of the religious and the ultra-religious to enforce legally all kinds of things that are details which have no moral force, but only in order to show that religion rules here, is counter-productive to real religious feelings.

LHC: We were over in Madrid and we saw Yitzhak Shamir sitting across the table from the Syrian Foreign Minister. Are you hopeful about what is happening now?

TK: I think it all hinges now around the next elections. You have two different attitudes, basically. The one is here. There is a promise by God to Abraham, and not an inch of the land will ever be given to the Arabs. They can live there, or some say they cannot, they have to be transferred, but not an inch ever will be given to them. With this attitude, you won't get very far.

And I don't think it's our need from point of view of security. I believe we should keep every bit of land that we need for our security. But all the rest, on that promise of God to Abraham, there was no dateline. And today, it means that money is being spent for safeguarding another piece of land here or there that should be spent on absorbing Russian Jews. And during the last few months fewer Jews are coming because there are less possibilities for work than they had hoped for, and in Russia, apparently the danger isn't so great, so it's gone down from ten to twelve thousand a month to about five to six thousand a month. This can be a permanent loss, and I think it's the greatest danger for us.

The country has been created as a Zionist country and Zionist means, first of all, a home for every Jew who wants to come and to attract every Jew that you can to Israel. This is our first and primary task, and nothing else. And everything else has to be subordinated to this. Everything else at the moment is subordinated to getting another piece of land on the West Bank, getting another piece in East Jerusalem, or another building or another shop. I think it's the wrong priority.

It will be decided in the next election, what the priorities will be. I am as anxious to have a large Israel as anybody else. But this isn't the point. We don't want to rule a million seven hundred thousand Arabs. It will destroy us; it will not strengthen us. It is a wrong view.

You have an example next door. Up until 1920 you had a strong Christian enclave in Lebanon. Then came the French, and the Christians in Lebanon were all so full of themselves, so then they created La Grand Lebanon, the great Lebanon, and they included the Druse, and the Sunnis, and the Shiites and everybody else, and then in due course those became the majority and you see today the result of what's happening in Lebanon is not our action there. We may have done some things we shouldn't, or we didn't, never mind. But at the moment we are only concerned with our own security, and therefore we keep a piece of the Lebanon which is as large as, I don't know, a little piece of Park Avenue outside. So it's of no real consequence, geographically.

But we are in danger that the same thing that happened to the Lebanese will happen to us if we suddenly have a million seven hundred thousand Arabs. You cannot have a democratic country and keep these Arabs, or you have no democratic country. Or, you have a democratic country, and you keep the Arabs—the results are obvious, are foreseeable. It's a tragic misconception, I don't know if this is your view or not, but when I have a chance to put my views forward, they are these. I think we should keep Jerusalem and Israel within those frontiers that we absolutely need, minimum, to guarantee our security. And that is much, much less than anyone in the present government perceives.

LHC: Teddy, when there was talk during the Camp David period of the Egyptian peace treaty, one of Sadat's people threw out an idea that we don't really want to have Jerusalem sliced up, but what we would like is maybe our flag, an Arab flag on a mosque.

TK: That is ancient history and of no great importance today. Moshe Dayan at the time was willing to give them a flag on one of the mosques. It's of no importance now. What they want now is Jerusalem practically divided: two capitals in one city. This will never happen. If you have it, you would have the city divided by a wall in no time, because you would have two laws, two police forces, two customs directions, and in no time you would have the wall up again. It would be a very sad situation. Besides that, Jerusalem never was anybody else's capital.

In the year 1996 we will celebrate three thousand years of David the King having come to Jerusalem and making it the capital of his kingdom. And we'll commemorate this at the right time in the right way. But nobody ever else really, except for the Crusaders for eighty or ninety years, turned this into a capital.

Arabs didn't turn this into a capital when they could have. They started building a mount and neglected Jerusalem to the utmost. It was crumbling, there was no water there, there was nothing there, no social welfare, no good schools. It was all in very, very bad shape when we took over. We had to invest a great deal in order to put the city into comparatively good shape. Not only did they destroy fifty-eight synagogues; every civilization there always destroyed the previous civilization.

The Romans destroyed our temple and the Christians turned all the mosques into churches, and when the Moslems came back they turned all the churches into mosques. And they destroyed 58 synagogues because that was the symbol of the previous regime, that was us in the Jewish quarter for hundreds of years.

We were the only ones who once did something else: we left them the Temple Mount. It wasn't easy. Although the rabbis were all for it, and the rabbis told our children, get out of the Temple Mount until the Messiah would come, and it was forbidden to tread there, but there were people who were of a different opinion and they still exist.

Of no great importance, but you have these faithful of the Temple Mount who holler all the time that we should take the Temple Mount. I think we did the right thing. It was one of the basics to ever come to peace. But there are people who think they should drive the Arabs out. They will never leave. The Christians will never leave. And to go there and to take a shot here and a shot there and say Jews are entitled to live everywhere—of course Jews are entitled to live everywhere. The question is whether it is wise or not.

Why don't they start out, all these very famous and liberal Jews who are fighting for something, why don't they start out living amongst the Natori Karta? Nobody is penetrating there. We shall not conquer the city that way. We have to treat them as the sovereign to whom this belongs and who can decide on the laws of this, we have to treat minorities as we want Jews to be treated all over the world.

LHC: Teddy, you are very well-liked by a lot of Israeli Arabs who do live in Jerusalem. Do you think that most Israeli Arabs care if Jerusalem is their capital or not?

TK: No, no. It's coming out of Tunis, and some groups here. It's like our faithful at the Temple Mount. You know, you have such groups everywhere, but they didn't demand this thing. They could have done it until '67 if they would have felt strongly over it. It's a new-fangled thing, in order to put another obstacle to the peace process. There are some people who think the only way to do it is to do away with Israel altogether. They still exist. You shouldn't exaggerate peaceful intentions of the Arabs, wherever they are, not of Egypt, not of anybody else: they'll get accustomed to us.

It's a long pull. But you have to know that it isn't an easy job.

LHC: Are there any civil rights that are not accorded to Arabs who live in Jerusalem?

TK: Under the law, they have the same civil rights. They are not accustomed to the law. They are not making the best use of it. You have many Arabs who go to court against the government and against mistreatment by the police, and very often the courts decide in their favor. Sometimes they only go to court because they want to show off to their neighbors what heroes they are. But you know, there is a certain amount of terrorism. A policeman is attacked, and the policeman gets a stone thrown from a roof. His friends get excited over this. If an Israeli policeman treats an Arab roughly, it's a great story. You have enough civil-rights Jews who fight battles, instead of fighting for the rights for the Kurds who are gassed in Iraq, or for the for the few Jews who were treated badly in Syria, and I don't know what else. They are very worried about what will happen to the Arabs. The Arabs can take care of themselves. And while there are maybe, here or there, some things that I would wish shouldn't happen, it is on the whole a very reasonable situation.

It is not so on the West Bank. On the West Bank there are some tough dealings. And our problem is, in Jerusalem, that the West Bank is throwing a shadow on Jerusalem, so if you hear of something tough happening on the West Bank, here some stones were thrown, the soldiers reacted, in the end they had to shoot because they were attacked and somebody was killed. The frontier is not so far away, and people who sit on Park Avenue think that it's happening in Jerusalem. It isn't. In Jerusalem on the whole, civil liberties are observed, the courts are good for everybody; not everybody makes use of them.

LHC: Very few people understand that; that the law is open, but a lot of people don't know how to use it. It's somewhat akin to the blacks, by the way, in the South years ago, who also had the process open, but they did not know how to use it.

TK: You see, here you have another point. There was never such a law in an Arab country. They are accustomed to judges being appointed by the king, or by the dictator, and therefore only doing what the king or the dictator wants. They are not accustomed to our way of justice. They are not accustomed to democracy. Even if they know that democracy means voting once every four or five years; it isn't only that.

Democracy means compromise and it means taking on the responsibility, and they are far away from this. It needs education, and not only the Arabs, but also a great number of the Jews who come from Afghanistan and from Morocco, and gradually you make progress, but they also didn't know what democracy was.

LHC: What does the next twenty-five years look like?

TK: Rosy. We have today the best schools in the country, the best technical school in the country, and we have today a city that is well-built. We have built a cultural background. We have increased by far the religious schools as well. The tension between the religious and the less religious has, to a great extent, evaporated. We're building a City Hall, finally, for the 570,000 people that we are today. And we've built great shopping centers and industrial parks and other things, and industry is coming there.

It's all a slow process. We are a very multicultural city. We have Jews from a hundred and four different cultural backgrounds. They have a museum, and it's one of the great museums that has been created in the world over the last period since '45, and you have a symphony orchestra, and you have various other things, a film school and a theatre school.

I believe on that basis we can now attract industry. We have proven that some industries came to Jerusalem because of this, and particularly in the recent past. Small factories here or there. We have, as I said before, we have absorbed slightly more Russians than our share, and we have absorbed them slightly better than anywhere else. It will be a good city. Today, it's a good city. It will be an even better city.

Teddy Kollek recently celebrated his 90th birthday. Retired some six years as mayor, he is considered one of the key builders of Israel. From his position as a young aide of David Ben-Gurian he became mayor when the city was in despair. Through his personality, charm and hard work he brought Jerusalem to the forefront of the world's greatest cities. He was also admired by the Arab population.

GAD**YACOBI**

Gad Yacobi, Israeli Ambassador to the UN. He has been a constant force in mending Israeli–Palestinian relations.He has been a leader in establishing diplomatic contacts with emerging nations.

LHC: Let's start with what's going on at the UN. Basically this is a direct result of the Declaration of Principles, the DOP.

GY: First of all, it's a result of the DOP between Israel and the Palestinians. Secondly, it's a result of the joint agenda for peace that was signed between Israel and Jordan, and thirdly of course, it's a result of the new approach by the present government of Israel, and the global affairs, developments that all of us are witnessing every day. The United Nations already has changed its positions regarding the Middle East and Israel in a very dramatic way. Tonight the United Nations General Assembly just voted about the nuclear armament of Israel.

LHC: What's that mean, the nuclear armament?

GY: That Israel has to be controlled and inspected by the NPT [Nuclear Non-Proliferation] Treaty, and Israel has to stop any development of nuclear armament if it's not within this control and inspection. In former years, an overwhelming majority in the United Nations voted for this exact resolution.

LHC: So today they don't have to be inspected, is that it?

GY: No, today we are not inspected. We are not controlled. Israel refuses to be controlled as long as there is no control of the nuclear armament development in Iran, Pakistan, Iraq, and other places including Libya. Perhaps now there will be more inspections.

Gad Yacobi,
diplomat and former ambassador to
the United Nations

LHC: So the vote today did what?

GY: The vote today was that this resolution, which was to condemn Israel, criticized it and called for an international inspection, fifty-three member states voted against forty-five member states and sixty-seven abstained, which means that 70 percent refused to vote for this resolution which condemns Israel.

LHC: A great victory.

GY: Yes. Secondly, on Tuesday, the United Nations General Assembly took a positive resolution about the Middle East and Israel. It calls for comprehensive peace in the Middle East, for the continuation of the peace process, for regional cooperation between Israel and the Arab neighboring countries, for an international system to implement the DOP between Israel and the Palestinians.

For the first time in twenty-three years, since Security Council resolution three hundred and thirty-eight after the Yom Kippur War was accepted in the United Nations, and twenty-six years after the Security Council's resolution two hundred and forty-two was endorsed by the Security Council, that the United Nations has approved a positive resolution about Israel and the Middle East.

The other former resolutions, many of them, which criticized and condemned Israel in very harsh language, all those condemnations and criticisms were deleted, eliminated from the United Nations' General Assembly resolutions following an agreement between the United States, Russia, the PLO, Israel, the Arab Group, and the European Group. So sometimes, with certain elements, we still have differences of opinions, but the language has been changed.

LHC: I think it's great. Tell me, what is the practical effect of something like that. In practical terms, what does it mean?

GY: In practical terms, it doesn't mean an alteration of any operational move or step.

LHC: But it shows a movement—

GY: It shows that there is a new climate, a new atmosphere, a new political environment in the international community which has indirect, and direct, impact on the policies of many member states vis-à-vis Israel. It helps, for example, to enhance the establishment of diplomatic relations between Israel and member states which don't have diplomatic relations with Israel yet. We now have diplomatic relations with 135 member states of the United Nations out of 185 member states. Just during the last two months, since the signing of the DOP, we have established diplomatic relations with ten member states. Last week I signed with Laos. The week before I signed with others here. When the Minister of Foreign Affairs of Israel visited the General Assembly he signed with five. I signed with Mozambique about five weeks ago, and still there are four or five member states with whom we are having very enhanced, very progressed negotiations in order to establish diplomatic relations.

LHC: You have been UN Ambassador for a year and a half, Gad?

GY: One year and three months.

LHC: A lot of action since you came?

GY: A lot of action and a lot of change.

LHC: Any cause and effect between your coming and that, or don't we know yet?

GY: Yes, of course. There is a direct correlation.

LHC: Gad, you have told me of many things that have transpired at the
       UN, but I'm not sure the public generally understands it. Give us
       some more of those accomplishments. I think it's important,
       because what needs to be done is that people really have to weigh
       the long-term benefits vis-à-vis the short-term problems that are
       occurring today, and if they can get that into their consciousness,
       then maybe the peace treaty will have the ability to go forward.
       We've had people on this program who are very much against this
       peace treaty. You're saying something very positive, that because
       of this Declaration of Principles that was signed on the White
       House lawn, you've had such benefits in the UN which can have
       long-term beneficial effects for Israel. You said something about
       multilateral talks, bilateral talks, administrative things; can you
       elaborate a little bit so people can understand it better?

GY: The United Nations is involved in the Middle East and in the ter-
       ritories in two other ways. One is the peacekeeping forces, as you
       know, in Lebanon, in the Golan Heights, the multinational force
       in Sinai, and in Jerusalem. They are fulfilling a very positive role
       in keeping the security and providing Israel with a buffer zone
       between Israel and Syria and Israel and some of the forces who
       are fighting against Israel in Lebanon. But short of it, we have a
       very intense involvement of the United Nations' agencies in the
       territories. Last year, 1993, UNHCR, which deals with the
       refugees, relief works, and the UN DP, the United Nations
       Development Program, who are dealing with economic develop-
       ment and infrastructure development in the territories, and
       UNICEF, which deals with children, invested in the territories
       about three hundred million dollars. Next year, 1994, following
       the DOP and following the new atmosphere within the United
       Nations, they'll invest 450 million dollars, which may create a new
       environment.

           The people have to see some change, some hope, some dif-
       ference following the peace process, following the DOP, follow-

ing the agreement between Israel and the Palestinians. And the United Nations is very, very intensively involved in creating this change in the territories.

Short of it, we are gradually but surely being involved in the United Nations Administrative Executive Branch. Some Israelis have been accepted to work there, so we'll be involved in the Executive Branch of the United Nations.

The United Nations is involved in the multilateral talks which are creating progress and a sense of cooperation between the countries in the Middle East, the multilateral talks that are taking place all over the world from time to time in different places. Forty-three states are taking part in it, and of two of the next meetings, one is taking place in a month and Israelis will participate in this meeting. But we're going to an Arab country, which doesn't have diplomatic relations with Israel; it's some change, a substantial one, I would say. And the other one, a month later, will take place in Qatar about arms control, and the Israeli delegation will go to Qatar.

LHC: Do you have relations now with the Ambassador from Jordan?

GY: We are talking to each other.

LHC: That's enough. You don't have to go bowling with him.

GY: We are talking to each other, and we are talking to some other Ambassadors from other Arab countries, some of the Gulf countries, of course Morocco and some others.

LHC: There's a rumor that Morocco's made some real good moves towards Israel. I know economically, they've brought in some banking people to try to establish some banking relationships, and Morocco's always sort of been friendly.

It's an open secret, you can't talk about it, but Rabin has met the King of Jordan many more times than I have met old girlfriends, and a lot of things have been happening in the Middle East, it's all changed. The key question is how you are doing with Syria? It's a big one.

GY: I think that Syria is a cornerstone in the peace process towards the future. After reaching an agreement between Israel and the

Palestinians, and hopefully very soon, I believe that it will come and it will be reached and be achieved. Now the two parties are playing the game of brinksmanship, which is natural, but there is no better alternative.

LHC: But any better mood in the UN between you and the Syrian Ambassador?

GY: I would say that Syria is disappointing us, from this point of view. I didn't speak with the Syrian Ambassador. I have not had any opportunity to exchange views, so far. Syria, Lebanon, and Iran voted against the positive resolution in the General Assembly on Tuesday night.

LHC: Do you think, in your opinion, that they coordinate their policies, Syria and Iran?

GY: Lebanon is a colony of Syria now. But Iran is not coordinating its policy with Syria. Iran is against the peace process. Iran is a real threat to the Middle East. Iran is the main supporter of the terrorist groups, which Syria is hosting in Damascus. Ten of the headquarters of the most violent extreme terrorist groups are located in Damascus, but I hope and quite believe that the negotiations between Israel and Syria that will be resumed next January will lead, in a certain period of time in the future, to a positive conclusion.

LHC: The polls on Rabin have slipped, you know that. Obviously because of these terrible killings that are going on. Was that anticipated? When we were in Washington we all watched this great handshake. You knew that you were going to have reactions, right? Did they know how much? Did they predict, or was it impossible?

GY: I don't know that anybody could predict how harsh the situation will be, and how violent the situation will be. We, of course, are witnessing now a lot of violence on the Palestinian side and the Israeli side. Too many people were killed and many were injured, and I'm quite concerned about the aggressive elements among the Palestinians, mainly by Hamas and the Islamic Jihad, and some aggressive violence, small groups, marginal groups, among the settlers.

I think that 95 percent of the settlers are not giving a hand in these violent and aggressive operations, but as a result of the actions of very small groups, the violence is spreading over on both sides. But I believe that this proves that this atmosphere, which is quite difficult and hard, will gradually be eliminated and will be changed after an agreement is achieved. There is a big difference between the atmosphere before an agreement is being achieved and after an agreement will be achieved, by both parties. It will create a new kind of authority by the PLO, vis-à-vis their people, it will change the posture of Rabin and the government in the eyes of the Israelis, and if the implementation is successful, and I believe that it will be successful, it will take time. Perhaps a year, perhaps a year and a half—but the implementation will be successful.

I believe that the people of Israel will understand even better than they understand now that there is no better alternative but to reach peace agreement, a collaboration, and to prevent ourselves from a perpetual conflict in the future. The only alternative to the present move toward an agreement and peace is a conflict, which might cost a lot of human lives, a lot of economic burden and sacrifice, a deterioration of the Israeli position in the international community, preventing Israel from investing its resources and human energies in education and health and economic development—all these might be the cost of not reaching an agreement. Of course, the main result might be that Israel may become a bi-national state, and a non-democratic state.

LHC: So it's very dire. If the agreement is not executed, you see very dire consequences for the State of Israel.

GY: Yes, very much so.

LHC: What about the funding to the PLO? Arafat says that he cannot fund an army or a militia more than 20,000 people. I know that a lot of people who are working with the PLO are not even getting their salary. I think it's very dangerous, especially for Arafat, if his bodyguards—they have to be paid. Do you hear anything about

Saudi Arabia or the Gulf States being willing to fund these peo-ple? We know what Peres did. They formed this pact, so to speak, to fund these people. Are they going to get the funding?

GY: I hope that what was said here, humoristically, just a month and a half ago, that the pledges of $2 billion that were collected in Washington D.C. at the conference, will not be the sum of the pledges for the UJA, but I wish the Palestinians would be as suc-cessful as the UJA. I heard just today from the PLO observer, with whom I lunched to discuss the UN resolutions about the Middle East and the Palestinian question, that they are very, very tight on financial resources and they are concerned that they will not be able to finance the Palestinian police, and to make the first moves that will show the people on the ground that there is a new hope, there is a new difference. But I guess that those commitments that were made by the European countries, by the United States, Japan, and Germany, by some other countries including Israel, will be met in the future, and they would have the resources to establish the self-rule administration in Gaza and Jericho, and they'll be wise enough and sensible enough to meet the Israeli security con-siderations, which will not be compromised by us.

I think the Palestinians have to understand now, and I think they are starting to understand that Israel cannot give up its stand on security, and cannot give up other security considerations that are the main reason for the postponement of reaching the agree-ment between Israel and the PLO these days.

LHC: Is there any conceivable way that you can think of that this agree-ment will never come to fruition, or do you think that it's absolute, that it's going to happen?

GY: Of course, everything can happen, and might negatively, but I think the PLO understands very well that this is the only alter-native, and Israel and the government of Israel understands very well that this is the only imperative for our future. So I think that both parties are really committed to achieve the agreement and both parties will do their best to implement it.

LHC: So you're fairly hopeful.

GY: Yes, very much so.

Gad Yacobi was a very active representative to the UN. In the early seventies he was the youngest member of the first Rabin government. He had been heavily involved in the Entebbe rescue operation. He was the choice of the conservative wing of the Labor Party for the prime minister's job. At the time of his UN tenure the world level of Israeli standing improved. He constantly sought closer relationships with Arab diplomats.

ORI**ORR**

*Ori Orr, chairman of the Defense and Foreign Affairs Committee of the Knesset. A believer
in "trading land for peace" with the Palestinians. Wants a firm peace without the creation of buffer zones. Favors improving Palestinian living conditions. Believes two million Arabs will become Israeli citizens.*

LHC: About a year and a half ago we talked about the possibility of
peace and the peace process. Then along came the great
September 9th signing with Yitzhak Rabin at the White House,
then came the Egyptian Accords. A lot of people I'm not sure
understand everything, at least in America. The feelings are as follows, and you can question me one by one: people do not trust
Arafat. He has not shown himself as a great man. Two, they're
very upset about a speech that he made in Johannesburg about
Jihad. Three, there are some reports that there are secret documents made by the government with respect to Jerusalem, which
would infuriate a lot of the population.

OO: Let's start from the beginning. We don't have a peace treaty. We
have a declaration of principles. Some people, and many in the

United States, feel that we have a peace agreement. We don't have a peace accord.

LHC: It's not Camp David.

OO: No, it's not Camp David. It's a declaration of principles. I'd say we have less than 20 percent of a peace accord. Now, we have just signed the first phase: Gaza and Jericho. It's only the first phase. You asked if there was trust for Arafat. It's not a matter of trust or not trust. Arafat is not Nelson Mandela. He's not my favorite, but the Palestinians have only Yasser Arafat. We don't have another

Yasser Arafat,
chairman of the PLO at the signing
of the Oslo II Accord at the
White House in Washington

leader. I believe that the mainstream among the Palestinians understand that for their reasons, they need the peace. They need to go forward, step by step.

LHC: But is he a leader for them? Do they trust him?

OO: Some of them trust Arafat, some of them don't. But they don't have another option. And we don't have another option. But this is not the case. The main reason I joined the Labor Party is because I believe that two million Palestinians as Israeli citizens are our main chance for the future. So what this government did in the last year, we start to separate between the majority of the Palestinians and the Israelis. And you have just asked about Jerusalem. No change in his government about Jerusalem. Jerusalem will remain united as our capitol. No change.

LHC: Would you walk out of the government if there was a change?

OO: I'm not in the government, first of all. I am in the Knesset.

LHC: Would you leave the party?

OO: I don't believe that you should say and take steps like that, because our government and 95 percent of our population supports the government on the Jerusalem issue. In this case, the opposition tried to find these, you know, "secret documents." It is a letter. Nothing new in that letter. I agree that our government should show the public the letter. But that is not the case. No change about Jerusalem, in the government public opinion, in the Labor Party public opinion, in Israel public opinion. Arafat okay, doesn't agree with me. We didn't say we've finished the fight. As I said, this is a declaration of principles. We didn't agree about the border. We didn't agree about Jerusalem. We didn't agree about what kind of entity we're going to give to these Palestinians.

LHC: Do you believe that there will be any entity less than a Palestinian state?

OO: First of all, let's finish the first three years and give them a free entity. If you ask me, the Palestinian state is not the important question. The most important question is what kind of borders are we going to see with this Palestinian entity. For example, the Jordan Valley: is it going to remain under Israel's control or not? In my opinion, there are more important questions than a Palestinian entity.

But let's go step by step. Now we are in the first stage. I think that time is a very important factor in our area. To reduce hostility and to build mutual trust, we need time.

Check Arafat, check the other leaders. I would like to tell you that even the Palestinians understand that they should go forward with Arafat, and some of them even say without Arafat.

LHC: Who are people under Arafat that could take his place? Is there anybody?

OO: I don't like to say names here, on TV. But you can see, and look carefully, there is a new generation growing in the Gaza Strip, and West Bank. A new generation, in their thirties and forties, and they control the streets, even now. And Yasser Arafat should think about how to combine these people with the people who came from Tunisia and create a new administration.

I would like to see a Palestinian in Gaza and Jabalyah and they should see economic improvement. This young Palestinian from Jabalyah, he should see light at the end of this tunnel. I would like to see a better standard of living, better housing, better jobs, a better life. Otherwise, this will continue, this terror.

LHC: How many ministries does Rabin have right now?

OO: In the government?

LHC: In the government. Has he got a record number of them?

OO: First of all, Shamir has more ministers than Rabin. But I don't remember the numbers. Now, we don't have a lot. First of all, now we don't have Shas in the government, so we miss at least two ministers from Shas.

LHC: That's a good point, Ori. Basically, you have fifty-six in your coalition, plus the Arabs, which are five, so it's sixty-one, is that right? And you're making a major change in the country in policy. Is that enough to carry the country?

OO: It is not enough, but I believe that it will have success and that the public opinion in Israel will support us. Even now, I think we have a majority. And as you just mentioned, we have problems. Because a lot of people in Israel, and all over the world, say okay, now we are in the peace process and we're going to be finished with the terror, we're going to see peace and quiet.

We have the Hamas, we have the Hizbollah, we have a lot of Palestinian organizations that oppose any agreement. Some of them oppose the state of Israel. So we are, at the same time, in peace negotiation, and fighting the terror. You can feel some disappointment in Israeli public opinion, because they want to say, this is the end of the war. This is not the end of the war.

More than that, right now in Israel, we are in a crucial period of time. We are, let's say, since independence, we didn't have any dispute over our borders. Now we have real disputes over our borders. So we have these disputes, and at the same time, high levels of terror, and at the same time, uncertainty. Uncertainty for the people who live in the Golan Heights, who live in the Jordan Valley or in the Gaza strip, uncertainty for the Palestinians—some of them don't trust Arafat, some of them trust Arafat. So with all of these kinds of feelings, you can understand why the people in Israel feel it's not so good.

More than that, the people in Israel are very sensitive about the security issue. Some of them have the Holocaust Complex. Some of them, you can understand, that after one hundred years of fighting, don't believe that we are in the beginning of a new era. Still, I agree with you that we need more support. And I hope that Rabin can find a way to put more parties in the coalition. I hope so. I agree, we need at least one or two more parties in our coalition.

LHC: I want to talk about two other subjects. They're disparate. Chaim Ramon and Syria. Chaim Ramon is a young Turk who was in the Labor Party, left the Labor Party, was Health Minister, went out and tried to take control of the Histradrut [Federation of Trade Unions] elections, and took the Histradrut elections, which was a big political move in Israel, and a gutsy move, and was expelled originally from the party. Is he back now in the party?

OO: No, I don't think he's going to come back. But to conclude my answer, I would like to say that I believe in '96 Rabin will lead the Labor party, and more than that, in '96, I believe Rabin will lead all the parties in Israel, from the center to the left, as our Prime Minister. Not Ramon and not other people. That's my idea about it.

LHC: So Ramon is in the Knesset as an independent now?

OO: It's an unsolved problem. He is in the Knesset—

LHC: He votes with the Labor. Sort of a Talmudic move.

OO: It's a temporary situation and we will find some solution.

LHC: Was that a big revolution in Israel, this victory?

OO: Not a big revolution, but a change. Some people in Israel, after the election say that we don't need parties. I don't agree. I believe that in the long run, good democracy needs parties, like in the United States. Okay, maybe we'll change some of our system of how to elect our people, but we find out that we will come up with parties. I believe that if the peace process continues, we'll see in four or five years a major change in the structure of the parties.

Because in Israel now, right and left are related to the Arabs. Not like in Western Europe, social, economic situations, things like that. If we solve our problems with the Arabs, we will see a different structure, I believe. But not today. Today, the peace process, the Arab-Israeli relations are still the major issues in Israel.

LHC: Syria: any movement?

OO: I support our government's idea, that we are ready to compromise on the Golan Heights, but are not ready to give up *all* the Golan Heights. Assad doesn't buy it. Assad would like to see Israel give up all of the Golan Heights. His friend Mubarak keeps telling him all the time, "Follow me." I've got a peace agreement with Israel, I've got every square inch of land, and $40 billion, mostly from the Americans. Assad has still not gained public opinion in Israel, like Sadat.

LHC: He hasn't made any gestures.

OO: Exactly.

LHC: But Ori, you're an expert on that area. You were the Northern Commander. You know exactly what it takes security-wise to keep the country safe. If anybody had to call an expert witness in, if you were not in the government you would be called in.

OO: I don't like to see Syria thirty-five meters from the Sea of Galilee, but I'm ready to compromise.

LHC: Ori, are you tracking North Korea with the United States and what's happening here?

OO: We worry about it, about North Korea. You know, I don't like to give advice to President Clinton, but they should pay more attention to what happens in North Korea. From an Israeli point of view, we successfully stopped the North Koreans from supplying long-range missiles to Iran, with the United States' help. Nuclear capability in North Korea, and North Korea's attitude now, should be stopped by the United States. I cannot see another way of thinking or another mode of operation, other than to stop North Korea, because it's going to affect not only Japan and the Far East, but the Middle East. Iran can take this example.

LHC: The biggest problem facing Clinton today is North Korea. I don't think economic sanctions work. Japan today said they'll refuse. It starts to affect everybody. I'm sure that North Korea has some kind of alliance with Syria, too. I'm sure they supply them with weapons.

OO: The economic situation in North Korea is very bad, so let's start with economic sanctions. And do it step by step. I don't think that North Korea is going to war with South Korea after the sanctions. So my recommendation is let's start with sanctions. We'll see. We don't have another option. I'm not going to declare war against North Korea. Let's start with sanctions, gain more support in the United Nations, and we'll see afterwards what is going on. But don't leave them alone.

LHC: Let's scour the Middle East again. Has Iraq rebuilt itself? Has Iraq become a formidable power again?

OO: We are very happy with the situation. We prefer to see Saddam Hussein forever in Iraq.

LHC: Why?

OO: Because if you have Saddam Hussein in Iraq, the United Nations is going to chop him. The United States is never going to believe him. So we'll see a lot of teams who are going to check every step in Iraq, and one day in the future they will change Saddam Hussein, and they'll come up with a nice guy and the people will start to believe in this guy and believe in Iraq. In Iraq, they have the knowledge of nuclear weapons. And if the regime—this is the big "if"—if the next regime comes up with the decision to go for nuclear capability, they can do it. So I prefer to see Saddam Hussein and all the world will keep their eyes on Saddam Hussein. Otherwise—

LHC: Were you in the army when Begin made that historical move against the nuclear plants in Iran?

OO: Of course. I was Central Command Commander.

LHC: Did you know about it?

OO: Of course.

LHC: Do you think history will show it as one of the great moves of the Israeli government?

OO: Yes, but it didn't stop the nuclear capabilities, it didn't stop the process. Maybe delayed them a few years. And a delay of a few years is important. But you know, I don't believe in the long run that if states or countries or continents decide to gain nuclear capabilities, I don't believe that anybody can stop them. So, let's say that in the next century, we're going to see nuclear capabilities in the Middle East.

LHC: Would you be against the United States having troops in that area, in the Golan?

OO: Yes, I am against it.

LHC: I understand you made a statement against it.

OO: More than once. We are going through the peace process. Of Syria and Israel, or Syria and the Palestinians, I prefer to see common patrols.

LHC: You don't want a buffer?

OO: I don't need a buffer. Between two countries who are ready and willing to do peace, we don't need buffers. That's one. I don't like to see American troops in the Golan Heights fighting terror. I don't like to see the American women, or an American mother, with her husband or her kid in the Middle East. We have enough power to protect ourselves. We respect the law, we respect our agreements, so I don't need any army to protect us or to keep us— you know, as a people they sign agreements and we don't know how to keep it—we don't need that.

LHC: You're saying that if we really have an agreement, we have an agreement, and we don't need middlemen.

OO: We don't need middlemen and we don't need buffers. I prefer to see, as I said, common patrols. Okay maybe a few observers or maybe a few electronic intelligence devices, yes. But to see Americans, or any international troops, no. We don't need any buffer zone. I don't like to see international forces in Hebron. I don't think that's good for our agreement. We are going to stay in the Middle East forever. Let's find a way to reduce the hostility, to build mutual trust, and live together. Side by side. Not in a battle zone with other people that come from the United States or from Europe.

LHC: Is that the majority opinion in the Labor Party?

OO: To be honest, I don't know. I believe that a lot of people in the Labor Party think like me, but I can't tell you if it's the majority or not, to be honest.

LHC: An important point. Let's go around the world a little bit to Iran. What's happening in Iran? Dangerous.

OO: I'm very happy to say—well, not happy, but Iran is not only Israel's problem. You can find Iran's fingers in Jordan, in Lebanon, in Algeria, in Egypt. In Sudan, it's more than fingers, it's all their hands in there. It's the one big country in the world that uses terror as a legitimate political tool. But Iran, now, they're trying to get nuclear capabilities.

LHC: Where do they get their money? From oil?

OO: Only from oil. But you know, to gain nuclear capability is not a matter of money. You don't need a lot of money for that. To gain the knowledge and they have had some success, but not so much. A lot of countries together share the idea of how to stop or delay them, but I think now for Jordan, Morocco, Algeria, of course, and Egypt, Israel is not the first enemy. Iran is the first enemy, not Israel.

LHC: I know there's no concrete answer yet, but is there a possibility that the Palestinians can make a claim to return 1948 refugees?

OO: They understand. And this is the main reason you see a lot of refugees from Lebanon, from Beirut. They call Arafat a traitor, because they understand for the first time that no one is going to give them back their land from 1948 Israel. Some of them can come back to the Gaza Strip or to the West Bank, but not to Israel. And they understand that. You know, they are going to establish committees and check every name, but all of the names that they are going to check are about the West Bank and the Gaza Strip, but not about Israel.

LHC: So they won't come back to Israel.

OO: They won't come back. And most of them understand that.

LHC: What happens to an Arab who, in 1948 left Jaffa? Will they have a claim for reparations? Will they have a claim for money?

OO: We will see. You can make a claim for money. As you know, a lot of Jews who came from Syria, from Egypt, from Morocco—they can claim the same thing. As I said in the beginning, we have a lot of things to solve. Thousands and thousands of details. We are in the beginning. A very important beginning. A very crucial period of time, but it is still the beginning. For the first time, we are just starting to talk about these issues. One year ago, we hadn't even talked about it.

LHC: Are you doing joint patrols with the Palestinian police?

OO: Yes. You know, today, it's exactly three weeks since we have Palestinian police in the Gaza Strip. I am pleased to say that they are doing quite a good job.

LHC: Economically, has it been beneficial?

OO: That's a problem. That's a main problem. If Arafat was to ask me what to do, I would give him one piece of advice—pay more attention to the people than to the symbols now. Because without taking care of these people in Jabalyah or in the Gaza Strip, they're not going to see any future. The main problem now is an economic problem. There were those in the United States who were ready to finance them. But they need to see the tools. They'd like to see any kind of administration that can take care of the money. They'd like to see the people who can come up with the short-run plans, the average-run plans, the long-run plans, to give the people, as I said in the beginning, some kind of light in the end of this tunnel. What we really worry about is that if the average Palestinian from Jabalyah, and this is a big "if," if they were not to see any candle of hope, they would continue with the terror. Not the most complicated electric fence would help these people to find a new standard of living, a new hope. And this is Arafat's job. In my opinion, he does not pay attention to these people.

LHC: One of the problems that people speak of Arafat is that he doesn't delegate, and he's running this like an organization or a committee, whereas really he has a defacto type of government. He needs to get some kind of transportation person, and an economic person. I know a lot of good people, Palestinians, who don't want to join. They don't want to be associated with him. That's his problem.

OO: That's Arafat's problem. He is a good survivor. Some of the reason that he's a good survivor is because he uses the people all the time. I believe, and most of all, as I said in the beginning of our conversation, some people in Gaza, among the Palestinians, would take control of the area without Arafat, one day. Arafat is smart enough to understand it, and I believe we'll change some of his attitude.

Ori Orr, a former highly decorated general. He is currently retired from politics. He became inactive after being accused of making derogatory remarks about Israel's Sephardic population. Orr had been Chairman of the Defense and Foreign Affairs Committee. He is adamant about denying the return to Israel of the Arab refugees.

BENNY**BEGIN**
& DOV**SCHIFRIN**

Benny Begin, son of Menachem, former leader of the right-wing Likud Party. In quest of being prime minister he lost out to Benjamin Netanyahu. He distrusts the Palestinians and is concerned about Israeli security.

LHC: On this declaration of principle, it was signed in Cairo very reluctantly by Arafat but he did sign it and your prime minister did sign the document. What is the Likud's position on this today?

BB: We have to tell people what the situation really is. It was the chief of staff of our military, General Barak, who recently reiterated his assessment. We know, all of us, that Hamas stands for the destruction of the state of Israel. It was General Barak who assessed that the ultimate goals of both Hamas and the PLO and Arafat are identical—doing away with the state of Israel—and Arafat gave away a lot of ground to substantiate that assertion. He came to Gaza two weeks ago and he exclaimed and chanted with the crowd in spirit and blood "We shall redeem Palestine" which is the whole territory, including the part in Jordan, the state of Israel, Judea, Samaria, and

Gaza. He actually declared this September 15th, while shaking the hands of my prime minister on the White House lawn. On Jordanian TV he exclaimed "Long live Palestine—free and Arab" and every Jewish mother knows that in that free and Arab Palestine there can be no room for a sovereign Jewish state. This is what the future promises us and we have to be very, very careful not to do business with the chief of that terrorist organization.

Benjamin Netanyahu, former Prime Minister

LHC: There have been many people we have interviewed who have said that the prime minister and the foreign minister knew when they were signing these documents that ultimately there would be a Palestinian state and they did not tell the truth to the country. Would you say that is a correct statement?

BB: I never criticize my government while abroad or while using English in Israel for export, and I won't do it now. Formally, at least, on many occasions Prime Minister Rabin reiterated his very firm position that he objects to the establishment of an independent, Arab, PLO or Hamas State in Judea-Samaria-Gaza and I have reason to believe this is his true position.

LHC: OK, assuming there is a election in 1996 and I believe you have a new law where you have direct election of the prime minister, assuming that the Likud Party has the prime minister, assuming a majority in your Knesset, what could they do in 1996 to wipe out what has been done by this government, legally?

BB: In 1996, according to the Cairo/Oslo agreement, which Yasser Arafat refers to as a "nonagreement" according to Muslim history, none of the articles that relate to the final status of Judea-Samaria-Gaza will be in effect. There will be a lot of room and a lot of time to see to it that the basic interests of the State of Israel are kept in mind.

What has to be borne in mind is we don't know what will happen in two years or in two months in this country. We have business with a terrorist organization [the PLO] which is cooperating with the terrorist organization of Hamas. Prime Minister Rabin himself, who sent his liaison minister to the Knesset several months ago, stated if the PLO continues to breech the Oslo agreement we will all be back to square one and revert to the status quo ante. It was the legal advisement of the foreign ministry and the legal architect of the Oslo and Cairo agreements who stated formally about a month ago that Yasser Arafat's recent statements in Johannesburg calling for a *Jihad*—a holy war—against Jerusalem already voided the agreement. So with all the breaching of the agreement, none of the commitments offered by Yasser Arafat were actually delivered by him. Taking all of that into consideration you might say that the agreement is not there anymore, technically and substantially.

LHC: It's a legal position of the Likud that the agreements were signed by the government of Israel but they've been breached—

BB: By the PLO—

LHC: Because those are Rabin's words, "continuous breech," they have been breached, all you need is one breech to break a contract.

BB: If you so wish to do. If some people want to go on and on and on despite that—that's a different matter.

LHC: You can waive a breech, we're talking legalistically, but that's very important.

BB: I think it is more than a legalistic aspect, it is a political aspect. The PLO cannot deliver the so-called Palestine covenant. Their call, openly, is for the destruction of the Jewish State of Israel. Despite the commitment taken by Arafat September 9th in his letter to Prime Minister Rabin, all that is not there. These people want to see a free liberated Arab Palestine, including the whole state of Israel. Which will explain to you why Arafat was fresh enough and had the guts in Gaza to directly address the Arab citizens of Israel, promising them that they will inherit the earth and they will be made leaders in their nation. This is a very clear reference and a very dangerous one.

LHC: At the Madrid Conference, we spoke with Arab delegates. They told us they were taking direct orders from Arafat and Mr. Shamir attended that conference. Do you think that he opened the door for what has happened today?

BB: No, not at all. I think Mr. Shamir insisted that the PLO not be participant to the Arab delegation, the Arab delegation representing Arabs in Judea-Samaria-Gaza was part and parcel of the representives of the delegation of the King of Jordan, it was a joint delegation. We insisted that no Arab representing Jerusalem would be part of the delegation. When someone tried to monkey around and said formally that he represented the PLO, he was asked to leave and he left the room and he wasn't part of those negotiations. We were very particular about it and we are actually very correct on the matter.

LHC: Let's talk about the country, Rabin has fifty-six members of the government and five Arab seats so right now sixty-one, is his plurality. He's transforming the country with a minor authority of government. Would you agree on that?

BB: If freely elected, a government is a legitimate government, and is the only government. It is empowered to follow its policy and no one can interfere, physically or otherwise with that policy being executed. For us in the opposition, the thing to do is cultivate the public, to tell them the truth as we see it, to talk, to walk, to write, and to wait until the next election comes and we can replace the government, come to power, and see the interests of Israel the way we should.

LHC: Is there a Palestinian problem and what would the Likud do with the Palestinians?

BB: Actually the Camp David formula is the only wise solution that has any chance in bringing genuine change in the ill-relations between Jews and Arabs west of the Jordan river. It is based on the assumption that Jewish people have an eternal natural right to their homeland Israel which English speakers and the Arabs call Palestine. We have a right to the land.

However, we do understand and accept that there are many Arabs there, that they will be our neighbors and the inhabitants of Judea-Samaria-Gaza and Galilee for many generations to come and we have to extend our hand as we did in Camp David. The essence of Camp David, the wise element of it, is that we conceived of an experimental period of five years when the Arabs will have to prove that they are ready to coexist peacefully and in that period of five years they will run their lives on a day to day basis. They will run their lives as a political organ that is a functioning one, with an administrative council, but with no legislative powers, no mini-parliament, no embryonic version of a sovereign state, according to the Camp David formula. Israel should have jurisdiction over the territory and the Arab administrative council should have jurisdiction over the inhabitants.

Israel is, of course, responsible for the security and from that point of view the Oslo agreement is diametrically opposed to the Camp David Accord: no administrative council but a legislative one, no jurisdiction over the inhabitants, they would have jurisdiction over the territory too. They are responsible for antiterrorist combat called internal security. Under those conditions it will be close to impossible to help relations between Arabs and Jews.

LHC: What was your reaction to the letter sent by Foreign Minister Peres to the foreign ministry at Oslo about the ability of Arabs to pray in Muslim places of worship in Jerusalem.

BB: My friend and I had something to do with exposing the letter and it went far beyond religious rights of people to observe their religion. It actually reiterated three times the term "Eastern Jerusalem" thus indicating a tendency to sub-divide the city into two separate cities, eastern and western ones, and also committed the government of Israel to see to it, to encourage the operation of all

Palestinian, that's PLO, institutions in Jerusalem. Including, even, one should understand from the wording of the letter, all institutions even the political ones of the PLO. It is a very far reaching letter and it already caused a struggle here when the PLO said, "We have a letter of commitment, you cannot oust us from Jerusalem," even as Prime Minister Rabin tried to do so, justifiably, lately.

LHC: I'm a little confused about the letter—you found out about, this was not a public document?

BB: No, this document, as some people would know, was kept in secret for many months, it was not made public and took us some time to expose it and to have some government officials admit that such a letter exists and the severity of its significance.

LHC: Is that commonplace in government activity, that secret letters exist?

BB: Sometimes secret letters do exist; sometimes governments should be allowed to keep a lot of their diplomacy secret. I think sometimes it is a precondition for successful diplomatic relations and I would not complain that much about it. However, in that instance, we had business with Jerusalem, as my father used to call it Jerusalem DC—David's Capital—you don't monkey around with your internal capital city. That letter should have been made public, should have been made known to the Knesset, but it's all right. Now everything has been made known and rectified from this point of view.

LHC: Tell us about the Likud today—how united are you?

BB: As united as any Jewish organization can be. Jewish organizations in this country, have lately been split. In the Likud there's always some noise, but we have one basic ideology, a common platform. We all work to see to it that the public is convinced that Oslo/Cairo agreements do not prevail and that they entail a very great danger ahead for the State of Israel.

LHC: What is the Likud's position in regard to Jordan?

BB: Such meetings with the Hashemite King of Jordan is very important and very positive and we should look optimistically toward the future. However, I can state that this is a direct development ensuing from the Likud government under Shamir's initiative in October 1989, in which for the first time, an Arab delegation from Jordan and an Arab delegation from Syria met in Madrid and then Washington in order to conduct direct, open public negotiations among those countries. What we see now is an offshoot from that initiative and we should be still very careful about the details of the agreements the Hashemites would like to negotiate about the border of the Jordan River, north of the Dead Sea, this is still an issue. There are several other outstanding issues yet to be resolved, but let's hope for the best.

LHC: You think next week a peace treaty will be signed—or that's an impossibility—between Prime Minister Rabin and King Hussein?

BB: I think we're very remote from the signing of a peace treaty. The Prime Minister of Jordan indicated yesterday that what the area needs is a comprehensive peace treaty, signaling that he is reluctant to sign a peace treaty with Israel without first seeing a peace treaty signed between Israel and Syria. This is very remote. So, we have to be cautiously optimistic—this is good enough for that very troubled, tricky, muddy part of the world called the Middle East.

Benny Begin, a geologist by profession, was at one time considered a Likud Party candidate for prime minister. He remains vehemently opposed to the Oslo Agreement along with the creation of a Palestinian state. He favors the original Camp David agreement providing autonomy for the West Bank and Gaza. Begin's son, an air force pilot, was killed in a crash last year. Begin resigned from the Likud and formed his own ultra right-wing party as a protest against Netanyahu's leadership. Later he dropped out of politics.

Dov Schifrin, professor of political science at Tel Aviv University is an expert on Jordan. He objected to the Oslo Agreement which, he claimed changed Israeli–Jordanian relations. A Labor Party supporter of Rabin, he endorses the philosophy of land for peace. He refers to Israel as a first-world country and the Arab nations as third-world.

LHC: What do you think of their meeting? What happened yesterday with Shimon Peres and Prime Minister Majali and Warren
Christopher?

DS: I thought it was a very good thing that we are finally doing the
right thing with Jordan. We've had a strategic alliance with Jordan
for more than fifty years now and it worked very well until the
Oslo Agreement. In the Oslo Agreement we substituted an alliance
with Jordan for an alliance with the PLO and this worried King
Hussein. He had a very, very serious problem as a result of the
Israeli policy. And now we're finally trying to rectify some of the
things we did in Oslo and I'm delighted that we've done the right
thing now.

LHC: The Ambassador from Jordan to the United Nations said that they
thought it was scandalous, and they felt betrayed. The question
is this: can it be repaired?

DH: Well, to some extent. The major damage that was done was to
recognize the PLO as the legitimate representative of the
Palestinian people. Meaning, not the Palestinians in the West Bank
and the Gaza Strip—this would be only natural after Oslo—but
the representative of the Palestinian people. Namely, that Arafat
represents most people who live on the East Bank [i.e., in Jordan]
and not King Hussein, but the PLO who also represent most people who live on the West Bank. This makes King Hussein redun-
dant. We can still correct some of the damage but not all of the
damage. It depends very much on what we do with the West Bank
and the Gaza Strip.

LHC: How do we correct the damage?

DS: We don't let the Gaza Strip/West Bank/Palestinian state that we
have established in Oslo develop in a way that can endanger
Jordan. First of all, we don't give them a position in Jerusalem. If
any Arab should have a position in Jerusalem then it should be
the Jordanians and not the Palestinians. From the Israeli point of
view, it has a major advantage because the Jordanians have a capital city. The Palestinians want a capital city in Jerusalem. From a

Jordanian point of view, it is very important for King Hussein to be the guardian of the holy places; it will strengthen his position in his own kingdom and in the Arab world. The second thing is don't let the PLO get too strong because the only reason the PLO, for the moment, is not acting on its own irredentist ambitions vis-á-vis Israel and Jordan, meaning it—at the moment—isn't trying to undermine Israel and Jordan, is because it is weak, it is impotent. If we allow the PLO become strong, it will automatically take over Jordan and then try to undermine and then take over Israel. If the PLO takes over Jordan, we will have one hostile reality from Heran [an ancient city in southeast Turkey] to the middle of Jerusalem.

This from an Israeli point of view is very serious. You have the Iranians, the Iraqis, Jordan under the PLO, and the PLO and this is a very serious threat to Israel even as an existential threat to Israel. If between the PLO, Iraq, and Iran we have a strong Jordanian state, pro-American, pro-Israeli, moderate, this, from an Israeli point of view, is much better, from a Jordanian point of view is much better, and I dare say that for most Palestinians on the West Bank and the Gaza Strip is much better, because they don't want to go on fighting against Jordan and against Israel. They want to live peacefully on the West Bank and the Gaza Strip and the PLO may not make it possible. So we do anything we can that strengthens Jordan.

LHC: So I can say you're not too excited about this September 13th meeting between Prime Minister Rabin and Arafat?

DS: Well, it has one advantage. You know the anti-Semites have always said that the Jews are a smart people—now we have tangible proof that this is not the case. The Israeli government demonstrated this in Oslo. But I'd be delighted if things worked out with Jordan and Syria, this would be very important for Israel. And maybe in the balance between Jordanians and Palestinians in the West Bank we can get a better deal.

LHC: Isn't it too late?

DS: Well, it would have been nicer if we had done the right thing in the beginning but now we're being clever. You know the difference between a wise man and a clever person is that a clever person can weasel himself out of a situation that a wise person would never put himself in the first place. We are not being wise but we are being very clever and I hope we continue to be clever.

LHC: We were in the Gaza Strip when Arafat arrived and we sensed some jubilation amongst its population and I dare say these people sensed some sort of feeling of independence. I feel as though the prime minister could have been more forthcoming to his people and say, "Look, what I have done on September 13 is a prelude to a Palestinian state."

Now, I'm not sure the population here was told that, so from that point of view I agree with you. What I did sense in Jordan was fear. If I tried to interview a normal Jordanian, they were very fearful of talking, especially to the Israeli press. They sort of were deferring to the King. Now, obviously, if something happens between Rabin and the King in Washington, that fear might be alleviated.

It's not as beautiful as Shimon Peres points out, it's not this beautiful, wonderful fulfilling of the dream of Abraham, but yet it's a step forward.

DS: Yes, I very strongly agree with your observations. First of all, anything Shimon Peres says about the New Middle East or if you want to take it to the extreme, he's talking about Benelux. Israel, Jordan, and the PLO being like Benelux with Yasser Arafat being so much like the grand duke of Luxembourg, everyone in the Gaza Strip speaks fluent Dutch so we'll have Benelux. This is a very, very different ball game. This here is the Wild East. If you don't pack a six-shooter, you don't go into the saloon.

In Jordan, I think the atmosphere you've seen yesterday is going to change. It's perhaps going to take a little time. The moment the Jordanians see it's OK to be warm to the Israelis, they will, because after all, we have a common enemy. The Jordanians know about Arafat—they can tell us what Arafat is all about. When they realize how much benefit they could have with peace, without illusions about a New Middle East, there will be tangible benefits for Jordan and the most important thing is that the stability of Jordan depends on a strong Israel.

And they want a strong Israel. I think that this attitude will change, the Jordanians will be, perhaps of all the countries around us, the best allies we can have. The Syrians will continue to be bitter and hostile even if they do sign a peace treaty with Israel. The Egyptians belong to a different milieu. The Jordanians are very strong, very close, they know the Palestinians very well, and I think we'll have a very good relationship with them.

LHC: Are you a member of any political party?

DS: I used to support Rabin for the last twenty-five to thirty years and what he represents.

LHC: Basically, the Labor Party—

DS: Basically the Labor Party—until Rabin transformed. Before Camp David. But now when he struck a strategic alliance with the PLO, I can't continue to agree with him. What happened with him is a very, very major change. At the moment I don't have any political home in the Israeli political spectrum and I don't think many Israelis have. This is a very dangerous thing in Israel. You have the right represented in Likud, you have the left and radical left represented in Labor, and in the middle—people like me. I belong to the extreme center. Where people like me used to stand, where people like Rabin used to stand, there is no political party, and I don't think it's very good for the Israeli democratic system. It will get worse if we have these direct elections for prime minister.

LHC: Do you think Rabin knows where he's going now? I have a sense he's on a train and he doesn't know where it's going.

DS: I agree that at least he doesn't have the strategy laid out as clearly as before. The strategy that I supported until this very day is something Rabin adopted in May of 1989 and he followed it very consistently. Namely, an alliance among, Israel, Jordan, and the 1967

PLO, what they called the Jerusalem PLO, not the 1948 PLO. Because if you have an alliance with the 1948 PLO, you cannot answer their concerns. What they want is not Nabulus, what they want is Jaffa and Haifa.

Because they represent all the Palestinian people, millions of them, and they do not see the Gaza Strip and the West Bank as their home. Hundreds of thousands of them have lived in the Gaza Strip for the last forty-six years and don't consider it their home. So we don't have a solution for the '48 refugees and you can't strike a strategic alliance with them. There is a contradiction inside Rabin's policy and I agree with you, I don't think he's being systematic.

LHC: In your opinion, what transformed him?

DS: I don't know, I wish I knew. I really don't know. I can very easily typify what happened, I can explain the transformation, but I don't know why. I have spoken to many people who know Rabin closely—I, myself know him quite well—and I could never get a good answer. The answers I have are quite shallow.

LHC: Professor, are you not disappointed with the Likud?

DS: Yes, but you know I did not have many hopes concerning the Likud, so I could not be so deeply disappointed with the Likud. I supported the basic trade-off that the Labor movement proposed since the 1967 war, which is essentially '48 for '67.

LHC: Land for peace?

DS: Yes, land for peace if you want. The question is not the magnitude of the concessions. The question I have with the present government is that we are giving away all of the bargaining chips and we are getting very little in return on the Palestinian front. On the Jordanian front, the government is doing the right thing and on the Syrian front the government will probably do the right thing. But on the Palestinian front we've made a very major mistake, but you know Israel today is so strong that we can even afford to be dumb. This was not the case a few decades ago.

LHC: The big question is why did Hussein move now? Was it monetary with the United States, did he need U.S. support, did he have to get rid of the $700 million debt or internal reasons we don't know about?

DS: There are many reasons. The real question is not why did King Hussein move ahead now but what stopped him from moving ahead in the past and now is no longer there, and then you can add the incentives. The major problem that Hussein confronted for many years, was the fact that he wanted to make peace with Israel isolated from the whole Arab world. Before '77, before Sadat, it was totally impossible. And between '77, in the late 1980s, early 1990s, it was practically impossible because Jordan couldn't alone be the first, it also couldn't be the second. But, when everybody negotiates with Israel—and this is what we've been getting since the Madrid conference—when everyone is only trying to get better conditions from Israel, why shouldn't he do it? Particularly since Syria came so close to negotiating with Israel in a deal which seems—in the very near future I think—very close to working. Especially when the PLO has already negotiated with Israel.

He understands if he doesn't move now the damage with the Israeli–PLO agreement will be something that cannot be reversed anymore. Now at least part of it can be reversed. If he waits another three or four years they will establish a full-fledged state here, and he will not be in a position to reverse it. Add to that all the incentives you mentioned—money—and it isn't only money directly from the United States. It is American pressure on Saudi Arabia to giving him money he was cut off from after the Gulf War. So you have all these incentives.

LHC: Final question: are you optimistic about the position of Israel in the Middle East today?

DS: Yes, and let me tell you why. We are so strong we can even afford to make major mistakes, and it's not just the force of the Israeli army. Israel is a first-world country. The Arab world is a third-world reality. The third world gets worse and worse every day—they don't have the infrastructure to lift themselves from the terrible situation they are in—and Israel has a major gap vis-á- vis the Arabs because we managed to grab the coattails of the first world and we became a first-world state.

So it's the economy, education, technology, the army, and the strength of the society. So you can afford to try and not even succeed in everything. Succeed in most things. You just compare— immediately after the '73 war, people used to tell me, "In twenty years, Israel will be doomed and the Arabs will be at the peak of their success!"

Look at what happened in twenty years since the Yom Kippur War. There is not a single Arab state that is not much worse off today than they were twenty years ago. Look at Saudi Arabia after every hundred million dollars are in a worse situation than they used to be. And Israel is much better. I mean, you visit Israel every year, you know. You know that the Israel of twenty years ago and the Israel of today are two different countries. The Arab world has major problems. They used to say, twenty years ago, "One day, Kuwait will be a great state!" Well, look at Kuwait. Look at Saudi Arabia, look at Lebanon, look at what is happening to the outside world. So we really picked good enemies, we really couldn't have picked any better. We confront them—it's tough, but we can make it.

Dov Schifrin is a world class expert on Jordan. He was prophetic in that he did not believe in the Oslo Agreement and rightly predicted its failure which he believed would interfere with the Jordanian relationships with Israel. Professor Schifrin opposed Peres's concept of a new Middle East economy partnership similar to that obtaining among the Benelux countries.

AVIGDOR**KAHALANI**

Avigdor Kahalani, a prominent member of the Knesset, defected from the Labor Party to head his own Third Way Party, which gained four seats in 1996 but none in the 1999 elections. He was and is strongly against abandoning Israel's hold on the Golan Heights.

LHC: We're speaking to Avigdor Kahalani, a brigadier general in the Israeli army, and now a founder in a sense of the Third Way movement, which will become a new political party. And they hope it will become the center party that blocks the prime minister from going too left and blocks the other prime minister from going too right. They'll be in the center. You refused to go along with your Labor Party and vote for this agreement, Oslo II, they call it. Why did you vote against it and did you ever read the agreement?

AK: Of course I read the agreement, I read it very carefully and I can tell you I am from the Labor Party, but everyone knows what my point of view is about the situation with the security borders, about the situation with our country. When I came to the Labor Party, I demanded that I represent it in the Golan Heights to explain to the people that we should stay in the Golan even in peacetime.

This is exactly what was written in our platform. And Rabin sent me to the Jordan Valley to explain this is going to be our border for any situation in the future and he told me go and do it because people believe in you.

I didn't change my mind. I found my friends in the Labor Party—they changed their minds. They changed; they are ready to withdraw from the Golan Heights, immediately or maybe in three years. They are ready to withdraw maybe six months from now but I can feel from the agreement very soon. Then the Palestinians are going to build a state between us and Jordan.

LHC: But everybody knows there's going to be a Palestinian state. When the Oslo I agreement was concluded, everybody knew there was going to be a Palestinian state. Why doesn't Rabin come out and say, look what I'm doing here is creating a Palestinian state? Why doesn't he tell the people that?

AK: Because we wrote in our platform that we would never give permission to build a Palestinian state. Now what he's trying to do is to do it *de facto* and here is the reason why. I'm not so worried about a Palestinian state, what we worry about is that they will have the right to build an army, to have an airport, and to have everything, and maybe some day to have the right to invite two divisions from Iraq to visit. If you worry about the situation, and we don't know, but now we depend on the general of the PLO's decisions if we have Palestinians there, not on our government if they can block it.

LHC: It's a major change in the Israeli philosophy now that basically your whole existence rests on the good faith of a man called Arafat. Does that get you very nervous?

AK: Yeah, of course, you touched the point. I think that this is the main problem. We have to believe in this man when he says that Jerusalem is going to be our capital. And you are going back to the '67 border, from one side. From the other side, we have to trust him on the future of our country where we depend too much on this man when we can listen to him talking on the radio and the TV almost every day how he gives courage to his people, how to make terror in Israel, and to fight us for the future of their life. It's worrying that he doesn't control his people in the area. Forty percent of those people are Hamas, we know that.

LHC: Yitzhak Rabin has always talked strongly about defense and security, that's basically why he was elected two times to be prime minister of Israel. What happened to Yitzhak Rabin?

AK: I think something happened to him. I'm not going to tell you what he said, but I can tell you we will have new elections next year. We have to realize that people here in Israel can see forward one year from now and try and identify what the situation is.

Second, I think he depends too much on Meretz, the left-left wing. Those people they are willing to withdraw from most of our country and I don't trust them from a security point of view. His government depends on five PLO representatives in the Knesset, five Arabs, and they believe that we should go back to Poland and maybe to Yemen and to the United States; and those people live with us in the Knesset.

Too much depends on people you don't believe in, the way to keep the country together, and keep the safety of our lives. And something happened to him: three years ago he talked about the Golan Heights. Ten days before the election in the Golan Heights he said, "We're going to stay here forever, even in peacetime; we're going to stay here." Did he change his mind? I think so.

LHC: Is the Oslo II agreement reversible in any way?

AK: No, I don't think so. It's worse than you think. In the agreement there is a paragraph talking about three areas [A, B, and C], withdrawing from an area every six months and we don't know how far we're going to withdraw. They're going to negotiate. And we're [the Knesset] going to vote on this and the government can withdraw every six months from Area C to Area B, from B to A, and no one can block the government anymore. I asked Mr. Rabin to show me the map and how far you're going to withdraw. "I'm not going to show you any map." So I said, "Are you going to bring it to the Knesset?"

LHC: Wait, he refused to show you a map and you're going to vote on it?

AK: No map, because we're going to negotiate. It's like writing a check, signing it and the amount I leave to you to figure out.

LHC: You're telling me that the sixty-one people in the Knesset who voted for this agreement never saw the maps?

AK: The maps that we have now everyone saw. But we're going to withdraw every six months—it's a paragraph in the agreement. Every six months we have to withdraw from some area. What is the earliest we are going to withdraw? Nobody knows, but everybody signed it. The government, they now have the permission to withdraw.

I asked him, "Why should I sign this agreement if I don't' know how far you're going to withdraw? Are you going to bring it to the Knesset?" He said, "No." They are not going to bring the next withdrawal from the area to the Knesset.

I convinced him one hour before the vote to bring it back to the Knesset. It was a part of our negotiations between him and me. Finally, I refused to vote against the agreement and now he will not come back to the Knesset when he wants to start to withdraw.

LHC: So he made a deal with you that if you voted for it, he would go back to the Knesset and bring the maps. And now that you voted for it, he won't bring it back to the Knesset?

AK: Yes.

LHC: Tell me, Avigdor, how much pressure was put on you?

AK: A lot, but I believe in what I am doing. It is very difficult. All my life I was in the army. I decided to join political life just to be involved and give my personality to the situation to protect the country. It's a lot of fun, but it's really difficult.

This is my office here, I'm the deputy mayor of Tel Aviv. I read in the newspapers they're going to kick me out of this job. Just two days ago I saw my name in the newspaper, they're going to kick me out of the committee for security and the foreign affairs committee in the Knesset—and many other things. But I don't care. I'm going to be a Knesset member and I believe a lot of people support my way in the country. This is my mission.

LHC: You found out the Knesset is a political arena. What was the role of Shimon Peres? Do you have many conversations with him?

AK: I talk with him, he attacks me all the time, because I'm a part of the Third Way—

LHC: The Third Way is a political movement that will probably transform into a political party.

AK: He attacks me all the time and he tries to make jokes about the Third Way movement. Peres is a very active man and he's really pushing. But we have only one prime minister [Rabin] and everything depends on him.

LHC: Aren't there enough people in the Labor party who felt like you about security?

AK: I don't know, I cannot explain that.

LHC: Do you ask the same question some times?

AK: Yes. On the day that we built the Third Way movement—it's a movement from the right wing of the Labor Party—and we built it with something like eighteen members of the Labor Party. The day that I proposed the Golan Heights law and tried to block the government from withdrawing from the Golan Heights, we had seven Knesset members together to sign on this proposal. And the last proposal we had like three. Most of them ran away. You have to know and I believe you understand, every politician in the world is looking far away. How far away? The next election.

LHC: It's called survival.

AK: Sometimes you have to change your mind about your future and sometimes it's about the future of the country.

LHC: Tell me about the Third Way.

AK: The Third Way is a movement. Why Third Way? The first way is to resort militarily to the '67 border. The second way is keeping our hands on all the area including the Arabs. And the third way we are willing to have some compromise between our people and the Palestinian people in Judea and Samaria. We don't think we should control their lives, but we think we should stay in the Golan Heights to protect the country. We think we should stay in the Jordan Valley and we think some areas in Judea and Samaria we should keep in our hands.

LHC: OK, if you keep that land, do you have any problem with the Palestinian state?

AK: No, I don't think so. I don't have any problem for them to kick around.

LHC: So, in other words, if people vote for the Third Way, the Third Way says I don't care if you have a Palestinian state, as long as we have this land, is that correct?

AK: We haven't agreed about the Palestinian state. I told you personally I'm not so worried about it for me, but I'm not going to encourage a Palestinian state. But if it's going to be a fact, my problem is to protect our country not to give them any time in the future to build an army or to have an air force that can bring weapons into their "state." This is the main problem we fear in a Palestinian country.

You don't have to be in Gaza and these other little villages and towns in Judea and Samaria, because we're not going to convince them to be Zionists. It's a difficult mission believe me. I don't believe we'll build some borders between them and us, like some fence. They can work in Israel. But they can keep their own land and they know it will belong to them and we will be in the Jordan Valley to protect ourselves. And, of course, we are not going to negotiate about Jerusalem. This is one town and the capital of Israel, forever.

LHC: Do you believe that Rabin feels the same about Jerusalem? He changed his lexicon, his language. He used to speak about greater Jerusalem. Now he says Jerusalem plus. What is Jerusalem plus?

AK: I asked him about a week ago, "What do you mean, Jerusalem plus?" And he did not answer me.

LHC: We know that if an Arab comes into Israel and shoots an Israeli and if he runs back into Arab territory under this agreement the Israeli authorities cannot capture him. Is that correct?

AK: In Area A you can never go inside to try to identify any terrorists.

I believe this is the future and now we can never go back, like we can never go back to Gaza. We can of course go with a lot of tanks.

LHC: I assume you said this to Rabin?

AK: I said, "Look, I prefer to see an agreement where we can sit together now with the Palestinians and try to find the final solution for the situation." Because there are some questions that can never be resolved. The question about Jerusalem. The issue about refugees the rights of return. The border between them and us. We can never solve these, from my point of view.

    And a few years from now all of those issues are going to be like big bombs in our room waiting to explode. Of course, no question about it. I told Rabin, "Let's get together, we'll try to solve the problem now." He said, "I prefer that we try to solve the problem a few years from now, even I know what you mean and maybe I agree with you."

LHC: He agrees with you it might blow up.

AK: Yes. Everybody knows it will blow up. Like the Palestinians—they want Jerusalem as their capital. Listen to them—they are saying it right to our face. Do you think that we can convince them to build Ramallah as their capital? Never. In the future, a man from the PLO will come from his country and bomb us and Arafat will say, "I'm sorry, what can I do, this man had a dream: Jerusalem as his capital. And now you stopped his dream—what can I do?" And this is going to be the situation in Israel.

LHC: Rabin told this not only to you, but I suppose he told this to all the other people, all the other generals in the Labor Party. How come we have no other profiles of courage. How come it's you?

AK: Well, with Rabin, he said that maybe the two nations have to live together to try to change their minds about each other and maybe then it will be easier. But he agreed about Jerusalem and about another issue that we talked. It may be worse. I don't know, I'm not going to explain the situation in the Knesset to explain what happened to my friend Yitzhak, you can maybe ask them.

    To do what we have done—it's very difficult. If you are a

Knesset member, you belong to a party, and, apart from our democracy is that you obey.

LHC: Party discipline.

AK: What happened to us it's unusual and we know it's unusual. But it came from inside. I couldn't do anything else.

LHC: Tell me what the reactions have been—have you heard from any of your Labor comrades? Have you heard from Rabin since this vote took place?

AK: I haven't heard anything from Rabin after the vote, but I can tell you that I read in the newspaper they are going to kick me out from the job that I have. I'm not sure it might be a stupid way, but if they do it—

LHC: —You're willing to take the consequences.

AK: Of course.

LHC: Did Barak call you?

AK: We talked before the vote in the Knesset and he tried to convince me we see eye to eye. He's a good man, Barak, I think our point of view on this situation is almost the same. But he has a problem —he's in the government. And in the government you can't refuse a vote against.

LHC: You can walk out of the government.

AK: Yes, but he's just started the politician's life.

LHC: Avigdor, when are you going to start the Third Way into a political party, when are you going to transform it?

AK: I think this month we're going to discuss about that at our council and we will see then—it's almost done.

LHC: And how many members do you have, do you know?

AK: We have a few thousand who just joined us, we didn't ask people to join us, but people write letters and people send money sometimes. We will start everything at the end of this month.

LHC: And you'll come out with a platform?

AK: We already have a platform. We did most of our platform and we showed the people what we are thinking about the situation. And we are going to elect a new chairman to the movement. I believe at the end of this month we'll know who the chairman is. And we'll move.

LHC: Is there any possibility that some people from Labor will join the Third Way?

AK: A lot of people from Labor have joined. If you're talking about Knesset members, I'm not so sure. But I have a friend who's a member of the Knesset—he supports me, I support him. Most of the people who joined us are Labor people and they refuse to stay in the Labor Party anymore. They found the Third Way movement is like a new home.

AK: Very critical election.

LHC: Do you think the people are split on this? 50–50?

AK: Yes, almost 50–50 this is the situation now. It depends on how it's going to be in 1996, the relationship between other Arabs and Palestinians and the future of the Golan Heights—many questions about the future and this will convince the people how to vote.

LHC: In 1997, tell me what this country's going to look like, who's going to be running the government. Who's going to win the election, what do you think?

AK: It's a different situation now. We're going to vote twice. Once for the prime minister it's never happened before, and second for the party. This is the reason why we maybe have a chance, the Third Way, in the future; because these people supported Rabin and they believe we can block him, and they don't want to vote for Likud, so they vote for the Third Way, this is the way.

My feeling about who is going to be the prime minister, is that we don't know who's going to be the prime minister. Now we can see from the polls Rabin and Netanyahu are almost the same. But my feeling is, in the future, the right wing will have more power and maybe Rabin will again be the prime minister. I know he's going to run. He hasn't said it formally but of course he's going to run again. Maybe we will have more power in the right wing, that is my feeling. We can see from the polls that the Meretz Party goes down from 12 to 7 seats and the Labor Party goes from 44 to 36 seats.

LHC: So you're saying a very important thing. You're saying look, we changed the law here, we're going to have direct election of prime minister. So let's assume Mr. Rabin becomes prime minister but we don't really like him but we really don't want to vote for Netanyahu, so we vote for the Third Way. And the Third Way can put a confidence or no-confidence in the government so Rabin despite the fact that he wins the contest for the election can be in a sense handicapped or crippled, he won't be able to function. So what you can do is call for another government again.

AK: First, we're not going to take sides about who is going to be prime minister. The Third Way is going to ask people to join us in our way. It doesn't matter who the prime minister is.

We will be in the center, we will try to control Rabin, we will try to continue to keep the Golan Heights in our hands. If he is the prime minister we will try to push him to continue the peace process. And we will not make our decision on who we will prefer to be the prime minister. But in the future if the prime minister does not have the power to build a coalition he will be out of a job. This is a very complicated situation but I believe the man who will be elected by the people will be able to build a coalition.

LHC: Would you be happy today with five seats in the Knesset for members of the Third Way?

AK: We will be happy to be in the center and control both sides and put our influence in the future of the country.

Avigdor Kahalani, a highly decorated soldier, leaped into the Labor Party after completing his military service. He bolted from Labor because of what he considered Rabin's conciliatory attitude toward the PLO. He heads his own Third Way Party. His desertion of Labor was based in part because of Rabin's change of view about a Greater Jerusalem. He believes the Oslo Agreement should be nullified.

In a recent conversation with the general he confirmed that he resigned from the Labor Party after Rabin refused to show him a secret negotiation with the PLO. Later it was revealed that the document detailed Rabin's Jerusalem Plus conception. This preceded Barak's alleged discussion at Camp David, for which he was widely criticized.

YITZHAK**SHAMIR**

Yitzhak Shamir, a former Irgun and Stern Gang fighter, Herut and later, Likud Party leader. He served as Prime Minister for nearly nine years. He strongly opposes a Palestinian state.

LHC: Mr. Shamir, please give me your feelings today about this Knesset vote that took place about expanding Palestinian rule in the West Bank.

YS: I am very disappointed today and I am very worried. Because I know where this agreement could bring Israel. My only hope is that this agreement will not become a reality, because otherwise we will lose—I don't want to say what—but we will lose. I don't like, to appear to the outside world with criticisms against our government, but I don't have any choice. When people ask me, I must say that our government is wrong. It is on a wrong course and we have to replace it. There's no other way.

LHC: Is it a Fait accompli? What can Israel do at this point?

YS: I don't think it's a Fait accompli. I don't think that there is such a thing in politics that you cannot change. Things done by people can be undone by people. But there will be damage—considerable damage. I don't know any government that conducts a policy that is against its philosophy, against its conscience. When, for instance, the Likud comes to power, they will not conduct the policy of the Labor party. It's very clear. And I think that they will find ways to change the situation.

Yitzhak Shamir,
former Prime Minister of Israel

LHC: You've had an illustrious career in this country, do you think that you can reverse something, an agreement that world opinion has in a sense committed itself to?

YS: Yes, I think that there is nothing that isn't reversible. If you study the history of any country, you will see it. You can change anything. It depends how much energy it will take, how much time you can invest in it. So I don't think it is irreversible. I know the opinion of the public, of course, but the public will see, I think, in a very short while that this agreement is not working.

LHC: What is the platform of the Likud in respect to the Palestinian issue?

YS: Well, I think we are still respecting the Camp David Agreements. Maybe not all the details, but the basic roots and the basic foundations. We are ready to work hard to give to the Palestinians full autonomy, as Begin said, but not a state of their own. And what they are getting now, or will get in the very near future, will be an independent Palestinian state on the same small territory on which Israel exists, and I think it's a disaster.

LHC: I believe that there is no doubt that there will be a Palestinian state. I've talked to some Palestinians who tell me it's absolutely going to be a done deal. Why doesn't the prime minister tell this to the people?

YS: Well, it's because he knows that the people are still against a

Palestinian state because everybody understands that on such a small piece of land there can't be two independent states together. [Henry] Kissinger said it once very clearly, that on such a small piece of land you couldn't have the existence of two states that are not in love with each other. Rabin says it will be some "structure," but not a state. Maybe de facto it will be a state but it will not be a state. Well, it's not clear, I think. The Palestinians themselves say that they want to have a state and they're going to get it and they want Jerusalem as their capital. Jerusalem could be a reason for a terrible war. Therefore, I'm sure that with these disagreements we are not going toward peace.

LHC: Do you think you could possibly move toward a civil war in this country?

YS: I don't think a civil war, because you don't have among the Israeli people anyone who is ready to go to a civil war. We don't want to have a civil war, it would mean war once again between Arabs and Israelis. It's not peace, it's war.

LHC: So you think if there's a document that they sign, it's not a document of peace but of war for the future?

YS: Not at all, because it doesn't lead us to peace. Because it doesn't work, it couldn't work. The Israelis may be on their side, they are willing to give up a lot of things. But the Palestinians will not change anything for them. It is a state-in-a-territory status for Arafat, and he is ready to go ahead with this concept. He is getting what he could get, and he will try to get more. This will be his policy all the time. His policy is not a policy of peace and he doesn't even say it. When there is an opportunity for him to talk to his people, his Arab friends, he talks about *Jihad*, about a war.

LHC: You were in the Knesset on Thursday when the prime minister spoke to the members of Knesset. He changed his tune, instead of speaking about a greater Jerusalem, he said Jerusalem plus. Do you understand that?

YS: Well, it's nonsense. He speaks for instance against the idea of the whole of Israel [i.e., the West Bank and other Israeli occupied territory]. He's the first prime minister to speak against the idea of the land of Israel—the only one. In the past we could understand that Israel couldn't be great—a small country—but not the land of Israel. They say they love it, they admire it. But for some political reason, for peace, for instance, they have to give up something that they couldn't accept. But to be critical of the idea of all the land of Israel, this is really disastrous. Rabin was the first to say it, I think he will regret it one day.

LHC: OK. Rabin worked very closely with you, and I understand had a good relationship with you in the National Unity government.

YS: Yes, but we never really discussed politics.

LHC: Never really discussed the future?

YS: Never. In the daily matters there have been differences of views and he was very interested in being the minister of defense and therefore decided to keep very good relations with me. But no, we haven't discussed the future and politics. And there was this gap between him and Peres that encouraged me at times.

LHC: Are shocked by the behavior of Rabin?

YS: No, I am shocked more by the behavior of the people. I'm sure half of the population shares my views, but we need more. But the position of Rabin, all these concepts are illogical and, I will say, not honest. Because it does not say the truth. He once said about the Golan Heights that he would not leave it.

LHC: Right. It's in his platform.

YS: How could he leave it? How can it be that the prime minister says the contrary from what he says a few days or a few years ago. But I am not shocked and I hope he will find ways to change the course of history.

LHC: Tell us the famous James Baker story, where Jim Baker, the American Secretary of State tried to hold up the $10 billion loan guarantee to Israel. This was during your tenure of office. What are the real facts of that?

YS: Well, of course it was the decision of [President George] Bush. He promised the Arabs not to give us this $10 billion until we change our policy, until we accepted this concept of land for peace. I was never ready to accept this concept. This was the thing. Jimmy Carter, who was not the greatest friend to Israel, once said to us if they have some disagreement with us, this was told by Mr. Begin, we will never use economic pressure on you, and he kept his promise. And no American President did it. Help from the United States, I cannot give details, a lot of help, politically, then defense matters, and economic matters. They have been always friends and the first time when there was some blackmail, some real brutal pressure, was in the time of President Bush. It was his decision and I hope he paid for it.

LHC: You remember the Gulf War. One of the issues I've always had trouble with was the Scuds falling on Israel. Were you bullied by Bush to allow the—

YS: No, I was not bullied. Maybe I was convinced, but I understood the position of the United States. After the Americans have constructed this great coalition with the Arabs it was very dangerous for them if Israel participated in the war actively and by this participation it could bring about a collapse of the coalition. It was in our greatest interest to have this coalition sound and strong; and as I was sure that a victory would be on the side of the coalition, I decided we would try and do our utmost to defend ourselves, but not to endanger the coalition.

LHC: Were you nervous that [Saddam] Hussein had nuclear warheads or something on his Scuds?

YS: Well, of course, but I didn't think that he had nuclear arms but other means. But, of course, after all the results, it justified our decision.

LHC: Would you say that was one of your toughest decisions?

YS: It was very tough, and well, it was a matter of time. It took less than a month.

LHC: Was it tough to hold back your military people?

YS: I don't think so, but there's some military people who think otherwise, not many of them. But it was not a matter of some issue with the general command. They understood my position and they supported it. This was the first case in the history of Israel that Israel didn't respond to such aggression. And well, sometimes you have to be the first.

LHC: What was your toughest decision as prime minister?

YS: Well, I don't know. There have been many tough decisions. I think I have been through some tough periods and this period that you mentioned before—the period of the Iraqi Scuds—it was a very tough time. And it was not easy to make decisions, but I think that my decision was right and it was justified by the events after that and now I think that the Israeli people, almost all of them, agree with it.

LHC: What was your greatest accomplishment as prime minister?

YS: Well, the greatest accomplishment was the immigration of the Russian Jews. It was a struggle for years. I was active in this struggle since the 1950s. It was lucky for us to get the great support of the United States to open the gates of Soviet Russia for the Jews to get out. I think President Reagan and Secretary of State Schultz worked for it very strongly, and they got it. And without them I'm not sure it would have succeeded. But it was a great accomplishment and it goes on.

LHC: I've noticed that they're very well absorbed.

YS: Very well absorbed, because of the special character of the people. You have many people among them with the highest qualifications—many scientists, many good professionals.

LHC: Where were you born?

YS: I was born on the border between Poland and White Russia.

LHC: So it's got to be a tremendous internal satisfaction for you to see 600,000 Soviet Jews come to Israel.

YS: I am really happy about it and I think it is ongoing and we will have in the near future one or two million of these Jewish people. It's a very great source of strength for our country. I hope we will have other Jewish people, too.

LHC: You told us Americans are immigrating too?

YS: I think one day American Jews will come here and invest their part, their qualifications. And we need them—very, very badly.

LHC: I know you're in a rush, we're running out of time. I want to talk about Secretary of State James Baker in Madrid.

YS: He was a very intelligent man and a very good Foreign Secretary. Very clever man. I had the impression that he was carrying out the policy of President Bush, because I spent a lot of time with him and I explained our positions and I cannot claim that he was tricky with me. While on the other end, he played a certain role with American policy to the Arabs. He gave them some promises and he came to the Madrid Conference because he believed that when it came to the stage of the negotiations about a permanent solution, America would be on their side. They hoped that Bush would always be the President and he would support their views.

LHC: Would you say that Bush was pro-Arab?

YS: He was pro-Arab, no question. He really believed that they were right. And he said it sometimes and other Americans supported his stance.

LHC: Why did you go to the Madrid Peace Conference?

YS: Because I wanted peace. We've been for a time in a very good situation in Israel and I think the quest for peace is necessary for a country to develop. To develop its economy, to develop as one unit. Of course, I didn't think going into this conference meant giving up part of our territory. I don't think it's a necessary price of peace. I don't know any other country in the world that is giving up its territory even for peace. But I wanted to get peace, peace with the Arabs. We have to live in peace here. But not at any price.

LHC: My last question—ten years from now, what will Israel look like?

YS: Well, it depends. It depends on if we succeed in nullifying this last agreement with the PLO, then I think our situation will be excellent. You will have here ten million Jewish people and Israel will be a very important country in all respects—economically, culturally, politically.

LHC: You see a good Israel in ten years.

YS: Yes.

LHC: But you have to nullify that agreement.
YS: Yes, of course.

Yitzhak Shamir was the longest serving prime minister in Israel's history. In his contacts with President George W. Bush he felt that the U.S. leader was more pro-Arab than even handed in his attitude. He considered James Baker, Bush's Secretary of State, a brilliant tactician but no friend of Israel.

Shamir made the momentous decision at the United States's urging not to retaliate in the Gulf War even as Scud missiles fell on Israel. He indicated that the decision was made at the personal request of under-secretary of state, Richard Eagelberger. He recently received the Israeli Prize, the highest award given to an Israeli citizen.

Shamir felt one of his greatest contributions was the immigration of 1 million Russians under his premiership. When I asked him who he considered his personal hero, I thought he would name one of the revisionist generals.

He said "Mao Tse Tung." When I aske why he said, "Mao fed a billion people."

SHIMON**PERES**

Shimon Peres, a former prime minister and leader of the Labor Party. In favor of a land-for-peace treaty, abandoning the Golan Heights for a treaty with Syria. He favors the creation of an Israeli constitution which Israel lacks and most politicians do not favor.

LHC: You're very traditional. Your background is tremendously traditional.

SP: Yes, yes.

LHC: Your grandfathers were rabbis and cantors. So why is the public so unaware of that?

SP: I don't know—what is the public? Half of the public voted for me; it's not a little, in a country that's so conservative. They have such a strong religious group. I am trying to introduce a change. People don't like changes. I say, "Be controversial, don't be popular." What is popular? They agree with everything that exists, they agree with anybody they meet. What is controversial? You want to change. It is not that people don't know me. They don't like some of what I'm trying to do. They can't understand it.

LHC: We were in the Knesset yesterday. I sense that this country's in despair. People really don't know which way to turn.

SP: Yes.

LHC: We interviewed people from Likud, some from Labor; everybody's
       in shock from the first one hundred days of [Prime Minister] Bibi
       Netanyahu. They don't really know what to make of it. The feel-
       ing's that he's put some strain on the relationships with Jordan;
       that he's put some strain on Camp David with [Ehud] Barak; that
       he's put some strain, obviously, on relations with Arafat. They look
       at you like the wise man, the statesman, and I'm talking about the
       political people; maybe the population didn't know enough about
       it, or maybe they did.

SP: Yes, the population has a much better understanding. And I got
       thousands and thousands of letters. I didn't get a single negative
       letter. Letters of support, of love. I have more problems from the
       top than among the people.

LHC: Where do you see the country going?

SP: Look. The Likud promised three or four things which were impos-
       sible. They said, "Why should you pay for peace? They should
       give you peace without a price." Free. Free lunch. Free peace. It's
       not honest. I am telling the people, as I'm telling you. Peace has
       a price. The peace process is not a book of poetry. It's a book of
       blood, of struggles, of disappointments. The Likud came in and
       said, "Have it free!" Then they say, "Why should we have peace
       with terror? Let's have security first, peace after." This is again not
       serious. Only peace may bring security. But if we would wait until
       we have total security, we would never have peace.

       Then they came in and said, "Mr. Peres was in a hurry. He was
       galloping, you know, he didn't do it." Again, it's nonsense. Because,
       if you come to horses, and you see all those galloping horses, and
       you say, my god, I can't stand their pace. I would like to become,
       say, a turtle. That's fine, you can become a turtle. But the horses,
       they will not become turtles. The horses of war, the horses of
       [Islamic] fundamentalism, the horses of missiles. And you are a
       fool if you think that the armor of the turtle on your back will be
       a compensation for the speed of the different horses.

       I'm telling you that in three or four years, we shall face a terrible situation. Fundamentalism will spread, they may win over some of the oil wells, they may have a nuclear auction, they will have missiles, and then what? With all due respect to a rabbi who has reached the age of one hundred years, what does he know about nuclear weapons? What does he know about missiles? What does he know about the dangers that are facing us?

I want to tell you again, straightforward: there are many wise Jews, [but] the Jewish people is not a wise people. We didn't understand what Hitler was, we didn't understand what Stalin was, we didn't understand in our first temple and second temple, the enemies we faced, the need for unity inside. And I don't want to depend automatically on what is called "the wisdom of our people." Everything is written on the wall, and I'm not afraid to say so. And nobody will fight me.

They said, with the Palestinians, what Mr. Netanyahu calls a "generous autonomy." What does that mean, a "generous autonomy?" Generous to whom? The Palestinians will never take autonomy as a generous proposal, instead of modern autonomy. We think that autonomy is a station on the road for a permanent solution. They think that autonomy is the permanent solution. Generous autonomy.

All of this was our mistake, that is one of the reasons we lost the elections. We say, "For peace," the Likud says "For peace." But as we said that peace has a price. For example, you have to withdraw from part of the Golan Heights, or more than a part. They say, "No, no, keep the Golan Heights." You see? And that is why we paid foolishly. Now, the last four years, the government founded by Yitzhak Rabin, and all the credit must be given to him, were the best four years in the four thousand years of Jewish history. Never were the Jewish people, or the Jewish state, as respected as today. Never did we have a better economic situation, never did we have a more political wisdom of strategic facility than we have today. And now, what are we doing? Nobody knows where to go.

LHC: People are in despair.

SP: Yes, but look, I can only tell a little. I am not looking for popular
        votes. Maybe it was the elections, I didn't lose my conscience.
        Maybe I am short one third of a percent, but I am not short of
        seeing what the situation, as I believe at least, is, and I don't have
        the slightest hesitation to tell you what I think and what I feel.

LHC: Do you have any problem with the Palestinian state?

SP: Look, I have a problem with autonomy for the Palestinians,
        because I think it's unreasonable. I shall give you, again with hon-
        esty, a simple example. We have the overriding responsibility. A
        person from our intelligence service comes to me and says, "Look,
        I have a piece of information that three infiltrators are trying to
        penetrate Israel. Put a closure on Gaza." What is my choice? I have
        to put on a closure. But to put on a closure of a million people, I
        affect their economy, maybe I push them to support hostile forces.
        I don't think it's right. I would prefer it if they had said, Jordanian-
        Palestinian Confederation.

        Now my full views, I shall never publish ahead of time. I have
        learned from experience that everything that becomes known is
        dead. When you and I are sitting together negotiating, you have
        your proposals, I have mine; there's no chance that you would take
        my proposals or that I'll take your proposals. The art of negotia-
        tions is to create new proposals. And if you publish them ahead
        of time you kill them. So I carry them in my heart.

LHC: Interesting story: Ezer Weizman dispatched me about eight years
        ago to see Mr. Arafat in Tunis, on a secret mission. He couldn't
        go, he was an Israeli, Mr. Shamir booted him out of the govern-
        ment, basically, and you people saved him halfway. I saw three
        people when I returned.

        I saw Yitzhak Rabin, who didn't want to hear anything about
        Arafat. He told me that he's a terrorist and he represents no one,
        and "I don't want to deal with it." I saw you. You told me to keep
        speaking, keep going, keep speaking.

        Ezer was in Geneva, and he said to me, "I just want one read
        from you, one read. That's why I sent you. Can we do business with

him?" I said, "Yes." That was eight years ago. Tell me how you view this peace process, and especially Yitzhak Rabin. You remember that story, by the way?

SP: Yes, I do. The problem is not if Arafat was ready or not, but if our people were ready to lead the majority. Arafat was demonized in our country. We have to face the situation as it really is or was. Now, when we formed the government, Yitzhak told me he wanted to conduct the negotiations with the Palestinians. And he said publicly that he hoped that in six to nine months, they would find a solution. He was referring to the negotiations that took place in Washington.

In our private talks, I told him, "Yitzhak, there is no chance that anything could come out of those negotiations. You have to do it differently." And so he didn't believe in what I was suggesting, he said, "Okay, try your hand." What happened was that the negotiations in Washington failed, and the negotiations in Oslo succeeded.

Yitzhak was honest enough to say that he didn't tell any of his friends about the negotiations in Oslo, because he didn't believe that anything would come out of it. Now, what I did, and what he did, and again, I don't want to belittle his decisions; we have developed a relationship that saved us. We were sitting, just the two of us, no notetakers, no witnesses; nothing leaked. The word didn't leak. We spoke totally open, we didn't fight for credit, and then when we saw that really the only thing that could happen was the Oslo story, he took it.

LHC: And you developed a very close working relationship with him.

SP: Yes. Look, there were differences, there were difficulties from the past, there were suspicions, and competition. You know, a person who lives by himself wins every possible subject. But when you have two persons, you have troubles. That's normal. I don't complain.

LHC: When you sit in this chair, and you think, and your hero is David Ben Gurion, no question—what do you think he'd be thinking now?

SP: I think he would tell me, "You did right." He would tell me to never sacrifice your position for popularity. If you put on a good fight, if you were honest, if you told the truth, if you fought coura-geously, this is what counts. He used to say, "I don't do what the people want. I know what the people need. A leader is not one who tries to see what the people want, but tries to answer what the people need."

LHC: I talk with the Americans, everyone respects you. What is the prestige of Israel today?

SP: Israel has a tremendous amount of prestige. I think by sheer rhetoric, we lost a great deal of it. There was no need to go before the Congress and say, "We give up foreign aid." When you don't give up foreign aid.

LHC: That's interesting, because I was at both conventions and I interviewed Senators Orin Hatch and John Kasek, the Budget Chairman, and I said, "John, what do you think about the prime ministers talking to Congress about giving back some money on the budget?" He said, "Off the camera or on the camera?" I said, "Well, give it to me, both." Off the camera, he thought it was silly. Because you were not ready to do it.

SP: If you do it, do it. Then to talk about mutuality, what is mutuality? It says, "I won't give you anything, you give me everything." Mr. Netanyahu quotes Begin. Begin gave back the whole land to Egypt. Begin was the first politician on the right of the Israeli political side to say, "Land for peace." Doesn't matter if he said it in words or in deeds.

LHC: But you supported him, I remember that.

SP: I did support it, because without us he wouldn't have had the majority, and in our party there was a division. And I stood up and said, "Gentlemen, we didn't negotiate the agreement, we don't like parts of it. But that's not the problem. Are we going to have peace or not? If yes, let's support it. This is our only chance." I had a very strong debate with Yigal Allon. He thought that we shouldn't agree to the dismantling of the settlements in Sinai. I told him that's not the problem. If you vote against it, that's like voting against peace. We must be serious.

LHC: I spent a lot of time with a fellow named Bruno Kreiskey. Your friend from the Socialist International.

SP: He arranged a meeting between Sadat and myself in Vienna. I was in opposition, I was not in the government. But he decided to give the same honors to me as to Sadat. So Sadat got twenty or thirty motorcycles, I got the same. Planes, everything. But I was in the opposition, so when I came to the airport, I didn't have a car. So the head of protocol says, "Mr. Peres, where is your car?" I said, "I don't have any!" She says, "What do you want?" I said, "I'll take a taxi!" She says, "Are you crazy?"

Bruno says, "No problem. He will have my car." So he sends me his car, and the whole time we're in his car, and believe me, he treated me like a father. He looked where I was having breakfast, he came for lunch. Really. So one day we went down to the vine-yards, and there they make the grape wine, and he was an expert, so he took me to a very nice place where you drink, and I said, "Bruno, why do they attack me all the time? Why do they attack Israel all the time?" And he gave me a very interesting answer. He says, "Look, if I shall not attack you, how can I help you?"

LHC: It's very true. Because I'll tell you a story. When Weizman was Defense Minister, Avital Sharansky was in his office, Weizman asked me to help free Sharansky. So I traveled to Vienna and asked for Kreisky's assistance. In a split second he picked up the phone in front of me and called [Aleksei] Kosygin. He was unbelievable. And he told me that he was of "Jewish extraction," whatever that meant. He says, "My mother used to go to the synagogue and light candles."

SP: Yes, he told me that he was, on several occasions, attacked in an anti-Semitic manner. He told me that, for example, after the debate of the party, people stood up and shouted, "Do you think it's a kibbutz here?"

LHC: You had four good years. Do you think that any relationship to those four good years has to do with the collapse of the Soviet Union?

SP: I can't know, really . . . .

LHC: Syria was a little bit deflated.

SP: Look, the fact that Soviet Union has collapsed, the United States remained the only superpower, opened a window of opportunity for peace all over the world, not only here. I wish it could remain, but I know it's not the case, and another five to ten years, we shall see another five or six superpowers. And we shall see a different world.

LHC: Five or six?

SP: Yes.

LHC: Name them.

SP: The United States. China, 100 percent. The United Europe, Japan, India, and maybe Russia. Look, Russia has two capacities that no other nation in the world has. Number one, the capacity to suffer. They are a little like Jews, you know. Jews are never happy unless they are unhappy. Suffering is part of life. Second thing, they are used to sick leadership. [Leonid] Brezhnev was sick, for a very long time, you know? Look at all the leaders after Stalin. Everybody was sick in his own way. Now again, Yeltsin is sick.

But this is an interruption in Russian history. Russian history will go for the first time, since Ivan the Terrible, after Stalin the Terrible, over to a democratic system. It will take time. The Communists killed the country from an ecological point of view, they made the people sick from a political point of view, but the Russians are basically very intelligent people. The great story about Russia is the contradiction between the intelligence of the people and the lack of intelligence of the system. Never did such an unintelligent system produce so many intelligent people as it did in Russia.

LHC: What is the effect of the Russian immigration to Israel?

SP: Great.

LHC: About half a million?

SP: More.

LHC: Prime Minister Shamir, said this was the greatest accomplishment of his administration, that he brought a half a million Russian refugees to Israel.

SP: I saw Gorbachev in San Diego, and he asked me how did the Russian immigrants vote in the last election. "Not so good," I said. "Oh, you have another issue to blame on me," he said. It wasn't Shamir who changed the subject, you know?

LHC: I believe that's true!

SP: I think it was rather Gorbachev. And Shamir did a good job, I don't want to underrate him, but let's keep a sense of balance, and a little bit of modesty.

LHC: By the way, it's interesting that Yitzhak Shamir said that the Oslo agreement should be voided.

SP: If Mr. Shamir could have stopped the turning of the world around the sun, he would gladly do it. He thinks all the movement in the world is a waste of energy. If he could freeze the whole world, all movement, he would be a happy person. For good or for bad, whatever it is.

LHC: I understand that Bibi Netanyahu, who may want to move forward with the Oslo agreements, and maybe wants to do things, is blocked by Uzi Landau and Benny Begin, who are really idealistic in the way they think. It's my impression that maybe the only way the country can move forward is by a Unity government. Do you think that's a possibility?

SP: Right now it's not on our agenda. What is, is a united effort for peace. A government is administrations. Administrations we have had already. I for one, I don't miss the government. For peace, I would do everything.

LHC: You seem to be much freer now. It's like you can say things that you couldn't when you were prime minister. Maybe those roles are more important than being prime minister at times.

SP: Well, you know, when you are prime minister, you have the instrumentation to make decisions. When you are out of the prime ministership, you have the instrumentation to think about what should be done.

LHC: What do you think should be done? Just go on with the peace process?

SP: A hundred percent. It is an existential issue.

LHC: Are you nervous about the fate of Israel now, personally?

SP: I'm not nervous, I'm worried. I told you, at the beginning, in four years time, five years time, we shall see more superpowers. The Arab–Israeli conflict was living on the world conflict. The end of the Cold War, for a while, enabled us to handle our own conflict.

Unfortunately, then the Iranians will try to spread fundamentalism, as they have in Afghanistan. Afghanistan became fundamentalist. They are also in other countries, in oil producing countries. They may have a nuclear bomb. We have to think ahead. We cannot talk about the wars of yesterday, and we should not talk about the peace of yesterday. Have to speak and act for the peace of tomorrow.

LHC: What do you think the role of the United States should be?

SP: Americans basically, are fair-minded. They really do a wonderful job. I know there is a lot of criticism here and there, but try to think about it. Here we have a superpower. Two hundred and ten years old. They went to many wars, not for their own needs. American boys were fighting in the First World War, Second World War, and many of them were killed. America won the war. Conquered countries. And you know, they didn't keep anything for themselves. Think about it. It's unprecedented in history. The United States conquered Japan. Japan won because the United States conquered it. They won democracy, they won freedom.

Basically, the United States supports peace. She stood on the side of Israel, not all the time, most of the time, when we were in danger, and now they stand on our side when peace is in danger. And I have full respect. You know, I'm too grown up to be impressed by another piece of gossip, what this one said, what that one said, it's not important. You should see the main courses of history, the main movements. I myself am a great admirer of a French historian, Ferdinand Braudel. He says that the real history is not the history of events, but the history of developments. For example, the moment they learned how to use the wind to move ships on the seas is more important than the length of Cleopatra's nose. And from that point of view, I think that one has to follow developments, and not gossips.

LHC: I'm an economist by theory, basically, in history. My theory is that if Israel loses its prestige, investment will go down, tourism will go down, your economics will fall.

SP: Right.

LHC: Will that theory work here too?

SP: Yes, one hundred percent.

LHC: If the baby doesn't have milk and doesn't have a roof, everybody gets upset.

SP: We will have milk, but skim milk.

LHC: I said this to the group Friday night, when I had dinner, and they said, right away they said that God would become, like a superman, would come and take care of them, but I don't think that's very realistic.

SP: You should have another Friday night with a different group. Don't take this group as representing Israel. For whom did they vote, by the way? They were Likudniks?

LHC: They were Likud—

SP: So....

LHC: The question is that you have many different societies in Israel now. Is that not true?

SP: Yes, and you do, too, in America.

LHC: But we're pluralistic—

SP: The program is different. The American [law] prosecution is great because it is based on tolerance. Only tolerance permits pluralism to coexist. We have pluralism, but we don't have enough tolerance. What we need is tolerance. The essence of democracy is made of two points. One is that everybody has the right to be equal, and the second is that everybody has the equal right to be different. But you have to organize the differences, not only the equality. And the greatness of the American Constitution, as I have said, is the introduction of tolerance as a major foundation of the American life.

LHC: Why doesn't Israel have a constitution?

SP: Because Ben Gurion was afraid that in the age of the in-gathering of exiles, some of them may introduce in the constitution elements that future generations will not agree with, including the religious parties. You see, America was a revolt, not an agreement. Israel is an agreement, not a revolt.

America is the legitimate daughter of Europe. A group of intellectuals from Europe came and said, "Europe, spoiled our lives with churches and intolerance, and hatred and discrimination. Let's build a new York, a new Amsterdam." And they wrote the right constitution. A constitution of revolt.

What is a right constitution of consent, we would have a disagreement. Because it wouldn't be consent, it would be compromises here—it would be a coalition of ideas. You can have a coalition of parties, provided that the foundation of this coalition is tolerance.

LHC: Did you discuss this issue with Ben Gurion?

SP: Oh, yes.

LHC: Aharon Barak, who is the Chief Justice of your Supreme Court gives a few rulings, which were civil rights, human rights, and right away he needs protection.

SP: He is a great man. Every person who wants to change needs protection. And they get it. Only conservative people who do nothing are secure. And Aharon Barak is an outstanding jurist, and he's courageous, and he's brilliant.

LHC: You've been around the block a lot. How do you coincide or bring together religious law and jurisprudence? You're probably one of the few who can answer the question.

SP: Look, religious law is not a problem. The problem is the institutions of justice. Can you have two, or can you have one? Can you have the institution which is the Supreme Court and the Courts of the State, or can you have a Supreme Rabbinate? That is the real problem.

We shall not give the Rabbinate the supremacy of our democ-

racy. No chance whatsoever. The Rabbinate is a matter of volun-
teers; the Supreme Court is a matter of law. That is the difference.
Because you have different Rabbinates—you have Lubavitch, you
have the Conservative, and some people say that the Messiah
already arrived, so he's dead, so he's alive. These stories don't make
any sense.

The greatest diplomat that the Jewish people ever had is the
Messiah. The reason why he's so great is because he never came!
And they are still expecting him, they are still looking forward,
they are still hoping. But there must be a clear distinction: the law
of the land is the law, the religion of a person is his choice. We
cannot impose religion or anti-religious feelings.

*Shimon Peres is Foreign Minister in Sharon's unity government. The two men seem to be
at opposite ends of the political spectrum but...perhaps not! Both were disciples of Israel's
founding father, David Ben Gurion. As of today, the highly intelligent, Nobel Peace
Prize Laureate, Peres, at 77, and the brilliant (and slightly younger), Sharon have an
excellent partnership. Interviews with other Israeli politicians indicate that Peres' intel-
lect might have contributed to the loss of the presidential office to Moishe Katzav. He
remains a staunch advocate of peace. He strongly believes that economics and trade will
be the ultimate resolution of the Middle East conflict.*

DR. JOSEPH**BURG**
& RUBY**RIVLIN**

Dr. Joseph Burg, a leading member of the National Religious Party, a former Interior Minister. Vividly favored the continuing building of Jewish settlements on the West Bank. Accepted the Palestinian Authority but it should be under Israeli rule. Against direct election of the prime minister.

LHC: Dr. Burg, you have seen all the history of Israel. Abba Eban, the Foreign Minister who served with you in many, many governments, said that this is the lowest moment in Jewish, Israeli history. Would you agree with that?

JB: That now is the lowest point?

LHC: Yes.

JB: So that means something good, because that means there can be nothing lower. We should not be too nervous. In Israel and for the Jewish people all over the world, after a two-thousand-year persecution, that would mean that now is the low point. Because after having peace, too much of a cold peace—better than a cold war, but a lot of question marks. The peace with the Egyptians didn't come out as warmly as we wanted. We are happy with this peace with Jordan but the Palestinians as such are getting their inspiration from Syria, from Iran, also it's possible from Russia but I'm not sure.

So it's a low point today, especially if the nation is divided, what should we do with peace and what can we do without peace. What price war we know. What price peace we don't know. But we are willing to try it. The nation is divided concerning tactics, policy, and strategy at this point.

LHC: The religious problem, which you really are an expert on, the country has really become divided between the secular and the right-wing. Your party, the Maudal [National Religious Party], is not like it was before. What happened?

JB: First of all, it happens. Our party is still pledged to the unity of the Jewish people. There's not too many extremists, like people of the very right-wing. What happened with us, well I'll tell you the good side of what happened. In 1967, Israel became larger than we were before, almost Eretz Israel. And many people saw God's hand in this happening and therefore believed in the Eretz Israel. The finger of God is here, and now we have to make settlements.

The word settlements I understand in the political jargon of Washington became a dirty word. But don't forget my dear Americans that you also had your settlements when you settled the United States. Before the Mayflower there were not too many Europeans in the American country. So settlements are part of history.

If you want to see idealistic young people, go to the settlements. That is the good part. But it's a very complicated thing—you need a majority in the parliament and they are a minority. And for the same reason they're too radical, but they understand that time and circumstances will bring my party to the middle of the road. It is my firm belief that the middle of the road does not mean mediocrity. Middle of the road is a constructive way to bring together Jews with Jews, and Jews with Arabs who don't believe that the idea of coexistence denies the possibly of our existence.

LHC: Do you have any problem with the idea of a Palestinian state?

JB: I would say yes. First of all I would like to be sure that there is not a redemand. That the Palestinians who are there should not come every day with a new demand. And here I am using Palestinian—Arabs—that are living in the territory of the state of Israel that they should be exploited.

　　　 You see I was there when Chamberlain promised peace for all the generations—not with sympathy, but peace with honor. And you'll remember the peace with honor lasted from September, more or less, 1938 to March 1939. And the Sudeten Deutsche were exploited in a pretext to take over all of Czechoslovakia.

　　　 So I am very fearful and we have to be very, very cautious concerning issues of security, Israel's security, if and when there should be a Palestinian state. I am not a die hard, I am a man of compromise. I know we have to pay something, but something for something, not getting something for nothing. I believe this is a little bit of chutzpah—little bit is an understatement—to ask on the behalf of the Palestinian Arabs. Jerusalem is a capital, a capital of a state that never existed in any Arab state—never in history. In history, there was a state of Jerusalem, when the Crusaders came here in 1099 to Jerusalem. In Jerusalem there never was any Arab state, Palestine. And therefore I believe you can see this is very complicated.

LHC: Menachem Begin, who I consider to be a great prime minister, said that he thought there should be autonomy.

JB: Full autonomy.

LHC: Full autonomy. What did he mean by that?

JB: I regret that you had no time to ask him. But I can only say that autonomy would mean a maximum of policy parameters. I would like to say this a simple way. We were—Begin, Sharon, Shamir, and I—we were in the Blair House. I was asked by the Americans, "What does it mean? Autonomy?" And I said everything except having external politics and without having an army of their own.

LHC: There are countries that have that—the Netherlands and Antilles.

JB: The only true autonomy I believe is in Sweden, in Lapland. But anyhow, there is no other possibility.

I believe in the possibility because as natural things there are things that arise in autonomy, by themselves—traffic, post, public works, internal matters—things that we have to be together on, fighting contagious diseases, water problems. Development problems we could do together, security we have to do alone. We cannot have a foreign army west of the Jordan.

LHC: Had you been in the cabinet during the Oslo peace arrangement, would you have voted for it or against it.

JB: First of all I believe that no one would want my advice but I believe a stronger attitude of the Israelis was not realized. Let me tell you, in about 1980, I gave a press conference with the chairman of our committee, it was in the negotiations in London. And I was asked would you be ready—1980—to meet with the PLO and Arafat. And I said, "Yes, under two conditions. One condition that the part speaking about abolition, about destruction, that this part be abolished itself, and second, there should be two or three years without terror."

And not only because terror's a bad thing because it kills people, but in order to know if Arafat can deliver, if he can stop the terror. If he can deliver, stop the terror, for this I would pay a price, but for goods that do not exist and goods that cannot be delivered I cannot pay. Those conditions until today have not been really realized.

LHC: I've said many times that Oslo was a historical mistake for two reasons. One is that Rabin should say, "OK, I agree to meet with you or recognize your Mr. Arafat, but the same day you must take away your covenant to destroy me." On the same day—you can't let it linger on. The second is that there was no economic infrastructure created for these people, so they gave them back land without an economic infrastructure—that's just a disaster.

JB: I accept what you're saying, but it only means that serious minds must meet. And what you say about economics is also true.

LHC: They have to make a living, they have to be fed.

JB: I accept that.

LHC: Your country's entered into a new political arena where they now have, which no other country in the world has, direct election of the prime minister.

JB: But you have direct election of the president.

LHC: But we have a different system, we have a check-and-balance system. You have a hybrid system. You don't have an executive portion of the government and you don't have a check and balance system set up. Will you agree with me now that the Likud Party is not what the Likud Party was before?

JB: I believe that no party is today is exactly what it was before. That goes for my party, that goes for Labor, that goes for Likud. There is a question of leadership. You see, leaders do not come by the dozens. And leaders do not come because you ask—either they are there or not. So you have certain historical periods with a lot of leaders and then you have a certain time when there is leadership. I personally am against direct election of the prime minister and you are right in your argument because it is a different system. I believe that many of the people who advocated the direct election are now unhappy and I wish them happiness in their unhappiness.

LHC: Dr. Burg, you headed the National Religious Party, is there a place in government to have a religious party?

JB: First of all, we are much more than just a religion. We are sometimes very complicated. But we are very interesting, in my eyes, a unique mix of national and religious elements together. What percentage is religious and what percentage national every Jew discusses with every other Jew.

But anyhow, when we came here to this country, we came according to the old convenant between God and Israel. It's our place or we could have called it Poughkeepsie, or something else. This state is interesting for the Jews all over the world because we have a lot of our traditional heritage with us. Therefore, we have to take a little bit of our heritage: religiously, spiritually, culturally, into one unit in this country, that's my answer.

LHC: So what's your feeling now with this law of conversion where the Reform and Conservative will—

JB: Well, I'm very unhappy about it, because it's a mixture of political and religious argumentation. It's meeting together but not always with justification. You see the discussion between the different currents in Judaism, it's an old one.

It started in Germany around 1845, these great figures, the Conservatives not moving together with the temper of the Reform in Germany. I'm very surprised that Conservatives in America are getting together with the reform.

Let me say, ideologically, there is too much of a marriage of convenience between Conservatives and Reform. I'm unhappy because this discussion which started in Germany 150 years ago should not bring an ultimatum as it has this week when the Reform Rabbi said they will stop sending money to the state of Israel if this or this law will be accepted.

Why should the newcomer who's come from Siberia to Israel suffer because the Reform Rabbi is not satisfied with the politics of the Knesset here. The thirty thousand, forty thousand Reform Jews you have here will get everything they want, but to dictate here what should be in a conversion, I believe is not fair.

LHC: So why are you against the law?

JB: I am in favor of, in this country that there should only be one kind of conversion, that there is only one recognized form, Orthodox conversion. You see, I am a little bit of an expert, for I am ordained an Orthodox Rabbi. I was fourteen years Interior Minister and I have had the Orthodox problem on a very low, low flame.

And then when Begin came he believed he could find a solution. He made a committee and I was part of the committee. The problem, I would like to say, without bragging, that I was the only man who left the government of the State of Israel in 1958 because of the "new Jew" discussion.

So I would like to say, you cannot have in your country three different kinds of conversion. Every country has a law and this should be one at least. Now, the Reform Rabbi in the United States, he accepts someone, woman or man, in his synagogue but not in Judaism. Because in Judaism we have for two thousand years accepted how a conversion should be done.

LHC: Do you believe it will cause conflict with the American Jews?

JB: I believe it will not. I believe it is overdone, the whole issue. I believe there should be a more tranquil atmosphere. You see the problems for us in this country is that religion is living, living every day. For many Jews living in the United States, the religious climate is a little bit less. In our country you have electricity of 220 volts, in United States you have 110 volts, here you have plenty of Jews going to schule three times a day, and then you have Jews who are going to schule three times a year. Three times a day, three times a year—there is a difference and the difference should be understood.

LHC: Did you work with Yitzhak Rabin?

JB: Yes, sometimes with the same opinions, sometimes without opinions. He was not as elastic as I would have liked. But he was a man of courage and I was very unhappy that it happened and very unhappy that it was exploited against religious Judaism. This murder came from a certain atmosphere.

LHC: Do you think it was only one guy who had it in his head to assassinate Rabin? Or do you think it was a group of people?

JB: A group, if as you say a group could mean up to ten people. Since Meir Kahane came there has always been a right-wing extremist group and I am not happy about it. What we do, what we teach is against this kind of violence.

LHC: How do you visualize Israel in the next ten years?

JB: Chaim Weizmann once said that it is very difficult to be a prophet in Israel because the competition of the old ones is too strong. I believe that will come. We succeeded in the last few years in gathering millions of people in a large, national revolutionary experiment. We also have to give an explanation for what we did, but first of all the question is of security, defense, and having between Israel and Ishmael a better understanding.

Dr. Joseph Burg had the distinction of being the longest serving cabinet minister in Israeli history. His most important task was as Minister of the Interior under Menachem Begin. A longtime diplomat, he oversaw Israeli–Egyptian relations after Camp David. He was a leading member of the National Religious Party but was considered an orthodox liberal who opposed right-wing extremists. Dr. Burg died in 1999. Burg's son, Avraham, is now speaker of the Knesset and a leading candidate for prime minister from the Labor Party. Should Avraham Burg be elected, he would be the first Orthodox Prime Minister.

Ruby Rivlin, a Likud Party member of the Knesset. Firmly against allowing Palestinians' formation of a state with a capital in Jerusalem. Believes Jerusalem must be a Jewish city that permits no negotiating.

LHC: Ruby, is there any compromise in the Likud in terms of allowing the Palestinians to have any sort of rights in Jerusalem?

RR: Well, if we are talking about autonomy, we have passed the point of no return; we are negotiating with the Palestinians. We know that the Palestinian Authority is doing something in Jerusalem as well. Here in Zone B they actually have their headquarters. And we know they are trying to do a lot. Nevertheless they understood and they got the message that once we got in power, they could not behave in Jerusalem as though Jerusalem is part of the Palestinian entity. They were convinced that they should postpone, without question.

LHC: When the Oslo Agreement was agreed to, Shimon Peres said to one of his senior aides that the problem of Jerusalem will be on the back burner. Netanyahu, your prime minister, said that we want to go to final status talks, that includes Jerusalem, I understand. Where do you wind up with Jerusalem on the Likud side?

RR: I really think this a consensus of the entire Jewish people all around the world.

LHC: I'm not sure that's true. We spoke to David Hartman over there, we spoke to other people who are willing to see a joint capital here, they're willing to see a borrowed type of situation, someone, I think from the Peres camp has come up with something to allow religious freedom for the Palestinians. I'm not sure everyone is wall to wall on keeping Jerusalem.

Reuven (Ruby) Rivlin,
Likud Minister of Communication

RR: That is the whole tragedy. Because we were trying to convince the people of Israel and all around the world, not only the Jews, but all the friendly nations of the world, that the Palestinian are really now going step by step. They have this step by step strategy and they will get to Jerusalem. They will get it by getting a Palestinian entity and then to a Palestinian state and then to Jerusalem. Everyone said, "No way" only ten years ago. To former Prime Minister Rabin, we said "Rabin, what will be with Jerusalem?" and he said, "Don't worry! No question! There is no way to discuss Jerusalem, there is no way to put it on the agenda."

When we asked he was the right hand of Mr. Shimon Peres at the time, when we claimed during the election that Peres was going to redivide Jerusalem, he said we were talking blasphemy, that we were saying something against him that was not true. Now everyone agrees that Jerusalem is the microcosm of whether we can live together, Jews and Arabs. Whether they are willing to give up and to give into a Palestinian state side by side with Israel, without Jerusalem, without the Jordan River, here we can see the whole problem.

LHC: But Ruby, not everyone is an ideologue like you. The world is full of politicians who have made statements that have broken the dreams of many. Prime Minister Netanyahu said he would never shake the hand of Arafat, yet he has. Your prime minister said that he would never do anything on the issue of Hebron but he has. Isn't there sort of a dramatic or slow process that's being carried out? Are you and other hardliners a minority or majority in your party?

RR: Well, we are now maybe a minority in our party. No one really cares for the strategy of the Likud. We believe that the land of Israel belongs to the children of Israel. That was our dream and we built it step by step and we were very stubborn and we got to the idea that we could build the Israeli state. Then after the '48 war, the Independence War, we said that those territories are occupied by Egypt and Jordan but we will have a historical chance to release them during one of those times when they stop warring against us. And the dream came true in 1967—everyone praised them. Everyone swore that Jerusalem would not be divided ever again.

And of course I understand that after Oslo we've passed the point of no return. I can understand why so many ideological people in the Likud party, the former Herat party, the Begin party, the Jabotinski party, they faced reality and they became people who understand that they have to behave according to the reality that was created de facto. So we are not pragmatists, because we really believe that the land of Israel belongs to the people of Israel according to the law, according to our belief, according to our promise, according to the promise that brought most of those people to be buried here. Because only two hundred years ago only two thousand of our people were allowed to go to Israel. Now we are a majority.

LHC: I go to Tel Aviv and I talk to a lot of secular Jews and they tell me that they would rather have a peace and a shared capital in Jerusalem than a united Jerusalem and they're fifty percent of the population.

RR: Tel Aviv [i.e., the Labor Party] lost the election because of Jerusalem. We had two ideas that could have kept Israel within the boundaries of Tel Aviv with three or four million Jews all around, separating themselves from all of the history of the Jewish people from all the history that brought us back into Israel. The Zionist idea of why we came here. Why do you think we didn't go to America?

LHC: Right, we understand your point. Behind me is the property that Dr. Moscowitz bought to build some housing. What about the outcry against it?

RR: No. I really think that you don't want to go into provocation once you want to build your state, once you want to build your ideas, once you want Jerusalem to be one and not divided ever. I really think we should postpone it, but there is a danger, and everyone has to understand that the idea was to build one section here immediately. Because once you enter into negotiations—we started the war the moment Oslo was announced, we started the war on Jerusalem. Because you see, the continuance of the Arabic section which will be the capital of the Palestinian entity—God forbid state—but the Palestinian entity, you can see it right there and there is a continuance between it and the Temple Mount. The only way to avoid such continuation between the Arab section, between the capital of the Palestinian entity and Jerusalem is here. That is the place.

On one side we have the cemetery where you have six million Jews—not six million, four million Jews—buried. On the other side you have the headquarters of the Palestinian police, the sovereign headquarters. We have this block that was owned by Jews during past years. Why shouldn't we build here? Not now, because it is a matter of provocation, but because there was a strategy when we released Jerusalem. There was a strategy, because until 1967, the Jewish population in Jerusalem was an isolated island surrounded by Arabs and now we decided to be all over.

LHC: People say to waste or to spend lives on accommodating that theory is just not worth it. You know, you talk about land for peace versus lives. I bring you another subject. You are about to agree to give an airport to the Palestinians, they're about to negotiate for a seaport. Do you think that's—by the way, your Interior Minister spoke to me on Friday and said it's a fact, it's a done deal. Don't you think that that's, in effect, establishing a de facto Palestinian state?

RR: No question. Once you ask why should we lose people because of riots about building in Jerusalem, this is the question that should be asked because are we going to peace or are we going to violence? Because the Oslo agreement gives us peace and to the Jewish people, to the Israeli people, that Jerusalem, according to the Oslo agreement, will not ever really be divided. Because you cannot have Palestinian policeman here and Israeli policeman there and run the city. The city of Jerusalem should be run under one authority and one sovereignty.

LHC: But you're doing that right now in Zone A and you're having problems with the Palestinian police. If a man is a refugee and he does something to an Israeli and he jumps over the border, you can't pursue him. What I'm saying is, and I admire your conviction, but isn't the government and the world starting to peel away from that conviction?

RR: First of all, I agree that Zone A and the creation at Oslo is a disaster that has put us on a collision course. I said so three years ago when we spoke and I am consistent with this idea. Because I really feel as though if someone can kill a Jew or an Israeli and run away and no one is going to give him to the Israeli authorities that is a conflict. As I said before, when we came to the position we were pragmatic, de facto, because that was the situation.

Now we are talking about further on, because you have to understand—if the Palestinians will have a Palestinian state and in it an airport, we demand that the terminal be under Israeli control, which will allow Israel to control anyone who comes in or out of the Palestinian entity in Gaza. And when we see the reports on Gaza it is something that is a breech of the Oslo agreement, because there is no way the Palestinian entity will not be surrounded on its borders by Israel. So you made your point and we see what is going on and we criticize our prime minister when he lets the Palestinians go on with the idea that they will have control of the airport in Gaza.

LHC: So will there be an airport or not?

RR: I really think that we should insist—

LHC: That they shouldn't have an airport?

RR: Of course not, because by giving them this sovereignty we announce the Palestinian state. If we do so why should we lose people? Why should we fight?

LHC: Would the government allow that?

RR: Oh yes, there's no question about it—we were elected to save Israel from the possibility that there will be a Palestinian state.

LHC: You will leave the government if—

RR: I would call for a vote of confidence of the government and the prime minister. I really think that the prime minister will never let the Palestinians have such an idea that they will have an international airport serving the Palestinian entity because by that he announces the Palestinian State—there is no question about that.

LHC: Dennis Ross, the U.S. Middle East negotiator, said it's a fait accompli.

RR: It's not a fait accompli, because when the parties, when Mr. Rabin, the prime minister, the ex-prime minister—unfortunately—said that there is no way that the Palestinians will have any kind of an international connection and these signs of statehood. And he was the one who kept the idea that the terminal should be kept on the Israeli side and it was because of this it was planned so, and it should remain as it was planned. If we give up step by step—even under a Likud government then we are giving up everything we believe in.

LHC: OK, your Prime Minister, Netanyahu, is being isolated now, many world capitals don't want to let him in, don't want to talk to him and if you take this type of position—has not Yasser Arafat jumped the gun public relations-wise on you people? Abba Eben said if Arafat wanted to declare a state tomorrow, he'd get up to 130 countries that would recognize him. Is it too late?

RR: I hope not and I have to believe, because we believed during the thousands of years before we returned to our country, to our home, to our homeland, to our promised-land and I must say if we did not believe then, then we are going to face real problems. I really believe that Jews and Arabs should live together in one state. I really know we have problems because of that. We created the idea of autonomy. We were talking about five or ten years. We always talked about the final stage and the final stage is always very important. We say to the entire world that the Palestinian state is a declaration of war on Israel. No way that the Oslo agreement will lead us to a Palestinian state. I have to realize the reality that we are talking about autonomy, very strong autonomy and that if we are to find a solution, we have to really negotiate. Because what will happen with the Jordan River that we can see from here?

LHC: What percentage of the country is with you?

RR: I really think that 60 percent of the Jewish population when they understand that we are talking, and the entire world is talking, about dividing Jerusalem and giving up and giving away the Jordan River and bringing up the possibility that the Palestinians will have a state with international connections and with boundaries not surrounded by Israel, most of the people of Israel will reject such an idea. Of course everyone, if you give them something bit by bit or step by step, and if you give it to them in really small quantities, then they swallow anything. But if you say we will go and we have to find a solution that won't bring about a Palestinian state, if we insist and we are consistent and we believe that what we have done until now is right, then we will succeed. People will start to think that maybe we are not on the right way and we should give up Jerusalem, but if you give up Jerusalem you give up the whole idea, because Zion and Zionism is Jerusalem.

Ruby Rivlin is a minister in the present government. He wielded strong influence in assisting Sharon to become prime minister. He is highly popular as a media personality in defending Sharon and his party. He has consistently opposed Palestinian statehood but he believes autonomy is the solution. He is respected as a democratic ideologue who favors negotiating a treaty with Syria.

RABBI AVRAHAM**RAVITZ**

Rabbi Avraham Ravitz, former chairman of the Knesset Budget Committee, one of the leaders of Degel Hal Torah, part of the United Torah Judaism Party. Believes in not ceding any land. He addresses the Palestinian problem along with the function of the religious parties in Israel.

LHC: You are one of the leading figures of Degel HaTorah Whose platform is basically no giving up on the West Bank, no giving up on Judea and Samaria. Is this correct?

AR: No, it's not correct. We believe that Israel is our promised land and God gave us the land, and to us the land of Israel is not just a place to live but a value. But as in private life, you sometimes share a conflict between values. We are also in a conflict between values and human life, which is a very important value. So that if this is the situation the alternative is to give up one value. We have to judge which one is more important in the historical moment.

   We wouldn't like to give away our land, our promised land, the land that it says in the Bible that God gave us, but we are also saying that we have to live. We don't want to kill our people, that's also valuable to us. So we have to judge.

LHC: So what would be the position of Degel HaTorah to the Oslo agreement?

AR: Well, we're not sure that the Oslo agreement was a good one. But we're talking today after it already had been signed. Because it's already signed by the past government, our position is that we are to go on with the Oslo agreement but very carefully.

Rabbi Avraham Ravitz,
Knesset member, a leader of the
United Torah Party

And our position is like a business, like in your private life if you go in one direction, you have to know the end of the road, where you are going to. I think it's very important for Israel to go in right now to negotiations about the final agreement, how would Israel look, like together or not together, the borders, all the questions that would be in our future. In other words, before we move, we have to know what the end of the story will be. Therefore, we support the position of Mr. Netanyahu, that we should go into negotiations right now with the Palestinians, together with America, to make the last agreement. And then after we know this we could move through the Oslo agreement.

LHC: You're well aware that the Oslo agreement was witnessed by the Americans. Do you think that the Americans are putting pressure on Israel now?

AR: Well, I have to tell you, first of all, that I agree that America is a friend that helped Israel all those years. They have a position and they put together an agreement as partners. They could have interfered and tell us what they think about the political situation. But they would have to do it in a minor way in order not to pressure, just to convince. To try to convince as partners, as friends, because I think if they apply pressure, it might bring a negative reaction from the Israeli population.

LHC: You're obviously very involved in all facets of Judaism and you know that in the United States there is a movement by the Reform and the Conservatives to try to facilitate themselves into a very strong position in Israel and basically they want a right to have what they think is equality. Obviously, I'm sure your position is different on that—can you explain to our audience the difference in the issues?

AR: Well, I could tell you that I'm in a dilemma because I'm a democrat and I think that's the only system that we could adopt, a system for living our public lives. And as a democrat, I believe that every group if they want to be in Israel and to live their own lives, as a democrat, I think we have to give them the opportunity.

I don't think that they have the right to force me as a religious Jew to believe that the Jewish religion is pluralistic—they can't. In the name of pluralism, they can't force me to give up my belief that the Bible is the word of God that we've been carrying more than three thousand years. Should I say that this is just like a supermarket? That everyone could just come and say that Judaism is something else? They could say it, but they can't force me to accept it. And here's the problem. They want us here in Israel we to accept the idea that the Jewish faith, the Jewish religion, is not definite. That it's something that you could move around to whichever direction you would like to. In other words, to make it like a supermarket. We don't believe in it.

We take religion very, very seriously as part of our life. We believe that the Jewish religion is to keep the commandments, which is in the Torah, and not just something that you do what you feel. We have many kinds of religions here in Israel. So if we had a group of people—they would have to be big enough—right now the Reform is a small group, but if it were a big group, they would say, "We want to do it our way." Of observing our faith, our religion—or not religion, I think Reform is not a religion—they would say we want to do it. As a Democrat I would say let every group do their services as they want. Remember that they can't force us to say that the Jewish religion is something different than what we believe.

LHC: You're saying that if the Reform had a majority of the country—

AR: Not even a majority, a minority, a group. If they wanted to have their own services, they could do it for themselves. But they can't force us to accept that this is the Jewish religion.

LHC: And force the state of Israel to accept—

AR: Israel has all kinds of groups, minorities, big groups, small groups. It's an open country and we don't want to change the system. But at the same time we don't want to someone to force us to leave our belief about the Jewish religion.

LHC: You think this is a very severe problem in Israel? Or is it overstated in America?

AR: It's overstated. It's not a problem of Israeli society.

LHC: I agree with you. I can't find many people who think this is a big issue.

AR: Well, I'll tell you what's going on. In Israel, it became the combination between the Reform in the United States and those who are far away from religion, the Meretz [left-wing secularist party], and they made a combination to fight against the religion [right-wing religious parties]. Everyone has their own reason why they are doing it, but they made a combination. Americans are bringing in the money and the Meretz group are bringing in the people and you have such a big noise.

LHC: In America it's a huge issue, but I can't find anyone who thinks it's an issue here.

AR: It's not an issue at all.

LHC: Is it exciting to be head of the budget when there must be fifty lobbyists outside telling you to put little things into the budget. How do you feel?

AR: Well, it's interesting, that's for sure.

LHC: A lot of pressure on you?

AR: Yes, but I don't feel that people are trying to put pressure on me and I know my way. I listen to every group, to delegations that come here. And sometimes I influence the government to change some paragraphs in the budget. I think it's very legitimate that delegations come to me to explain the different issues that they're close to. And I hope—it goes up and down about the budget—but on December 31st I think we'll have a budget.

LHC: Will you have a budget?

AR: If we don't have a budget, according to Israeli law, we continue for three months with the budget of 1997. And after three months if we don't agree on the budget, we go to elections.

LHC: There are people who told me that in the event that the budget is passed and if it is in any way tied into another redeployment, which in effect would give rise to the possibility of the Palestinian state, they would walk out of the government. The budget is the thing they would hang on. Everybody's threatening to walk here on December 25th, but you don't believe it's going to happen, do you?

AR: No, not going to happen. First of all, I admire that Mrs. Albright understood that she can't put on too much pressure until December 31st. So nothing will happen and the political issue until then wouldn't give a reason to Knesset members to leave the government.

But the budget has to go through with changes—we already made some very important changes in the budget. You have to be aware, you have to use all your knowledge, you have to be calm.

LHC: Is unemployment a huge problem today in Israel?

AR: It's an international problem today, I must say, because we are moving to a new generation of industry and in high tech we are probably the best in the world or close to the best in the world. But at the same time, we are losing the other traditional factories that are asked to move away to countries that pay a lower salary. Here in Israel we have a law about minimum salary. So if you have a system that you are keeping the minimum salary by law those factories that can't afford it, can't pay it, can't compete with other factories, they close those factories. We are now in the middle of changing generations in our economy and this is a big question here in Israel. In a year or two how will we handle this changing of generations?

LHC: You'll have to retrain people.

AR: We have to retrain the people and this will cost a lot of money and it's not only a money problem, it's an organization problem. You may have to move people from cities also. We have to have much better roads to move people to other cities. So we are in a moving situation and we are really do hope a year from today Israel will reach the very high level of most of the rest of the countries in the economy.

LHC: What is your relationship to the PLO at this point?

AR: Well, this organization is probably the biggest organization of the Palestinians, so if you want to do something, if you want to negotiate with someone, probably the address is the leaders of the PLO.

LHC: So, if a delegation of the finance committee of the PLO came here and they wanted to meet with you would you have any reluctance to meet with them?

AR: Well, I will ask the prime minister what he thinks about it, because he is the leader of negotiations. Or if it was against the policy of Israel, I wouldn't do it.

LHC: There is a de facto Palestinian state right now. Abba Eben said that they are basically a de facto state. That if Yasser Arafat wanted to declare a state, 140 nations would recognize him.

AR: I say yes and no. Because according to the agreement, they don't have a right, we could stop them from bringing in the refugees, which is maybe another two million, to this little country. They have to be demilitarized. So this is not actually a sign of an independent state.

This is very important to us. We can't agree that next to Israel and Jordan there should be a another little state with so many millions of Arabs who really don't accept us.

LHC: You told me that the perception that Netanyahu is being torn apart and is not well-liked and is in trouble is not true. That you think that he's doing a pretty good job. Is that correct?

AR: Well, I can tell you that when I have a meeting with him together with other groups, with ministers, he's doing a very good job. He's understanding, he's fair. I know people are saying he's not telling the truth. Could he tell the truth? When he's asked to negotiate at the same time with the Palestinians on one side, Mrs. Albright on the other side, and also front the right wing, the third side—could he tell the truth? Allow the truth to be told to everyone? It's not easy.

LHC: It's not easy being the prime minister of Israel, I can tell you.

AR: He's not in a yeshiva, he's not a Rabbi, he's a politician. And he has to go around to all those different contrasting groups to survive in Israel. So I never heard of someone in our government who tells you the truth about everything.

LHC: Why the necessity for all these religious parties? It used to be that the National Religious Party was really running the show now you have a lot of different parties. Is that because you have different thoughts about how the religion should be viewed in the country?

AR: Not so much about how religion should be in the country, but we ourselves are different in expressing our religious values. Like if you take the National Religious Party, they're different than us, but it's not such a big difference. But Jewish people, if they are a little different, they like a lot of synagogues. But we are working together in the Knesset with all the religious parties and some of my friends are non-religious.

LHC: You know that the country's divided about fifty-fifty today. I mean, it was a very close vote for Netanyhu. How do you overcome this split in Israeli society?

AR: Well, if you take America for instance, would you say America is split between the two parties?

LHC: America is based on pluralism, because that is what we stand for. Israel is the Jewish state.

AR: Yes. So there always will be two parties here. Two parties and in between these two parties will be the religious parties. And that's why God made us, to be, during this time of history, a good Jewish influence on Israeli society. And no matter which government it is, I can tell you I had negotiations with Mr. Rabin and Mr. Shamir, they want to accept us and to listen to us. Also let us have a kind of power in order to influence Israeli society. I think it's very important if we want to survive as a Jewish country.

LHC: So what you're saying is that you people in the middle, the religious parties, don't control, but influence how the country's going to move?

AR: We will influence, if we didn't have an influence, we might not be able to survive as an independent country in the Middle East. Because the only reason why we could survive many, many years from now, many, many generations from now is because we are a Jewish people in a Jewish country. If we would, God forbid, lose our identity as a Jewish people, you wouldn't be able to survive here.

LHC: What's a Jew to you, rabbi?

AR: He's Jewish because he belongs to the Jewish people. If he has a Jewish identity and he wants to continue with us.

LHC: Can you be a Jew without following the Torah?

AR: Oh yes. If he feels that he belongs. If he's not following all the commandments, so his children will do that. He belongs here and he is Jewish.

LHC: One of the questions that always bothered me as a youngster when I came to Israel is that the religious parties were in politics and they'd compromise—let's say the buses in Haifa could run on Shabbat, but in Jerusalem, no. How do you bring that together as a religious experience if you're a politician?

AR: Well, as a politician, I know that the first commandment is to be smart and to know how to make compromises. You have to live together with all the people. Not everyone is religious, not everyone understands what it means to be Jewish, even if he is Jewish. So you can't force the individuals. You could try to influence the public life. You can try to teach people about Judaism, but you can't force people.

Rabbi Avraham Ravitz is a pivotal and forceful figure in the orthodox political wing of the Knesset. He is a Talmudic student and a believer in a greater Israel. As quoted in the interview he has little faith in any politician's version of "truth." He has many questions on the division between religion and politics.

EHUD**BARAK**

Ehud Barak, leader of the Labor Party, a former foreign minister and future prime min-ister. Favors any rational agreements with Palestinian and/or Arab countries which would bring peace and security.

LHC: Ehud Barak has declared that he wants to run for Prime Minister of Israel through a primary in the Labor Party, and, in a sense, to dethrone Shimon Peres. Why do you want to run so quickly? Do you think the government is in trouble here?

EB: The constitution of the Labor Party says that if we are defeated in an election, which unfortunately happened, then we have to choose our chairman and our candidate for the premiereship within fourteen months. So that's exactly why I intend to run against Netanyahu in 2000 or earlier, if possible, to attain the leadership of the Labor Party and its candidates for premiership.

LHC: The last time I met you, it was in the White House, and I said to the people there, "This is the future prime minister of Israel." Do you remember that meeting in the White House?

EB: I remember. I hope that you will be a successful amateur prophet.

LHC: At that time everyone thought that the Labor Party was really going to win this election, and that Shimon Peres would be the prime minister, and probably you would have been defense minister or foreign minister again, and everybody thought that it would happen. Why didn't it happen?

EB: First of all, this is the verdict of our public. In my judgement, the major mistake is our party being perceived by the public as being dragged by Meretz, which is the party to the left of us, and as a result, being perceived as giving too much too quickly to the Arabs. That was the perception of Peres, and that we are in a way, not just secular, but anti-religious, and elitist in terms of representing only the very high socio-economic echelon of society rather than the whole public.

Ehud Barak,
Prime Minister of Israel prior to
Ariel Sharon

LHC: Is it a little ticklish for you to see Bibi Netanyahu as prime minister?

EB: As a citizen of Israel and a leader of the opposition, I feel that within the first hundred days he accomplished a major journey backward to the past in every possible area.

LHC: So you would say that he had a major catastrophic journey for the first hundred days? You want to outline some of these catastrophes for me?

EB: There aren't yet major catastrophes, but the direction is very clear. We have once again been successful in uniting the whole Arab world against us. We've made a real blunder with the Palestinians and with the death toll, which is not low by now. We have major problems with the Egyptians. We feel for the first time in years a cold shoulder from King Hussein and we have military tension along the Syrian border, and all this has been accomplished in just one hundred days, accompanied by a very amateurish decision-making process.

In the economy, we are looking downward. In a way, the stock exchange in Tel Aviv and the same on Wall Street reads the right way; but that the inability to go ahead with a crippled peace process and a successful or flourishing economy: the flow of foreign investments into Israel is slow, and tourism is slow, and there are signs of a recession all around us. We witness very high tension between secular and religious people and we see the rule of law at the lowest point in years. The President of the Supreme Court became the object of threats on his life.

LHC: Ehud, follow my scenario for a minute. Bibi Netanyahu becomes very stubborn and he says that we have to void the Oslo Agreements. You void the Oslo Agreements, so therefore all the world is against you and then the economic consequences start to hit. Tourism is off, foreign investment is not there, the stock market is down: isn't that sort of a formula for a revolution?

EB: We are not in a revolutionary regime. It's only the public that will decide through the ballots who will lead it. But it's my judgement that the scenario that you have described is not the worst possible one. The worst possible one includes both friction vis-à-vis the Palestinians, with us shooting at each other, and also high tension and friction with the Syrians, and maybe even a much tougher conflict with the Egyptians.

So in a way the prospect is quite disturbing, but at the same time, let me tell you, that in my judgement, Mr. Netanyahu can avoid it quite easily by making the right choice. His two alternatives are either to stick to Likud-ideological kind of policies and break his head on the rocks of reality, or to adapt with a slight kind of cosmetic modifications our basic policies of pursuing security and peace and go ahead and adopt our policies.

If he doesn't, there is no doubt in my mind that he will lead us into a deadlock, into a kind of Belfast or Bosnia situation and no security, no peace, more terror, and a kind of bloodshed that I don't like, both as an Israeli citizen and as a candidate for prime minister in this country.

LHC: The right wing of the Likud, people like Benny Begin, Uzi Landau, and Ruby Rivlin, tell me personally, that if there is a Palestinian state they will not support Bibi Netanyahu. So Netanyahu is then, in a sense, really without his right side. Would the Labor government enter into a unity government with him to eliminate the prospects of what you told me might happen?

EB: First of all, I don't like a Palestinian state, either. But the truth of the matter is that we don't fully control it. At least half of it is in the hands of the Palestinians. I would prefer to see a kind of federation emerging between the Palestinian entity and the Hashemite kingdom in Jordan, but let me go back to your question.

In my judgement, the problem is not the content or what the government consists of, but the policies that it takes. And in my judgement, unless he breaks from the right wing, people like Benny Begin and Uzi Landau, and adopts our policies basically, we cannot consider joining a unity government.

Even if he does it, it will not be simple, since there is a real need for a clear say in the leverage to influence the policies. In my judgement, it will not happen in the foreseeable future.

LHC: Many people in America do not understand this direct election of the Prime Minister. It's a hybrid that does not exist anywhere else in the world. As you know, Yitzhak Rabin and Bibi Netanyahu were the proponents for this law. In order for people to bring down a prime minister, except if he gets nuts and you want to impeach him, then it's 75 or 80 votes, but now 61 can vote him out. Provided they also leave and run for reelection. Is there a possibility that everybody in the Knesset would leave his chair and bring down the government, if things got a little bit out of hand?

EB: It is quite improbable. The reason is what you have hinted toward at the end of your answer: that it is not just a vote of no-confidence for the prime minister, but the whole Knesset will go back home and the general election has to choose once again the members of the Knesset and they are not sure whether they will be elected even within their own party primary. So it makes it quite important, even with the old law where a normal majority of 30 against 28 would send a prime minister back home without touching the members of the Knesset. Even in that situation it was very rare for a non-confidence to be successful. Maybe one in twenty years or something. So I don't think that will happen very easily, but the real possibility is that the people, within a certain time, when it becomes clear not only that Netanyahu is inexperienced but in a way somewhat blind to some of the new realities, or maybe even worse, an ego suffering from a kind of mental or psychological fixation, and cannot operate with the realities of the Middle East. They will rage in a way—and force him to change policies.

LHC: Bibi Netanyahu shook the hand of Yasser Arafat. In your opinion, when he had political capital, twenty-four hours after he was elected prime minister, should he have, could he have gone to Arafat and said, "Look, I have problems, but I want to meet you and I want to talk to you." Would many boys have been saved?

EB: I would not expect him to have done that within twenty-four hours, but let us look at the last few weeks in Israel. What has been accomplished in Washington last week: Netanyahu sat down with Arafat for four hours. He could have easily done it a month ago. He recommitted Israel to the Oslo Agreements. He could have easily done it a month ago. He committed himself to end the negotiations about Hebron within a certain time limit and I can promise you that both Clinton and Arafat know that the time limit is only a few weeks from now. He could have easily done it a month ago.

Now, if he would have done it a month ago, we could have saved the lives of fifteen Israelis and seventeen Palestinians, but beyond that, if he had done it a month ago, he could easily have opened the tunnel without any kind of eruptions. I cannot see any reason for what we have experienced in the last few weeks.

LHC: Ehud, you are part of the Labor Party. Your Party did the Oslo Agreements. They are international agreements. You cannot revoke them, no matter what anybody says, and with all due deference to [Former] Prime Minister Shamir, you cannot revoke those agreements. Are those agreements not a de facto recognition of a Palestinian state, and if not, how do you envision the fulfillment of Oslo?

EB: I don't think that it should include a Palestinian state. I see the major element in the Oslo agreements as being the decision to separate ourselves from the Palestinians, to decide to not control them anymore, and to have their political entity outside the domain of our sovereignty. This is the major dividing line, and the Oslo Agreement still leaves a kind of latitude for a long type of plan, namely for our presence not just inside Jerusalem, but in the perimeter of Jerusalem, which will be united and sovereign under our sovereignty, with a wider corridor to Jerusalem, with a lot of modifications along the green line and with the blocs of settlements, and other blocs in Samaria, and of course including a presence, both of security and settlement, along the Jordan Valley.

But beyond this kind of geographical description, we should insist on not letting any foreign army be deployed west of Jordan, and we expect most of the settlers to be under our sovereignty, even in permanent status. This is the basis of our approach, and I believe that it is achievable and I am fully confident that it will be our starting point when negotiation of permanent status occurs.

LHC: Ehud, a lot of us worked on Camp David. Is there any danger of Egypt running off on this agreement? Mubarak's made some very tough statements lately. The feeling in the United States is that Netanyahu made some promises to Mubarak and he did not keep them. Do we have a danger of real problems with Mubarak and if President Clinton wins the congressional elections, what's your assessment? How do you think he'll be treating Israel?

EB: I'll begin from the last question. I don't think that any American president will ever exert pressure on Israel. I don't think that it will be appropriate. I will say that one of our major strategic assets is our close relationship with the United States. But of course, it demands that any Israeli prime minister behave responsibly in terms of his approach and being able to listen very carefully to the American perspective and the American interests in the Middle East, which ultimately serves the security of Israel.

We should not create a kind of contradiction between our interests and the American ones. About Mubarak, I hope that the answer is on the negative, that nothing will go wrong. But it depends on Netanyahu's responsibility and, of course, Mubarak. Moreover, let me emphasize, that at the starting point, the one who should be held responsible for this whole eruption is not Netanyahu. In our judgement, the original source of irresponsibility is Arafat, who ordered the strike and then the demonstration after the opening of the tunnel and was unable to control his policemen.

Our prime minister contributed by the clumsy decision-making process that led to the opening of this tunnel at the worst possible time. I compared it once to someone who has an open gasoline barrel in his living room and he uses his right, maybe his duty, to empty it out but at the same time he wants to try his new lighter just over the gasoline. Of course, anyone has the right to use his new lighter, but to do it over an open barrel of gasoline, is something totally irresponsible.

LHC: Ehud, a very crucial question: people are critical of the fact that arms were given to the Palestinian police. Is that a fallacious argument or is that a real constructive criticism?

EB: It's kind of criticism that is built on the fact that some of these rifles were used in the shooting of our people, and it's really something irresponsible on the part of Arafat, and he should be held responsible and action should be demanded from him in this regard to make clear that under no circumstances no Palestinian policeman would ever raise his rifle against an Israeli or an Israeli soldier. But, let me tell you that they were allowed to enter with a few thousand rifles in order to live up to the commitment made by the late prime minister Menachem Begin as part of the legitimate right of the Palestinian people to let them establish their own strong police. And the emphasis is in the original statements of Camp David—strong police for the Palestinians. You would not expect a strong police to come with sticks and rice or flour.

In order to suppress the Hamas and to make sure that Hamas who have automatic machine guns will not be active, they should have rifles. The whole problem brings us back to the attempt to try a new lighter on the open gasoline can before they empty it out.

What we had in mind was to make the two communities adapt to the new situation of gradually separating ourselves from each other and to get the two armed forces, our armed forces and the police, acquainted with the new situation before we put it to the test. And what happened here, unfortunately, without taking the advice of the chief of staff and the military commander of the region and some other high level officials, Netanyahu decided to open the tunnel and to indirectly ignite this whole eruption.

LHC: Let's take another look at another important area. What's going on in Syria today, and what do you think should be going on?

EB: I think that what's going on is very bad. You know that the Hizbollah, after their failure in the election in Lebanon, in order to show that they were still alive, they raised the profile of their activities. The Syrians, listening to some, somewhat uncareful, statements made by our prime minister, deployed their forces.

Now, when we respond to the Hizbollah activities by attacking them, we might find ourselves attacking very close to Syrian ground forces deployment. Now, when they come to respond to it, they might deploy their surface missile systems, either along the border of Lebanon or elsewhere. All this new deployment of Syrian forces leads to high level tension along our northern border, which is not healthy for the peace process and might lead to actual friction, if the leadership on both sides is not fully responsible.

Ehud Barak was the former Chief of Staff of Israeli Defense Forces . . . and the country's most decorated soldier. In the 2000 election he defeated Benjamin Netanyahu. After a mere fourteen months in office his government collapsed. Barak resigned from the Knesset and quit his post as Chairman of the Labor Party. Some think his career is over; others feel a comeback is inevitable. In recent days Barak has begun to surface with frequent media interviews.

DORE**GOLD**

Dore Gold, Israel's Ambassador to the UN. Calls for a joint Labor-Likud coalition to solve problems "realistically and reasonably." Objects to Russian meddling in the near East. Claims that Palestinians are not living up to the Wye Agreement.

LHC: Now, Dore, tell us what happened with Jerusalem and the European Union.

DG: Simply put, the European Union sent a response to a request of ours not to hold political meetings with the Palestinians in Jerusalem. Our request to the Europeans was based on the Oslo Agreements and the note for the record of the Hebron protocol, which stated very clearly that Jerusalem is under Israeli jurisdiction. The Palestinians maybe want to get it eventually, but it remains under our jurisdiction, and there can't be political activity by the Palestinian Authority or the PLO in Jerusalem.

The Europeans suddenly came back with a response to our request to stop these visits to Orient House, by saying, well you should know that the European view is that Jerusalem should be a *corpus separatum*. Those of us who learned a little bit of history immediately recognize those Latin words. That's the reference in resolution 181 of the General Assembly from November of 1947 stating that Jerusalem should be internationalized. So suddenly what the EU was saying is the debate isn't just over the West Bank, it's not just over East Jerusalem, it's over West Jerusalem as well. And when Israelis heard that, they were astounded.

Dore Gold,
Israeli Ambassador to the
United Nations

LHC: So what happens?

DG: What's happened is that we made a very strong response. Actually the first response to this came from David Ben Gurion in 1949 before our Knesset. Ben Gurion's position on resolution 181 and on the *corpus separatum* for an internationalized city is that recommendation was made null and void back in 1948, whereafter these UN recommendations were made, Israel was invaded by five Arab armies. Jerusalem was put under siege; our people were cut off without food and water; and the UN *corpus separatum* and the UN General Assembly did nothing for the residents of Jerusalem.

The only ones who saved Jerusalem were the Haganah, the Palmach, the Etzel with convoys that broke the siege and brought food and water to the residents of the city. So I think Prime Minister Netanyahu and Foreign Minister Sharon simply repeated the sentiment of the founding fathers of Israel, David Ben Gurion and Moshe Sharett, who rejected [UN resolution] 181 back in 1949, and we rejected it again.

LHC: That's a serious issue, because it's a very emotional issue for every person in Israel who cares about Jerusalem. That's one thing that's wall-to-wall. Dore, how many people are running for prime minister in Israel today?

DG: There may be some additions by the time the show is over.

LHC: If I get fifty thousand signatures, and I move over there and become a permanent resident, I can run, too. Let's see, we have Yitzhak Mordechai, he's running—that's correct?

DG: That's correct.

LHC: The Center Party, let's call it. Then we have [Ehud] Barak, obviously, the Labor Party; Benjamin Netanyahu, from the Likud, Benny Begin, Moledet what's he running on?

DG: It's a new combination of right-wing parties.

LHC: Anybody else?

DG: Yes. I read about an Arab candidate as well.

LHC: Is Kalahani still in the race? Does he have a party?

DG: He has the Third Way.

LHC: They're running? I don't hear very much about them, that's why I ask. Kalahani is now the Police Minister in Benjamin Netanyahu's cabinet, and he runs the Third Way Party, which is basically against giving back the Golan Heights. And he has a couple of seats in the Knesset, doesn't he?

DG: Yes, he does.

LHC: He helped form the government.

DG: But my job here is to talk about the interests of Israel, not to talk about politics, but about principles. In that respect, we still have tremendous challenges ahead of us. The Middle East is changing. It has changed completely from the period in which the Madrid Peace Process began, and the Oslo Process started, 1991, 1993.

      Prior to when this peace process began the Soviet Union was falling apart and there was no assertion of influence from the direction of Moscow. Since January of 1996 we've seen Russia active across the Middle East: from Cypus, with the transfer of air defense missiles; the renewal of contracts for military supply to Syria; activity in the Security Council to tear Iraq out of the sanctions regime and out of the monitoring regime; and of course, the greatest concern to the State of Israel, the supply of advanced missile technology and nuclear technology to Iran. Which is not just a problem for the state of Israel and the Middle East. It's a problem for the United States of America, which is why there's talk about renewing the Star Wars missile shield, even with the support of the Clinton Administration.

LHC: I asked President Clinton the question at a press conference, "Why are you not disturbed by the fact that Russia's giving nuclear armament to Iran?" And he said, "Well, from the United States policy" —I nearly flipped on this one, by the way—"they are so far away from the United States it would have no effect." I looked at him like he's nuts. I mean, first of all you have these nuclear terrorists all over the place, and they're funded by the Iranians.

DG: Let me also bring in one very important point here. We've already seen the test of a 1,300 kilometer-range missile by the Iranians called the Shihab-3. We know about a Shihab-4, which is under development, that will give Iran the capability of striking Western Europe. But we're also talking about a Shihab-5. This sounds astounding to most people. Does it make any sense?

Our intelligence people have reported this to the United States and I think it's taken very seriously—that there's an Iranian plan to have the capability in the not too distant future of having an intercontinental-range missile capable of striking the eastern seaboard of the United States. Which is why those who have missile expertise on missile defense in Washington are saying, given rogue states like North Korea or Iran, the United States must develop a missile defense. And we're doing it in Israel with the aero system, and we're, of course, cooperating with the United States to make sure that you can protect your cities as well.

LW: I thought that was very important that President Clinton, finally, changed his mind on missile defense, in support of missile defense this week.

DG: There's always been this debate, going back to 1972 about the ABM [Anti-Ballistic Missile] Treaty and it sort of became the holy of holies in arms control and something you couldn't touch. But the main point is we're obviously in a different strategic world in

1999 than we were in 1972 and we have to reconsider many of these issues.

LHC: What's going on with Jordan? Are you satisfied with the relationship now?

DG: We have confidence in Jordan. Jordan is obviously a country of great importance to Israel. We have our longest border with the Jordanians. Jordan is a country that has been under threat by many of its neighbors. Syria to the north looks down to Jordan, and views Jordan as basically part of southern Syria. They even use the word in Arabic, which refers to Jordan as part of the greater Damascus area.

To their east, since 1995, when we had the defection of Hussein Kamal, the son-in-law of Saddam Hussein who brought all the secrets of the biological program to Jordan, and they killed him for it, but since that time the Jordanian–Iraqi relationship changed, and now you have fire fights along the Iraqi–Jordanian border and Jordan is under threat from the East. To the south, you have the old rivalry with the Saudi royal family that goes back to the 1920s when the Hashemites used to rule down in Mecca.

LHC: Jordan was a spinoff of Saudi Arabia.

DG: So given that constellation, Jordan has a series of threats around it and looks to Israel as a partner. We still extend that partnership. We've had some difficulties dealing with the Palestinian issue, because we want to secure peace and can't always make the concessions that perhaps Jordanians would want us to make, but ultimately a strong Israel is also the best guarantor for a strong Jordan.

LHC: But does the ousting by the late king of his brother make Jordan essentially a weaker country?

DG: Well we had great respect, and we still do, for Prince Hassan. He was a great partner in making the Jordanian–Israeli peace process work.

LHC: What's his role? Does he have a role now?

DG: Absolutely. Many elements of this peace treaty were done in his house down in Al Aqabah. He was a critical player and I think he's a man of great vision and has a great deal to contribute to the Middle Eastern future.

DG: Obviously it's been reduced.

LHC: You know he changed his whole cabinet.

DG: We look forward to working with King Abdullah and we are extending our warm contacts and political relations and whatever strategic understandings we've had with Jordan in the past under the rule of King Abdullah as well.

LHC: What's the status of the peace process now, Dore?

DG: Well we've got a problem. The problem is very simple. The Palestinians haven't lived up to hardly anything in the Wye Agreement, with the exception of the famous change of the covenant. But I'll give you a specific example.

The heart of the Wye Agreement is security for land. Security meaning a detailed security plan for breaking the infrastructure of Hamas and the Islamic Jihad. We were supposed to have regular meetings between our security people and their security people and go over a work plan. Every two weeks you're supposed to meet and say well, what did you do in the last two weeks and what are you going to do in the next two weeks. Since Wye was signed, how many times have these meetings occurred?

LHC: How many times?

DG: Once. I won't go on with the whole list because it simply gets tedious. We put in a mechanism in Wye, because we had a problem. We had situations where Palestinian terrorists were killing Israelis, running off to Jericho, having an instant trial and getting out two days later and smoking cigarettes and drinking coffee at a café.

We said that we had to end the revolving door. And that was recognized in some of the side letters we received from the United States. What happened after Wye? What happened after mid-December?

We had about 200 Palestinian prisoners released, a good number of whom were hard terrorists, who were deputies to key cells of Hamas and Islamic Jihad. These people were released without the American vetting mechanism being used. In other words, the United States was supposed to review these releases. They just were let out.

So under these conditions Israel will not make more territorial transfers until we obtain Palestinian compliance. That's the way the Wye agreement is set up. Palestinians fulfill their obligations in every phase, then our responsibility to turn over more territory kicks in.

LW: You're saying that they haven't done anything?

DG: On these elements they haven't done anything. On the first phase it worked. And we gave them the benefit of the doubt. We opened up a Palestinian airport, we turned over about 9 percent of territory—that's about 7 percent of [Area] B to A, for those who know, and about 2 percent of [Area] C to B—we did these things. We made tangible concessions. But what followed was a complete breakdown.

LHC: What is the United States saying on this?

DG: We have a bit of a disagreement in terms of our public positions. The statements we're hearing out of Washington are that the Palestinians did some of their obligations in phase two, Israel has done none. But we're saying that that's the way it was constructed, the Wye agreement. In other words, until they complete all their obligations, our obligation to turn over land doesn't kick in. That's our understanding of Wye.

LHC: Wasn't it a three-month process, essentially?

DG: Yes, you're right, but there's phases, every month.

LHC: Wasn't it a danger for Israel in essence, that Israel would turn over a certain amount of land in three months and then the Palestinians could stop complying? At least that's they way I read it.

DG: Yes, and that's why it's very important to us, that weapons be collected. You know, you have a problem in Ireland as well. We have a lot of illegal weapons out there, and that whole arrangement in Ireland could collapse—if illegal weapons are out there. I'm talking about rifles, I'm talking about anti-tank missiles. If that stuff is out there, and not collected and destroyed, you've got a serious problem.

On the matter of principle, the vast majority of Israelis agree with these two points: one, that the peace process should continue, but two, that Israel shouldn't just give away land for nothing, that there must be Palestinian compliance. And on those two points, I think there is a wall-to-wall sense of agreement in our body politic.

LHC: What do you think is going to happen on May 4th, when Arafat has said that he would declare a Palestinian state? Is he going to do it?

DG: Well, the signs are that he's reticent. But what he's trying to do is gain a prize for not doing it. For us, this whole situation is absurd, because basically, the unilateral declaration of a Palestinian state on May 4th is a fundamental violation of the Oslo agreement, which says that neither side shall change the status of the West Bank and Gaza prior to the completion of permanent status negotiations. It's a clause in the agreement.

So what he's trying to do, he's threatening, saying "I'm going to violate this agreement," and then he's running around Europe and also coming to Washington, and saying, "Now, if I don't violate this agreement on May 4th by declaring a state, what are you going to give me for not violating the agreement?" So he's asking a price. And that's the current state of play.

LHC: And what's he trying to get?

DG: I think he's trying to get guarantees that if he puts it off six months he's going to get recognition down the road or certain support in the United Nations, as well as financial support.

LHC: Isn't his nephew the Ambassador at the United Nations?

DG: Yes, that's Dr. Nasser Al-Kidwa.

LHC: And how's your relationship with him?

DG: We meet. We speak. But the UN isn't a place where you build peace. It's a place where people try to attack Israel, and I have to fend off those assaults.

LHC: You're still feeling a lot of that now?

DG: Let me tell you something. Even when the Oslo Agreements were signed, on September 9th, 1993, within three months and one day of those agreements being signed, in December 1993, a whole slew of anti-Israel resolutions were passed in the UN, condemning Israel, demanding that Jerusalem be given up by Israel—even within three months of the Oslo agreements being signed—by majorities of 155 to 2. So nothing has changed at the UN.

LHC: After the Oslo Agreements were signed Rabin flew to Morocco, he had all the Gulf States, everybody was doing business.

DG: Something much bigger has changed here. And it's not just governments and Israel. It's that that situation we had in 1991 where the Soviet Union collapsed and America's the only player in the Middle East is changed. Russia's back. Even France is active in Lebanon. It's a different situation.

Iraq, which was a defeated power—it was the defeat of Iraq in the Gulf War that started this peace process—Iraq has been coming back. In 1996 they re-entered Kurdistan, they begin throwing their weight around in the region, and slowly but surely, they eroded [Executive Chairman Richard] Butler's inspection system of UNSCOM [United Nations Special Commission], and they're eroding the sanctions regime.

LHC: Is there a solution for Lebanon?

DG: Well first of all you have to understand the structure of what's going on in Lebanon, and it's very simple. Every few weeks an Iranian cargo plane flies from Iran to Damascus International Airport. It unloads military equipment: advanced mines, shoulder-fired missiles, you name it. And that stuff is shipped from Damascus International Airport to the Hizbollah in Lebanon, where it's used against Israeli soldiers and against Israel itself.

LHC: And they've got modern, up to date equipment.

DG: So we've got a whole set of interests here. We have Hizbollah fighting in Lebanon, for its own domestic interests, claiming it wants to liberate Lebanon from the Israeli presence in the South. We have Syria, which is interested in using Lebanon as leverage to get the Golan Heights, and we have Iran, which is seeking, especially now, with its newfound missile power and greater sense of support and strength, seeking to assert its influence all over the Middle East by penetrating Shiite minorities in different Arab countries, like Lebanon, like Bahrain, like the eastern province of Saudi Arabia. That's what's going on now.

Because you could ask: what if Israel got up tomorrow and left Lebanon? Maybe it would all go away. But does the Syrian interest of getting the Golan Heights disappear? No. So Syria would push Hizbollah to attack northern Israel. Does the Iranian interest of penetrating Shiite minorities throughout the Arab world disappear? No. So we have a fundamental problem. We have a problem that's local in Lebanon, but we have a regional problem involving Iran and involving Syria.

LHC: What's your policy?

DG: Our declared policy, which Prime Minister Netanyahu basically updated in early 1998, said that we're willing to accept UN Security Council resolution 425 to withdraw from Lebanon. But 425 says three things. It says that there should be a United Nations force created for southern Lebanon to oversee the Israeli withdrawal, to oversee the re-establishment of security along the border, and finally, to oversee the re-establishment of Lebanese sovereignty in southern Lebanon. We're for all three. Not just one, not just for withdrawal.

How do you get security? We need to have security arrangements. We have to have some kind of dialogue, direct or indirect, with the Lebanese government to put in security. And to also make sure that we don't have a vacuum in southern Lebanon like you have in northern Iraq.

LHC: It's a troublesome thing for the population of Israel to see so many deaths come back.

DG: Of course. We make an offer to the government of Lebanon that we're willing to withdraw if you just give us security, and you reassert control in the south. And do you know what the response of the Prime Minister is? No security arrangements, no discussions with Israel. Just get out.

LHC: So don't you think that you might have to do something offensive?

DG: The status quo is obviously very difficult. But Lebanon is increasingly making itself into another state that supports international terrorism.

LHC: I agree with you.

DG: Because the threat is not just to northern Israel. And this is an untenable situation. We're not interested in taking Lebanese territory, we're interested in getting out of Lebanon. But we're just insisting on certain basic elements.

Now a lot of people aren't interested—a lot of countries don't really care about these larger regional trends. They think because there's a President Hatami new winds of change have come to Iran; it's time to be nice. The same frequency of Iranian deliveries to Hizbollah from Damascus International Airport has been preserved. There hasn't been a reduction of deliveries, a reduction of support for terrorism; it's remained at the same level.

LHC: Can the United States do anything on this?

DG: I think what we have to do is have a comprehensive approach to the Middle East. You can't just try to figure out how to make the Middle East more stable by getting Israel to make more concessions. You have a much larger regional problem occurring, involving Russia's interest in the region, involving Iranian activism—

LHC: France is in there, too.

DG: France, the question of the future of Iraq. And unless we begin to address the Middle East strategically as a whole, and not just a question of, "Is Israel going to give up 13 percent, 11 percent or withdraw from here or withdraw from there...." We will never reach stability in the Middle East.

LHC: Is any other country agreeable to that? Do they want to do that?

DG: Well I think that what's important is that countries be aware that the problem is not just for Northern Israel. Bahrain has a Shiite population with a very active terrorist network operating there. Bahrain, which is right next to the major oil fields of Saudi Arabia, can be affected by this terrorism.

LHC: Does the United States have the power to convene a comprehensive Middle East peace conference? Do they have that power?

DG: I'm not talking about a conference. I'm talking about a comprehensive strategy. You won the Cold War in Europe because you had a comprehensive strategy called NATO. You didn't just try to say, we'll adjust the borders of Czechoslovakia and that way we'll solve the problems of Europe. That was tried in the 1930s and that didn't work too well. When you have a comprehensive strategy towards a region, you can begin to neutralize the threats to stability; not by just adjusting the borders of Israel.

LHC: How do we do that?

DG: First of all, you have to define the problem. We're looking at what should be the future of Iraq. What do we do about Iran's missile programs in support for terrorism? Should it be a coalition effort to try and change those policies or do we have countries operating with mercantile interests just to try to get their businesses in there and make more money?

Let's go back to the Gulf War. The Gulf War succeeded because there was a coalition. Everyone recognized that Saddam invading Kuwait was a fundamental violation in the Middle East and the countries of the world grouped together to take care of this problem. Just like you solved the problems in Europe through a coalition effort, you have to solve the problems of the Middle East through a coalition effort.

But the problems aren't just the questions of where the borders with Israel are or whether Yasser Arafat's in a good mood or a bad mood. The problems are much larger.

LHC: I agree. And you've got to get an Israeli government that is politically able to lobby this question to these countries so this thing can be identified and taken care of. It's not simple.

DG: But a lot of people in the west don't want to hear that argument.

Because it's hard to get [Russian Prime Minister Yevgeny] Primakov to change his policy of technology transfers to Iran. It's hard to get Saddam Hussein to conform to UN Security Council resolutions. It's hard to stop the support for international terrorism. It's easy to put pressure on Israel. And therefore we're always the fall guy.

I think all of us have to understand what are our joint interests for the protection of the western alliance. And here we have to have a much more comprehensive approach, and not an approach that just fingers Israel on what percentage of the land it's going to give up.

Dore Gold, American born, was appointed as Ambassador to the United Nations by Benjamin Netanyahu, of whom he was a strong supporter. After the unilateral withdrawal from Lebanon under Barak's administration (popular at the time but disapproved of by Gold) now is the subject of considerable debate, especially after the Lebanese abducted three Israeli soldiers. He now has returned to Jerusalem to work with a foreign policy institute and appears frequently on the international media on behalf of the Sharon government.

LALLY**WEYMOUTH**
& TOMMY**LAPID**

Lally Weymouth is a senior writer for Newsweek *and* The Washington Post *who is deeply involved in the study and coverage of the Middle East. She discusses Israeli elections and predicted a Barak victory in the 1999 elections. Believed that Netanyahu was responsible for drawing the United States and the PLO closer together.*

LHC: So, you had an exclusive interview with Bibi Netanyahu. And an exclusive interview with Ehud Barak. And you talked to Mr. Deri!

LW: I did. I had a two-hour interview with Deri, the leader of the Shas [Sephardic religious party; in 1999, the third-largest party in Israel].

LHC: I assume he didn't touch you—shake your hand.

LW: That's correct.

LHC: In your opinion, is he influential in the election in terms of the fact that he has been convicted, he's on appeal, and he's been sentenced? Is that affecting the election?

LW: He is influential. One of the things that made me want to interview Deri is that I was in the State Department before I left for Israel and a senior U.S. official said to me, "You know, the smartest

politician in Israel is Aryeh Deri."
And I heard that over and over
again from different people.

LHC: I told you here. Yitzhak Rabin said
that he was the smartest politician.

LW: Of course. He's had a great hand in
making and breaking governments
in the last twenty years. And he's a
very young man, he's only forty
years old. So it's an intriguing story
for Americans, I think.

Ariel Sharon,
current Prime Minister

LHC: Did he look repentant? Did he
look upset? Did he look frightened that he was going to go to
jail? Or didn't he think about that at all?

LW: He talked a lot about why and how he came to Israel from
Morocco, what he had thought he had done for the Sephardic
Jews, and he said that he personally wanted to resign as head of
Shas, but that Rabbi Ovadiah Yosef, who is the spiritual leader of
Shas, told him not to resign. That's why he was staying on, for
the moment, as the leader of Shas and would remain the leader of
Shas as long as Yosef ordered him to do so.

LHC: Did he say whether he was backing Bibi or Barak?

LW: Yes he did. He said he was backing Bibi Netanyahu. For obvious
reasons, I would say, which is that I asked him also about how he
felt about Ehud Barak attacking the religious throughout this campaign as he's been doing, and he didn't feel terrific about it. Barak
as you know has been saying that he will take the Ministry of the
Interior, which has belonged to the Shas for many years, and give
it to the Russians. I think that's a make or break issue for Shas.

LHC: Tell me about the mood of Barak. How much time did you spend
with him?

LW: I spent an hour with him, at his house, late at night.

LHC: Nice place! Right near the Green Line, by the way.

LW: It's about an hour from Tel Aviv. It's quite—very near the Green Line. And the thing that struck me, as an American, was how simple, how modest this house was.

LHC: I bet he had a piano there.

LW: No, no longer. He moved it. He used to—

LHC: Really? He's a great pianist, Ehud Barak. And one of the reasons, by the way, that they say that he might get 40 percent of the Russian vote is that Russians like classical music and they know that Barak plays music.

LW: I thought that it was very impressive that this man, who has had such a career in Israel, you know he's been Chief of Staff, Chief of Military Intelligence—he's living by American terms, in such a simple house. You know, it's perfectly nice, but very casual. I thought, imagine, he's going to become Prime Minister of Israel, I think, this week—either this week or on June 1st.

LHC: It's your prediction that Barak will be the next Prime Minister of Israel?

LW: It is my prediction. I think it'll be a close race, but I think that Ehud Barak will be the next Prime Minister. I could be wrong, of course.

LHC: Anybody could be wrong on this one. Where did you see Bibi?

LW: I saw the Prime Minister in his office, and again, I saw him for quite a long time—I saw him for about an hour. I've known him for years. I've known Barak for years, too. I had a very interesting interview with the Prime Minister. I thought he was very defensive.

There is a book that has been written in Hebrew about Barak, and it's been translated into Russian. There's a passage in this book that the Likud is saying that Barak wants to sell land in Jerusalem. Now, the Barak camp says that this passage is invented and put there, and our *Washington Post* reporter, for example, who reads Russian, also says it's a plant. The Prime Minister says that it's not a plant, and it's what he really thinks.

It's interesting because I met both Barak and Netanyahu when they were friends. The prime minister was trying to persuade me that Barak is really a leftist. Which I personally find hard to believe, frankly. He said, "Well, you don't really know his views anymore. And he went to America and said he wouldn't expose them." He basically kept insisting that now we know he's a left-winger, and he's allied with Yossi Beilin.

LHC: Did the prime minister get personal towards Barak?

LW: Well he didn't get personal, except in the sense of saying, "Well, he's a leftist," which I deem to be untrue, of course. So I guess you could say he wants to win, and so does Barak, so what do you expect? I think they're each trying to present the other in the worst possible way.

LHC: That's obvious. But what does Barak say about Bibi? Did you get to that point?

LW: I didn't really. I was discussing with Barak, where he would take Israel. He made some very interesting points, I thought. I said to him that the U.S.–Israeli relationship is at one of the worst points I've seen it, and I've been covering this for a long time. He said, "Yes, it's at one of its worst points. Netanyahu has actually driven the Americans into a warm relationship with the Palestinian Authority.

Barak made a persuasive case that this relationship is going to damage Israel, this relationship that Netanyahu has forced the Americans into. And that it would be harder for Israel to bargain in the future, in say, final status talks; you know, in the past, there had been negotiations, "We give this, you take that," with the Palestinians, but now that the Palestinians knew, from the letter that President Clinton sent them on May 4th, that ultimately they would have de facto U.S. recognition. At least that's what Barak argued.

Barak's argument was that they're not going to be so anxious to negotiate with Israel because they know that ultimately the U.S. will recognize their state, and that Netanyahu has actually weakened Israel. That was Barak's argument, which is persuasive.

LHC: They went two steps backward. I know Barak's argument. And it makes sense, if you think about it. What happened with poor Bibi, is that he lost so much political capital around the world that he was forced to make these little sorts of crazy deals. By the fact that he made these crazy deals, he put a cooler on the relationship between the United States and Israel, thereby, in a sense, forcing Clinton to do things that maybe he would not have done if Rabin was around or Peres or somebody.

LW: I remember Rabin telling me that Clinton was the most pro-Israeli President ever elected. And to turn him into someone who actually can't stand Benjamin Netanyahu, it seems to come down to the personality, really, this election seems to come down to the personality of Benjamin Netanyahu, more than any issue, I would say.

LHC: Obviously, it's character. What about Hillary's comment about the PLO? Hillary Clinton made a statement that she thought the Palestinians should have a state. Is that affecting anything out there, or is nobody talking about it?

LW: I asked [Faisal] Husseini when I met with him about it, if he thought that she meant it. And he said yes, he did think so, which I thought was interesting.

LHC: Of course he would.

LW: But no, I wouldn't say that that comment in itself is affecting the race. I think what's affecting the race—as you know, the key element in the race is the Russian vote. The reason that the Russian vote is leaving Netanyahu and going to Barak is that Natan Sharansky, the famous dissident leader of the Russians, was always friendly to Bibi personally, admired him, liked him.

        But Bibi undercut him by asking his chief of staff, Avigdor Lieberman to form a party to cut his power down. Now, the Russians took this very badly. The prime minister, when I was there, denied this, denied having forced Lieberman to form the party.

LHC: On the record?

LW: Yes, on the record. Because people in his campaign persuaded him, and the last weekend I was there, he finally admitted to them that he knew that he was in trouble. They persuaded him, "You must remarry Sharansky," is what they said to him. And so he held a press conference with Sharansky, and said, "I never urged Lieberman to run against Sharansky." But you know, the question is will it work? Even the prime minister's polls show the Russians leaving for Barak, and as you said, it's the key swing vote for this election.

LHC: I think that if you took a poll of the nervousness of both candidates, on a score of one to ten, Bibi is probably an eight or a nine. He's very nervous. I'm not sure Barak is that nervous now. What is your sense?

LW: I think that's right. I think that Barak looked like he thought he was going to win. Obviously, I agree with you, that anybody's nervous. You don't know which way an election is going to go. Bibi Netanyahu is a formidable politician, a good campaigner. You don't know how it'll turn out. Yes, I agree with you.

He sat behind his desk when I was leaving, and he looked up when I was at the door and he said, "Won't they be disappointed if I win." And I thought it was a very telling comment. And I asked him at the end, because so much seems to come down to the fact that he's alienated his ministers, who are now running in the opposite parties, like Dan Meridor is running in an opposite party, Yitzhak Mordechai whom he fired in January, is running in an opposite party, David Levy is gone—

LHC: Everybody who worked with him has really abandoned him. It's not a healthy situation for Bibi. And Barak seems to have done a good job in organization. Barak's a very clever guy, very well-organized.

LW: And has run a very good campaign.

LHC: He won't be accused of having too much charisma, either. He's not a charismatic guy. I'm sure one-on-one he is. I know him well, he's been at my house. I also know Bibi very well. Bibi has more personality, is more telegenic than Barak. But it's not selling now. People have really awakened to Bibi. One thing we don't know— the Haredim [ultra-orthodox Jews], when you do this polling, I'm not sure they tell the truth and I'm not sure that you can poll them. A big pollster in Israel says that if Bibi doesn't get 70 percent of the Russian vote, he's finished.

LW: And he's already way below that.

LHC: He's around 60 percent now.

LW: And falling.

LHC: And falling. I'm going to talk about [Yitzhak] Mordechai—did you get to him? What did you hear?

LW: No, but Mordechai was going up in flames, basically. The Center Party.

LHC: You mean falling?

LW: Yes, he was basically. Everybody was discussing was he going to withdraw before the first round or not? I met with Uri Savir, our friend, who was the person who made the Oslo Peace Agreement—

LHC: But he doesn't want him to withdraw because he might lose his seat. He's number five on the list. But I smell a deal between Barak and Mordechai. I can't tell you why, I just smell it. There's a deal there. If you look around and if they get together, Mordechai will be a defense minister under Barak if he folds at the right time. If he doesn't, he's out of it. The polls say he's only 6 percent now; he's falling.

LW: I think if he were smart, Mordechai would make a deal with Barak. Because he would be the key.

LHC: The lynchpin. These are both army guys, and I think there's something there. I'm not sure how or what, but it wouldn't surprise me if they made a deal. What is interesting to me in Israel today is that you have 32 or 33 parties. Prina Rosenblum is going to get 2 seats or one seat, that's the prediction. Kahalani, who ran and had about five or six seats, has fallen off the map totally. He ran on a platform of not giving back the Golan Heights. Everybody knows that the Golan is in play right now. It's an open secret.

LW: And the prime minister told me that he would like to restart talks on Syria.

LHC: Really? How is [political consultant Arthur] Finkelstein playing out over there? He predicted that he would lose, that's what I read. Finkelstein told Bibi that if things don't turn around, he's gone.

LW: Well I'm not sure that this election is really about Arthur

Finkelstein, who is Benjamin Netanyahu's campaign—

LHC: American campaign consultant.

LW: And I think that Ehud Barak told me that James Carville, Bob Shrum, and Stan Greenberg have been very helpful in his campaign. I think Benjamin Netanyahu is a great campaigner. I don't think that's the issue here. It's not the campaign. It's what happened over the last few years. Here was a young man, he was enormously brilliant, enormously impressive; he had the world at his feet. And what did he do? When he came to power, he alienated many of the people who should be his allies, and are now sitting there dying for him to lose.

LHC: You're right, Lally.

LW: As you say, anything can happen, but I asked the prime minister, "If you could do this again, aren't there things you would do differently?" And he started telling me, "I brought security...." and I said, "No, no, not security. Personally, aren't there things you'd do differently?" And essentially, he wouldn't say yes.

LHC: Hubris! It's called hubris. You know, about ten Israelis told me that they would've voted for Bibi if he hadn't smoked a cigar on television. It looked cocky. He takes the cigar out and he always looks cocky with that cigar, and I can't stand it. That's not the way to win votes in Israel.

LW: But if he does lose, it's sort of a sad story in a way, because here you had this young man who rose so fast and had every promise of greatness and blew it. If he loses. If he doesn't, of course, we're wrong.

LHC: You know, he's had a troubled marriage, and we don't know what will happen. Who knows?

LW: And she seems to be very involved in the campaign—

LHC: Big mistake.

LW: She seems to be his only ally. Alone at the top.

LHC: Big mistake. Nava Barak is wonderful. She's very photogenic, she's very reserved—she's Barak's wife. She's attractive and she's calm—

LW: And she's Sephardic.

LHC: And she's Sephardic. It's beautiful. The contrast is really stark, and very tough.

LHC: There was a big decision in Israel on the Orient House. The Orient House is the house the PLO uses to greet diplomats. Bibi tried to shut it down and the Supreme Court of Israel ruled that they had to keep it open. Big move, wasn't it?

LW: Yes. I went there, actually, to see Faisal Husseini—

LHC: Really? But you're not a diplomat.

LW: Right, exactly. Well, I've never been there before.

LHC: What does he say? Is he backing Barak?

LW: Yes, I suppose so.

LHC: But they don't get along.

LW: As much as he's backing anyone. The prime minister made a remark about how Assad and Arafat and all the Arabs were backing Barak.

LHC: They all say that. But a very important thing happened in Israel the other day. The head of the Muslims allowed the Muslims in Israel to vote. And they had always been forbidden to vote, I think. And they think that this will also give a group of votes to Barak. Also, you know that the Arab party's folded in under Israel One. I don't think Azmi Bashara who's running for Prime Minister, did. We have an interview with him. We can play it post-election, because I don't believe he's going to win the election, but it'll be interesting to hear what he says and how he attacks the other parties and their program. You have to know what it says.

There are two things that happened in Israel concerning Bibi. Bibi funded some money to Jerusalem, infrastructure money for about a hundred-fifty million dollars. His hand-picked Finance Minister, Meir Sheetrit, voted against it because it really wasn't in the budget. And there was no way to fund it. The cabinet voted for it, and they outdid the vote of Meir Sheetrit. So people are saying that Bibi's trying to spend some money to buy some votes.

He also declared a national holiday for Russian veterans, for the allied invasion of World War II, and he's also declared benefits for Russian veterans—40,000 Russian veterans—what that has to do with Israel, I'm not clear.

LW: Starting when I was there, and before I got there when he made two trips to Russia—he and Sharon are definitely courting the Russian vote. It just hasn't been that successful, apparently.

LHC: He went to Russia, to do cable television shows so they'd be broadcast back here.

LW: It's interesting, in the campaign ads, which run every night with the two candidates and the various parties, some of the ads are actually in Russian with Hebrew subtitles, which is really extraordinary.

LHC: Lally is predicting victory for Ehud Barak—will he be able to form a government? By the way, do you think it will be first round or second round?

LW: I can't say. A lot depends on Mordechai, a lot depends on how many right-wing voters turn out that we don't know about. I think too much is up in the air to say right now. If he goes to a second round it's definitely looking a lot better for the prime minister. That's one thing I'll say!

LHC: You have guilt now, because you want to feel good about Bibi, right?

LW: No, actually, I'm a journalist all the way. I just think it's an interesting election. And I happen to personally like both people. I don't happen to agree with the policies of one, but I won't get into that. I think it's an interesting election and just want to say what the issues are.

LHC: My prediction is that it's going to be a very close election, except I don't know that everybody's polling correctly. That always bothers me about Israel. But I think you may wind up with a Unity government or an all-encompassing government. So you may see Bibi as a foreign minister in the Ehud Barak government. That's a very strong possibility. Don't be surprised about these guys. Both were in the army together, they don't have any animosity toward each other, there's great respect.

LW: I asked the prime minister, "Do you have too much animosity toward Barak after this campaign to form a unity government?"

He said, "No, I don't hold grudges, because if I did, I'd need a warehouse to hold all the vitriol that's cast against me."

LHC: Alright, we'll see Bibi here in a couple of weeks trying to rent a warehouse to get the animosity out.

Lally Weymouth has been a frequent interview subject over the past thirteen years. The daughter of The Washington Post's *Katherine Graham, she is a frequent visitor to the Middle East and has close contacts with both Israeli and Arab leaders. She interviewed Arye Deri, considered one of Israel's brightest political figures and former leader of Shas, the religious party. After a lengthy trial Deri was sentenced to three years in prison for malfeasance. Despite the conviction he is still considered a strong political leader.*

Tommy Lapid was the editor of An Israeli Daily, Maariv. *He heads the Shinoi (a secularist) Party. Shinui was organized to stop Jewish fundamentalist religious groups, whom he sees as a threat to liberal democracy. He firmly believes in the separation of church and state. He is against funding religious parties with government money.*

LHC. Tommy, a man of your diverse background in the media—what happened? You got tired of listening to the politicians puff?

TL: No, I got tired of writing a million words and having no impact on what's really happening in this country. The country's getting out of hand, so I thought I may as well try to influence things where they are being really done, in parliament and perhaps in the government. You know this frustration of journalists, who know better, and write clearer things and find that there is nothing to say at the very end. It's a frustrating job.

LHC: I think so. I think that reporters and journalists are voyeurs, don't you?

TL: Yes, but on the other hand, we are playing in the same thing. You know, now I am in politics a month, and nothing in my life changes. I am meeting the same people, having the same talks—on the other side. It's a double-way mirror in which we are posing.

LHC: What happened? What really impelled you to go into politics?

TL: This is a party which basically has one issue, on which I am focusing sharply. You said we are a secular party but the idea is not only to be a secular party, but to stop the fundamentalist trend in Israeli politics. It used to be a curiosity like the Amish in America, and became a real threat to the liberal system of our democracy. It's not a joke anymore.

Yosef (Tommy) Lapid,
journalist and leader of the
Shinui Party

LHC: I think it's come to the forefront now with the conviction of Deri. And a lot of people are now examining the whole record, the whole concept of the Shas. I had reporters on my show last week who told me that the Shas organization was basically a fundamentalist organization funded by the Israeli government. Would you say that's a correct statement?

TL: Well, Deri is now in court for a second time, this time for using government funds to run his party. This is the litigation against him. But the point is not only corruption, which we have succeeded somehow, to drive out from the old system, and now it's coming back, but it is also mental corruption. We are going back into the ghettos. We are becoming a medieval country again.

         The rabbis are playing a major role. You know, the founder of this country, our Washington, Theodor Herzl, said that the rabbis should be kept in the synagogues. They are doing immense harm to our connections with American Jewry, because they are ultra-orthodox, and they are dividing us from the Reformed and Conservative Jews in American and a great majority of American Jewry. So they are causing damage not only in the country, but are causing damage to Israel by losing our best friends.

LHC: Do you think the answer to this problem, the problem between the secularist and the religion is a constitution? Do you think there should be a separation between church and state?

TL: If we had separation of church and state like you have in the United States, it would solve many problems, and mainly it would solve the problem of financing these religious movements with the taxpayers' money.

On the other hand, it's difficult to make this total division, because after all, Israel is a Jewish state, and in Judaism it is very difficult to make a precise division between nationality and religion. And then we would have a problem with keeping the Jewish character of the country.

Therefore, even I, who am considered the most secular of all the secular politicians in Israel now, I don't think I would take from your constitution this total division. I would still have this country as the Jewish state. But I would dry up the financial sources of the state for religious purposes. I think religion is a private affair and people should finance their own religion.

LHC: So you're not really anti-religion. You just don't want them meddling in the affairs of the state.

TL: I think that this is a dangerous mixture. Religion and politics create a very dangerous chemistry that is now about to explode in Israel. The reason I went into politics—I have nothing to win personally from politics. I am an old man who has no real future ahead. I don't need whatever they pay in the knesset to a member. I'm probably much better known as a journalist than I'll ever be known as a politician, so I really have an honest reason to go into politics. I really think that this fundamentalist strain in our political life is a dangerous factor for the future of Israel as a democracy, a liberal democracy, a Western democracy, part of the Western world. We don't think in the way of medieval ghetto Jews.

LHC: If you win four or five seats, you would have to make a decision to join a government with Ehud Barak, or Benny Begin or Bibi Netanyahu or Azmi Bashara.

TL: I don't know if everyone gets your jokes; if they are well versed in Israeli politics. The decision would be between Ehud Barak and Bibi Netanyahu. I'm not saying who I'm going to join. I'm going to join anybody who is elected prime minister provided he takes me instead of the fundamentalists into his government.

Now, people say that there is more of a chance that Barak would do that than Netanyahu would. But I am open-minded about this. I think that whomever the majority of the people of Israel elect for prime minister is good enough for me. What I am going into the government for is to prevent the fundamentalists from having further influence and prevent them from destroying the basic fabric of our society. This is what I want to do.

LHC: Are you surprised by the amount of votes that you seem to be able to get? You've just turned into a political figure, and bingo, you've got three seats.

TL: Victor Hugo said that there is no army that can stop an idea, that it just comes. I think that there is such frustration, at least in the thinking circles, that it was an idea that was looking for a politician to carry its flag. I'm carrying this banner now, and the response is overwhelming. I'm very well versed in Israeli politics, I dealt with it from the other side all my life. I'm surprised by the overwhelming response, as if people were waiting for somebody to say it. And this reflects not only on the fundamentalists. It reflects on the major parties of Israel. On the Likud and Labor, which don't dare to tackle the problem, because each one is afraid that the other one will make a—

LHC: Make a booboo and not be able to gain a coalition.

TL: And I want to provide an alternative. I want to say, "Listen, you don't have to be afraid of the other guy going with the ultra-orthodox. If you take me you have a majority."

LHC: What has been the reaction of other journalists to you?

TL: Friendly hatred. On the one hand, you know, they are colleagues. There is a little bit of a collegial pride in it, and a great deal of envy. Each one is saying that he should have done it, and that he would do it better than I do it. But on the other hand, they don't really refuse to give me a hand and interview me and write about me.

LHC: On this fifty-first anniversary of the State of Israel give me a projection, twenty-five years from now, on the seventy-fifth anniversary—what will this country look like?

TL: I think that in twenty-five years we will have overcome our present problems with our neighbors. I hope we will have peace sooner than that. Then Israel will be on its way to becoming a highly developed technological entity. You know that we are now supposed to be the second Silicon Valley of the world, partly because five thousand Israelis already work in the real Silicon Valley in California. And I think this is where the Jewish genius is returning to Israel. High tech.

The only impediment is that the Arabs have to become not only more peaceful, but they have to accept the basic tenets of Western civilization, which they haven't reached yet. You cannot really live in full peace with a neighbor who lives in peace with you only because he is afraid of you, and not because he believes that peace is the best way between people. So this may take twenty-five years.

Tommy Lapid remains a media personality. He is the leader of the new Shinoi Party, which has become a factor in Israel's political landscape. He has proven himself an able political tactician and negotiator. Some elements claim he is racist and anti-religious. He denies these allegations and maintains that he entered politics to stop fundamentalists' drives in Israeli politics. He is against the growth of Shas.

NAOMI**BLUMENTHAL**

Naomi Blumenthal, a Likud Party member and deputy minister of the Knesset, she wants a referendum to decide the fate of the Golan Heights. She believes Barak's expansion of ministerial posts is illegal.

LHC: We're speaking with Naomi Blumenthal. She was interviewed a year ago, and she made a terrific appearance. People wrote letters and they wanted to know who this beauty was who was in politics. Secretly, she was in Bersheva, years ago as an actress, and she won the Actress of the Year or something like that, right, Naomi? But we did get many comments. I predicted months ago, that Bibi Netanyahu would make a come back. Is that true?

NB: Yes, I think he will. He has such support, even inside the Likud. If in the inter-election that we have now for the leadership of the Likud, and we have like three candidates—Arak [Ariel] Sharon, Ehud Olmert, and Meir Sheetrit, the surveys show that if Bibi Netanyahu would've run on the 2nd of September, he would have won by and large—

LHC: To be the leader of the Likud.

NB: With 75 percent.

LHC: Wow. He's a very popular guy.

NB: He still is very popular, and it seems as if people identify themselves with him being the underdog. As if he never got a real chance to be the leader. He was the prime minister of Israel for three years, but the media and a lot of left-wing people didn't leave him one quiet moment from the day that he took office as prime minister. So Likud people and other people in Israel feel as if everything is against them. I suppose the majority of humanity feels that they can't proceed because things are against them, so they identify with the fate of Bibi Netanyahu as prime minister.

Naomi Blumenthal,
Likud Knesset member

LHC: Naomi, we've got to be honest, though. There was this, perception out there that Bibi didn't always tell the truth. And you would hear it from his own people. You told me that that's basically politics, that's the way it works. I need a hundred million dollars for my budget, and the next guy needs two hundred million for his budget. So you tell both that you're going to work with them. So one guy who gets hurt says, "You screwed me, you didn't take care of me."

NB: Or the treasury tells you, "We don't have the budget." You, as a leader, you mean well, you want to give as much money as possible, for the poor, for all kinds of projects, etc. But then the treasury comes and says, "Cut, Cut! We don't have the budget for it."

      It happens very often with politicians. I don't think it's only politicians. You can say that the politics or the circumstances brought about the situation that he didn't tell the truth. That situation came up for Bibi all the time, and they just started to say, "He's a liar, he's a liar." It became so easy to say, "Ok, he's a liar."

However to be prime minister and a liar is not a very good image.

LHC: Bibi said he'd never shake the hand of Arafat. He said that, right? Before he became prime minister.

NB: He said that, and Barak said that he would nominate more women to the government than any previous government in Israel and he hasn't done it yet. So there are things that you say in a campaign. But then, you have certain circumstances that you just can't resist.

I can show you other politicians that said that they would not take certain steps, and what do you expect from them? You expect that they will follow their way, their ideology, and I believe that Bibi Netanyahu didn't want to shake Arafat's hand because he thinks that he did too many bad things and he doesn't deserve his hand. He doesn't deserve my hand, either. But I had the privilege not to be in that situation, to be together with Arafat, and Bibi, as a leader, didn't have a choice. Maybe he made a mistake. Maybe he regrets it.

LHC: What about the Wye agreement? Was that a mistake?

NB: I think it was a mistake. I don't understand why he went to Wye. I don't think that the United States has to interfere as much as it interferes. We have to decide our own abilities, our own fate in Israel. This was our policy over the years, and America knows it. We never asked American soldiers to fight for Israel and we asked for some support, but never more than that. Economical support, and moral support, which we really appreciate very much, but I think he shouldn't go to the States—

LHC: Do you think Bill Clinton was rough on Bibi Netanyahu? You think he was tough on him?

NB: He was very tough on him. I think the people that surround Clinton, would be identified in Israel as left-wing people. They're Shalom Achshav. They are people who would be identified with Peace Now. They still surround Clinton today. They have their own beliefs about how Israel can achieve peace. But as you can imagine, being Likud, being now in the opposition, and I think to give back land for papers is the wrong way. I still believe it and I will fight for getting peace, but with security in the right way.

LHC: Do you think that Arthur Finkelstein was necessary in the election campaign of Bibi Netanyahu?

NB: I think Carville, or the others, what do you call them, the advisors, American advisors—

LHC: Carville versus Finkelstein!

NB: I think we really have enough people in Israel who—

LHC: I think so, too. I don't think it looks good for Israel to keep bringing these American consultants in and trying to do it. I mean, Israel's a different culture totally. So think Arthur Finkelstein could stay home, James Carville could stay home, [Bob] Schrum, [Stan] Greenberg, whoever—

NB: I don't think really that we need consulting from abroad.

LHC: Naomi, why did the Likud lose the election?

NB: We were not good enough. The agenda from the last election was different from former ones. I mean the ideology didn't play the roles that it had played before. And the direct election procedure that takes place in Israel—and a lot of Americans don't know exactly what's happening. I will try to explain.

You have two votes. One vote is for the party and the other vote is for prime minister. So Bibi Netanyahu, among Jews in Israel, still had the majority [in reality, a plurality]. He got 44 percent, it's nearly half. You can look at it that way. But the Shas [Sephardic religious party] people, the majority, they are basically like Likud supporters, they are right-wing people. They are in the national camp, I would call it. But there are factions—factions, and factions, and factions. It's bad for politics, it's bad for democracy.

LHC: So should they change the law and go back to the old non-direct election?

NB: Of course.

LHC: That would be better? Are you going to pass that in the Knesset?

NB: I'm not sure, because what happens is once the prime minister is elected, he is in love with the system!

LHC: You know who wanted that system originally? Bibi and Rabin.

NB: But if you remember, all of the Likud voted against it. Bibi Netanyahu was the only one to vote for the direct election of the prime minister. And he was right for his cause, but now we see that we have fifteen factions in the coalition—I think that no American citizen can imagine what that means. It's very hard.

LHC: Are you on your way to a peace treaty with Syria?

NB: I hope. I think it will be easier to have peace with Syria because it's an existing state that can sign agreements, and it will be easier than with the Palestinians, which is a much more complex situation. But Assad has to understand that we cannot just give up, because of our security, and whatever was in Israel, and how small the country is, how high the Golan Heights are and whom they're overlooking—they can't understand that it's kind of, maybe not suicide, but it's asking too much of Israel. Barak said himself, in one of the interviews before he was prime minister that giving up the Golan Heights would mean having problems with the security of Israel.

LHC: It seems, though, that it's happening. I think your friend Ruby Rivlin, who's a faction head, was ready to accept a condominium deal or something, with Syria, with the Golan. I'm sure they're trying to work out the details, but it looks to me, that Syria's really on the move also. I think it may happen. And that hopefully would solve the Lebanese problem for you, where a lot of boys are getting killed. Is that the feeling in Israel? Are most people in agreement with Syria in Israel today?

NB: It depends very much on what concessions we have to make. Then there will be a referendum. As we saw, the media and public relations make a lot of difference. I'm sorry to say it, because it shouldn't be the case, but still, we will see which campaign will be the winning campaign.

There will a campaign against giving up the Golan Heights, for peace. Every campaign is for peace. It should be understood, we want peace. My son was in Lebanon.

LHC: Really?

NB: Yes. There are too many young boys. They're wonderful. They don't want to fight. We don't want to fight. We never wanted to fight. So there will be a referendum. It depends on what it will look like. I'm against, basically, any referendum, but if it will keep the majority of the Golan Heights in the hands of Israel, or to keep our security; if this passes, maybe we can keep peace with the Golanis.

LHC: One of the interesting things that happened in the elections was that Natan Sharansky was basically given a great portfolio by Bibi Netanyahu. They're allegedly close friends; they play chess and checkers, and who knows what, together. In a way, there was a betrayal, wasn't there? Between Sharansky and Netanyahu? Because that was a real turning point, possibly, in the campaign. What happened there? Do you know?

NB: Anyway, he's playing the price. I like Sharanksy. I'm very sorry about what happened. He had in his party a member who was in the Labor Party before, it was [Roman] Bronfman, and he dragged him into supporting Barak. I saw it on election day, I went around the country, and I saw how the Sharansky party, the new immigrants party voted for Barak and Yisrael Baalyia. And now they pay the price because Bronfman has left the party with Alexander Tsinker. They are now a party of four. And I must say that [Avigdor] Lieberman, who is also in the New Immigrants Russian party, has four mandates [i.e. seats in Knesset], so....

LHC: Was his platform against police and justice or something?

NB: It was against justice. I saw that Barak, for the time being, is the first one, without any necessity, who changed the basic law. There should be outrage in Israel. In the basic law for the direct election of the prime minister there are eighteen ministers in the government, which everybody thinks is enough—

LHC: And now he expanded it.

NB: He expanded it, just like it was nothing. So I'm very cross with him. I hope this will be the only issue on which I am cross with him, but I think he shouldn't do it. There was no necessity. Let's say, two million new immigrants come to Israel—there is so much work for the government to do that he needs more ministers! There was no need for him to have more ministers. It's expenditure of money, he promised 300,000 jobs and the first thing he did was give some to members of parliament. Is it justified?

LHC: I think for the carpenters it is, because they have to build a big table!

NB: They don't need it. The table, it should be a table for them to eat! It should be a table to make a better Israel.

LHC: It was a big move for him. And what he did, he expanded it to twenty-three ministers?

NB: It's twenty-three now, but he still has another—

LHC: More ministers, really?

NB: Yes. We have—half of the parliament, out of the 120, then you have deputy ministers as well. It shouldn't be. I'm ashamed.

LHC: It's so the whole government is half the Knesset, practically.

NB: More or less.

LHC: What do you think about Arab members of the Knesset joining the Defense and Foreign Affairs Committee.

NB: We have to change the question, I'm sorry, Leon. It's not the Arabs. We have nothing against the Arabs, not the Likud—whether we are in the coalition or in the opposition. We are a very open party, very liberal. I think that Jabotinsky is a good example with what he led us to and there is nothing against Arabs. We are very democratic.

The question is whether an Arab member of Parliament should sit in a committee for Foreign Affairs and Security, when he often incited against the State of Israel. Where are the red lines of democracy? This is the question. And it's nothing against Arabs. It's the person.

LHC: So you're saying that because they espoused the rhetoric that calls for the destruction of the State of Israel, how can you let them sit on that committee?

NB: It's incredible, how open we are. It's too much!

LHC: Well, it's obviously politics. He promised that Arabs would have some kind of role in the government and he had to deliver. Is that correct?

NB: But there should be, as I said, some red lines, to what you agree to do for votes.

LHC: You're chairman of the immigration, and the absorption and the Diaspora.

NB: We are doing a great deal of work in my committee, bringing in the new immigrants. We have a rise of new immigrants coming over from the former Russia.

LHC: And you're going to get more, by the way. Because anti-Semitism in Russia is blowing up again and there's a lot of criticism against the government of Russia that they're not trying to hold back on this.

LHC: What's the future of the world, Likud?

NB: Wonderful. You know, it can't be worse! So we're looking to a bright future!

LHC: In how many countries do you have branches?

NB: Very many but you know, there are some countries that we're not in yet. Still, we have a lot of support around the world. We have veterans, we have new members and youngsters, and the Betar youth movement.

LHC: So you're hopeful.

NB: Yes. Very much.

In addition to her government position, Naomi Blumenthal—formerly a nationally known actress—is a chairperson of the International Likud Party. She complained about Barak's creation of additional ministries. However Sharon has now expanded that number to twenty-three. Ms. Blumenthal was a devoted Netanyahu supporter. That is probably the reason for Sharon awarding her the post of deputy minister rather than a full ministry. Along with others, she believed the desertion of Natan Sharansky from Netanyahu in his contest with Barak brought the Russian parties tilt toward Barak.

YEHUDA**LANCRY**
& RAGHIDA**DERGHAM**

Yehuda Lancry, formerly ambassador to France, currently Israeli Ambassador to the UN. Admires the bloodless Israeli withdrawal from Lebanon. Looks forward to a rapprochement with Syria. And is optimistic about a settlement with the Palestinians.

LHC: Explain why Israel was in Lebanon from the beginning. What was the reasoning?

YL: As you know, we do not have any territorial conflict with Lebanon. We don't have any aspiration to a so-called Israeli imperialism over the Arab land in Lebanon. Our main concern was and remains the security of the citizens and the laws of Israel. If this issue is settled, I think that we can have a chance to enlarge the era of peace which started with Egypt, continued with Jordan, now in current implementation with the Palestinians, to Lebanon. That is our hope. And even to Syria.

LHC: You called it a tragedy that you were in Lebanon. If it was a policy of the government, why was it a tragedy?

YL: Because the story is really tragic. We lost a lot of people. More than 1,500 Israeli soldiers killed.

LHC: 1,500 in Lebanon?

YL: Yes, since '82. So that is a tragedy. I think that our government took a great step in order to put an end to this story. And I hope that with the cooperation of our neighbors and the international community we can restore the security and the confidence between all sides.

LHC: You pulled out earlier than Barak, your prime minister, said you were going to pull out, is that correct? Did he have a date in July?

YL: Barak always said that we would resolve by July, but he never gave a precise date. So it's accelerated, but the final outcome for Israel is generally positive. We left Lebanon without any Israeli soldiers getting killed, finally we are in the current process of integrating the South Lebanese Army, the ex-South Lebanese Army, their families. I think that we have to make sure that there is an alternative to their situation. We offered the SLA, two or three months ago, such a solution.

LHC: The SLA is the Southern Lebanese Army that was basically funded by the Israelis. It's run by a man named General [Antoine] Lahad, whom I've met. We interviewed him a few times. He's an interesting character. You might have found him in Paris sometimes. He liked to go there. Where is he today?

YL: He is in Israel, not far from his country. I know him personally. When I was Ambassador to France, from time to time, we shared some moments.

LHC: He was an Ambassador from Lebanon to Paris?

YL: No, he just visited. He has family in Paris, his wife and his children.

LHC: Will he live in Israel now?

YL: He personally lives in Israel now, but I don't know what the final decision will be.

LHC: You're saying something very important. Are you saying that Israel, in a humanitarian gesture, offered the SLA or most of the SLA refuge in Israel?

YL: Yes, absolutely.

LHC: I don't think that's widely known. I think people think there was a selective basis for the way these refugees were coming in.

YL: It was made widely public in Israel. In our current negotiations and contacts with the United Nations, we made it clear. But we can understand that those people are at a different stage, they prefer to remain in their villages, in their country. It's a natural feeling and a natural link that we respect. But while events turned out as they did, I think that there is no other choice than to give them the shelter they require and all the attention they deserve.

LHC: What do you hear at the UN about this withdrawal? Are you getting support from the other countries?

YL: It is clear from the report of the Secretary General to the Security Council, there are requirements, I think, from all the sides; from Israel, from Lebanon, directly from Syria, and as far as we are right now, Israel has operated in full accordance with the UN requirements. So now we expect that the UN force could play its own part....

LHC: That's the United Nations troops, by the way.

YL: And help, according to the 425 and 426 resolutions, help the Lebanese government restore its sovereignty and its authority in the area.

LHC: What do those resolutions actually say? I know Israel, when they said they were going to withdraw, they probably reported it to you, to [UN Secretary General] Kofi Annan. You probably delivered some notice to Kofi Annan that your people were withdrawing, correct?

YL: This resolution fixes all the borders, provisions and stages of its implementation. Right now the United Nations has to confirm the Israeli withdrawal. The division is along the internationally recognized border, without any ambiguity. And that is the situation right now. The two other requirements were the dismantling, disbanding of the SLA. It has been done. And the liberation of the prisoners. It has been accomplished also. So now we are in full accordance with those requirements and we expect that the Lebanese government could convoy its civilian and military infrastructure to the area and to contribute to the implementation of this resolution with the international community and the UNIF [United Nations Interim Force (in Lebanon)].

LHC: Wasn't the theory of the Israeli policy that the withdrawal of Lebanon would put much more pressure on Syria to, in a sense, leave Lebanon also, and that there would be international pressure for everybody to relax tensions in Lebanon and let the Lebanese people take care of their own destiny?

YL: That could be an interesting outcome of our withdrawal. As you know, we first tried to settle our situation in south Lebanon and to withdraw with an agreement with Syria, a peace agreement. Unfortunately we didn't succeed in this, so far. Now we are creating a new reality where the only occupier of Lebanon is Syria. No more Israeli occupation. So Syria has to face this situation, to face the Lebanese claim, maybe the international claim. But that is, I think, a problem that concerns Syria but not Israel.

LHC: Tell me, when you meet the Syrian Ambassador at the UN, will you talk with him?

YL: We never met. I didn't have the opportunity to meet him and talk to him. I would be very pleased to do so.

LHC: We're not sure how he would be on that. Nobody knows.

YL: I think that in principle, since our prime minister met their foreign minister, the door is open for some talks between all the representatives. So that is my wish.

LHC: Maybe we'll interview them, put you all together.

YL: That could be a good possibility.

LHC: There were reports that Prime Minister Ehud Barak was supposed to come here last weekend. And at the last minute he cancelled. Why was that?

YL: Now it is clear. Maybe a week ago, it was not so clear. As he explained to President Clinton and to Secretary-General Kofi Annan that the situation in Israel, the security one, the political one, was really intense and he was obliged to be in Israel. I think that, in light of the Israeli withdrawal, he was totally justified.

LHC: So he stayed because of the withdrawal. Arak [Ariel] Sharon, the leader of the Likud, called the withdrawal a disgrace.

YL: If you keep in mind some pictures, you can really feel a time of shame. You can't really conceive of withdrawal as a triumph. There is no possibility. What really matters is the final outcome. And we did that without any injury or loss of human life. We now have a calm situation and that is most important.

LHC: How are the residents up in the north? Are they calm, the Israeli residents?

YL: I think that they will get more and more confident. I was mayor of a city—

LHC: Which one?

YL: Shlomi, located exactly on the Israeli-Lebanese border.

LHC: So you know the area very well.

YL: I can evaluate the situation exactly .

LHC: Are you speaking to people there?

YL: I am in permanent contact with the mayor of Shlomi and others. I know all their hopes, their fears.

LHC: You lived there, you know better than anybody. You were there.

YL: I was there, and in my heart, I am still there.

LHC: Of course, you had a home there. So you really can speak about what the northern residents feel. Easier than a guy in Tel Aviv.

YL: Absolutely. I am part of this reality, I was a part of this reality.

LHC: Do you have family there?

YL: I have family there. Only two weeks ago, there was shelling in Shlomi by Katusha [rockets].

LHC: So the fact that you're in Lebanon didn't help the shelling of Katushas, right? I mean, if you look at it in a sense, mathematically, you were still being shelled, you had an army in there and boys were getting killed, so it's sort of logical that you withdrew. But it's fascinating that you were a mayor up there. So you really know the temperament of what's going on.

YL: During many, many years, I really believed that the only possible situation was to have our army in this security zone.

LHC: In Lebanon.

YL: In Lebanon. Despite the fact, which we can't neglect, that that was a kind of occupation, whatever you say. And the paradox was even harder when we always stated that we had no territorial conflicts with Lebanon, but we were there. But after many years, and even as a former mayor and a resident of this area, I came to the conclusion that we had to change our modus operandi in this area. You can't be prisoner of what the French call the *pensée unique*, the unique thought. A fixated one.

    You have to be in an era of peace and negotiations and change, a logical change in our region. With all its risks and dangers. We also have to be creative and to normalize the situation. I think that our army should be and could be able to provide us with security from our area, from our international border. That should be the role. We considered, Mr. Barak stated it, that any attempt to violate the—

LHC: You mean attack Syria?

YL: —Israeli sovereignty will be considered an act of war.

LHC: I worked on that at Camp David, as to what an act of war is.

YL: So you are well informed?

LHC: I am well informed. I understand it. Menachem Begin had a huge fight over that. And that was one of the key points before we completed Camp David. Because what there was, was a pact between all of the Arab countries that if Israel attacked them, it would be an act of war and they would unite against Israel. And Begin insisted on having a definition of "act of war."

YL: Fascinating.

LHC: You think that any residents will leave Shlomi because of this withdrawal?

YL: No, I can even tell you that some major cities in Israel, like Netanya, and we have an inter-alliance between Netanya and Shlomi, proposed to entreat people from Shlomi to come to

Netanya for a week, two weeks, or whatever is needed. The offer was obviously appreciated, but the children of Shlomi are still in Shlomi, decidedly, and I think that there is beauty in hope and courage.

LHC: The PLO and Israel—are they going anyplace?

YL: You mean the Palestinian Authority. What I think about this Oslo Agreement is that it's not based on the political grammar. It's very important to have an interim agreement, and then a final one. I think that the originality of this Olso Agreement is its grammar of coexistence, for the first time.

LHC: There's no defined borders.

YL: For the first time, we've reached with the Palestinians what we call "mutual recognition," and we came before '93, before Oslo, from an area of mutual rejection and mutual negation. That is an old story. But I do know that you can't move from an ancient order of mutual rejection to a new order of mutual acceptance and admission without dealing with some huge contradictions. Sometimes violence, sometimes killing people, the assassination of a prime minister.

It reminds me of a statement of François Mitterand, the former French president, who commented on the collapse of the Communist world, and he stated that you can't move from this ancient order to this new order without some violent contradictions. But this mutual recognition is really the driving force of our process, which permits the process to remain irreversible.

The best evidence is Benjamin Netanyahu. When he came to his post of prime minister from, in principle, a negation of the Oslo process, the Olso logic, in the spirit and in the word, he found himself very quickly signing the Hebron Agreement, and what is more significant, the Wye River Agreement. For a man who has been nurtured in the Likud ideology—

LHC: It was a big step, obviously, a huge step. Because in his program, when he was running for prime minister, he said he would never talk to Arafat, he would never recognize the PLO, but there are

modern techniques of making people forget about political statements, and they go forward.

YL: I think it is due, in the philosophical root of the process, to mutual
recognition. Mr. Netanyahu came to the conclusion very quickly,
that there is really a new genesis between us and the Palestinians.
And that he has to adhere to all the limits, as well as to adhere to
its logic. So this makes me optimistic. Basically optimistic. I think
that we are, Israelis and Palestinians, in opposition, where we can
meet and compromise, we come together and compromise.

LHC: You do it in a casino in Jericho, I can tell you that, I was down
there. We filmed that. And there were far more Jewish people than
there were Arabs in that casino. There was a lot of camaraderie
there. On the jackpot. It's ping-pong diplomacy with gambling.
Are you friendly with the Palestinian Ambassador to the United
Nations?

YL: We shared lunch, a dinner, we share views from time to time. We
meet at the United Nations. When I served as Ambassador to
France, I worked very closely with the Palestinian representative.
I met Palestinians, elected people, when I was a member of the
Israeli Parliament, in a variety of conferences. And the dialogue
is there. I personally, not only represent the official Israeli policy,
but I think that the Oslo Agreement, with all its contradictions,
difficulties, limits, the Israelis hope to reach an agreement and to
exist side by side in security, peace, and coexistence.

LHC: By the way, an aside, on France: how involved are they in the
Middle East?

YL: I think that the involvement of France is felt mainly through the
French influence on the Lebanese side. I think there is a durable
affinity between France and Lebanon, but France is also really pro-
active in the EU [European Union].

LHC: And they want to be involved in the Middle East?

YL: Of course. And right now they have a golden opportunity to be
involved. They are considered a key factor. So they can contribute.
But they are waiting to see how things are settling; if Lebanon is

quite ready to fulfill its obligations. But we do think that here, for France, it is a good opportunity to be more and more active and influential.

LHC: So it's a good time for them to get in. When we used to interview people from the UN, and we'd ask this question, "Do you meet with the Arab Ambassador?" and they would say, "No, the PLO, no. Nowhere near us. If we meet them in the elevator, we go the other way and they go this way."

So you really have to be hopeful. Because here we are, the foreign minister of Syria is meeting with Israelis, and the UN Ambassador has lunch with the representative of the PLO. I'm sure the Jordanian Ambassador is very friendly with you.

YL: He gave a lunch in my honor.

LHC: Three weeks before the peace treaty we had the Jordanian Ambassador on this show, who would not even touch an Israeli invitation. He didn't want to hear about it—their mortal enemy. We like to speak to you because you sound very hopeful. In the foreign policy region, things look hopeful and it's nice to hear.

Yehuda was elated at the time of the interview when Israel withdrew from Lebanon. The unilateral withdrawal continues to be condemned by many as border problems have resisted solution and the Lebanese continue to attack northern Israel. Public opinion is still divided over the withdrawal and obviously people are angered by the abduction of three Israeli soldiers, Adi Avitan, Benny Avraham and Omar Suwid, on the border of Jordan.

Raghida Dergham, a popular journalist for the Arab newspaper Al-Hayat. Concerned that, despite the Israeli withdrawal from Lebanon, no treaty has been signed with the Lebanese. She decries the failure of the Clinton peace talks in Geneva. Believes that a solution of the Jerusalem problem would result in a peace treaty.

LHC: And we are now talking to Raghida Dergham who is the premier journalist for the Al-Hayat newspaper out of London. I think it's the largest Arab newspaper in the world. Am I correct?

RD: Most influential, we'll say that.

LHC: What is the Arab point of view about the withdrawal from Lebanon. How is that perceived in the Arab world now?

RD: Elation.

LHC: Elation.

RD: Yes. Lebanon is now free of occupation. The Ambassador of Israel didn't shy away from calling it an occupation. It was a failed policy, really. Regrettably, it had to cost so much on both sides. Not only 1,500 Israelis soldiers but lots of Lebanese have died, civilians on top of it. So twenty-two years later, the land is freed of occupation, the land is getting back together.

LHC: Will the Lebanese take control of their own destiny or does Syria control Lebanon?

RD: Right now, there is a government in Lebanon. There is a president, a prime minister, they both have been to the south; they are making all the arrangements so they can deploy their authority all the way to the border. Now, the United Nations is in charge of taking interim steps.

LHC: Are they going to put troops there?

RD: They have UN troops. They have about 4,500 UN troops. The idea is first to confirm the withdrawal, that it happened, all the way to the international borders. So they would draw sort of the practical life of the withdrawal, confirm that the Israelis have completed it in accordance to these two resolutions, 425, 426, and then assist the government of Lebanon in restoring its authority in the south all the way up to the borders. There are troops to do that, they may have to increase them, but Lebanon will not be a buffer. The United Nations will not create a buffer zone in the south of Lebanon, nor is it going to be another Kosovo.

LHC: It's going to be integrated.

RD: Yes, it's clear—help the government take over.

LHC: And what are the Lebanese going to do to Hizbollah?

RD: Hizbollah as you know, is also a member of the Parliament. Hizbollah is also a political party, not only a resistance party.

LHC: Are they going to be armed and allowed to roam?

RD: Right now, the reaction of Hizbollah so far has been quite admirable. For example, towards the men who had worked with the SLA, they didn't just take care of the victory and say, "Alright, let's eliminate these traitors." In fact, they were very clear and very cooperative and they said "We are not going to sit in for a government. There is government, there is law," and they turned them over. So the government would take care of those men.

LHC: So you're saying two very important things to me: Number one, that the Hizbollah is only a political organization. Basically, the Lebanese army will take control over that area and they will be more integrated, and maybe more importantly, is that Lebanon will stand on its own feet and withstand Syrian influence in that area.

RD: There is still a lot of Syrian influence.

LHC: I don't mean "influence," let's say "takeover."

RD: There is no Syrian takeover. There is an invitation by the Lebanese government to the Syrians to come in and help them out. That invitation was issued quite a number of years ago.

        Right now we have a new situation on the ground. There is no longer an occupation of southern Lebanon. There are Syrian troops still in Lebanon. Eventually, in my view, they will have to leave. I don't think it will happen automatically, because there is no pattern or no comparison. You don't say there was an Israeli occupation and a Syrian occupation as two different things.

        But now that the occupation of Lebanon by Israel is over, there will be an eventual withdrawal of the Syrians from Lebanon. Again, as I said, eventually, and it will be in a gradual way. But also it depends, on the Syrian-Israeli track on negotiations. I still think it will happen. I don't think that right now negotiations are dead. I don't think there's no hope of a Syrian-Israeli peace.

LHC: I'm going to shock you, but I feel the same. I don't think it's over. Give me a little bit about Assad. Is he sick? There were rumors that he had another stroke. His prime minister just assassinated himself because they found out that he stole a few cookies from the cookie jar that weren't his. What's going on here?

RD: How many times have we heard reports about the state of health of President Assad?

LHC: Many, many.

RD: So I'm not going to get into that. Let me tell you what I think is happening in Syria right now. They're taking many steps to take care of their internal house, if you will. The son of President Assad, his name is Dr. Bashar Assad. So the first important step in making it official that he is part of the team that will be running the country will happen June 17th when he will be elected to the regional leadership of the Bath Party.

LHC: You're not claiming that Syria's a democracy, are you?

RD: I never said that. In fact, I said that I am against sons inheriting their father's positions. But my point is that the Syrians are taking many steps, within the Syrian house, to correct the wrongs that have been practiced in the past, to put Syria on a new map, if you will.

       Right now they're issuing laws for investments. They're taking care of correcting old ways that need to be corrected. They're sending signals that they're ready to resume the negotiations. That they are ready to find a solution for that one outstanding issue between the Syrians and the Israelis—

LHC: The water rights, and the border of the lake [Lake Tiberius i.e., the Sea of Galilee]—

RD: For me, it's a shame that we arrived at this, and it takes courage by both the Syrians and the Israelis—

LHC: You can't claim that [Ehud] Barak hasn't been a courageous leader. He's been pretty courageous.

RD: You know what, Leon? Explain something to me. How is it possible that one can't understand, if they solve this problem of the lake, if there is that solution, and the formulas are there, Israel would have gotten not only a retreat and a defeat from Lebanon, it would have gotten a peace treaty with Lebanon. It would have gotten a peace treaty with Syria. And still could, by the way. It puzzles me, why Mr. Barak wouldn't have all of that because of the lake.

LHC: Well, he probably has internal reasons, conflicts within Israel, the parties. I tell you, the Likud people all want a peace treaty with Syria. There's no one in Israel who doesn't want a peace treaty with Syria.

RD: I was very clear in saying both Syria and Israel need that bit of courage to go for it. It's there. It's done.

LHC: I agree with you, but Assad comes from a minority sect in Syria. Can he shove his son in there to run this country?

RD: It's the Bath Party. The party that runs the country, rules the country, and governs the country is the Bath party. There are twenty men in that leadership, the regional leadership. I said that Bashar will be elected as one of these twenty men. I think he is clearly being prepared.

LHC: I was just curious. You know why I think there will be peace with Syria? You'll blow me out on this one. You know why? Because of the Internet.

RD: I've heard that. And by the way, Bashar is big on that.

LHC: The country, the young people are getting into communications. There was a lot of censoring in Syria, about what people could do and not do. But the satellite and the Internet are going to absolutely open up that country.

RD: And they really are taking the necessary steps. To compare them to what's in the United States or other parts of the Arab world, you say, "Where are they? They're way behind." But the fact that they're issuing laws regarding investments, regarding openness, changing the way of reacting to what's happening in the world, Internet and otherwise, they're sending signals.

LHC: You're right. They are. I know a Jewish person who does a tremendous amount of manufacturing in Syria, and it blew me out. I didn't believe it. He said it was the best place to produce his goods, and he's doing business there, and he's Jewish.

RD: When we have an agreement between the Syrians and the Israelis, remember that Lebanon, the government, and the government of Syria, are committed. They will not sign peace treaties separately with the Israelis. So right now the Lebanese track is pretty much ready. The withdrawal is completed. The commitment is to sign that peace, and it's important.

LHC: The Israelis have always said the Syrians, when they make a commitment, they don't breach it. They have never breached a commitment.

RD: That's right. And it's unfortunate, right now, that things are stuck on something so small. However, I think there will be the momentum of the Israeli withdrawal. The fact of the matter is that this is the first time Israel withdrew from an Arab territory without preconditions, in accordance with a United Nations plan, with resolution 425, and without a peace treaty. Israel had withdrawn from other Arab lands through a peace treaty. This is not. This is a retreat. Not a peace treaty. So there is still something to be done on the Lebanese level, and that happens through Syria.

LHC: You follow the Arab world every minute. What's the reaction in Syria?

RD: In the beginning, when there was talk of a unilateral Israeli withdrawal from Lebanon, the Syrians were saying, "Well, this is a trap, and the Israelis are playing." But then it became clear that the Israelis were really determined. So the Syrians, said wait, to see if they're going to do it in accordance to this resolution that I mentioned, 425. Now that it's happened, without conditions, now that it's done and clear to the world, awaiting confirmation by the United Nations, the official one of course, then it's a different ballgame. The Syrians are saying, "Fine."

LHC: You read the editorials in the Syrian papers, or your own papers? What do they say?

RD: The editorials are about elation. You know, May 25th is declared a national day in Lebanon. And all the Arabs are saying it's incredible this has happened. But they're not saying now that because of that, let's say resistance will always be the only solution, the only way to teach the Israelis. They're saying that the resistance in Lebanon made a point and won it. But let's go back and see how we can use it through the peace process. Let's see if we can use these developments right now to usher the region into a new relationship.

LHC: So you're saying something very important. You're saying that the withdrawal from Lebanon, which is part of the Israeli policy, would stimulate the world to understand that Israel's not there any longer, that Syria should also not be involved there, and that they should really knock their heads out and do a peace treaty.

RD: The Syrians will be in Lebanon for a short while. Eventually they will not be always in control or influence Lebanon. It cannot happen overnight. It will not happen overnight. It should not happen overnight.

The Syrians helped the resistance, the Hizbollah and others, in southern Lebanon accomplish their aim, which was to get rid of the occupation. That's done. It's a defeat of the occupation. Again, the page of peace is still open, but it behooves both Mr. Barak and Mr. Assad to get that magic formula.

LHC: And Mr. Clinton.

RD: And Mr. Clinton. But Mr. Clinton, in Geneva, you know, there were many mistakes. He meant well, but—

LHC: You're talking about the meeting with Assad and Clinton. What happened? Were you there, by the way?

RD: I was not there, but I have pretty good information about what happened. See, I know President Clinton would love to arrive at a peace treaty between the Israelis and the Syrians. It would be a fabulous thing for him. I think he came late with his concern about the peace process for the Middle East. Eventually, the mistake that was made in Geneva from my point of view is that he went in thinking that if he presents Mr. Barak's view, then the Syrians were ready to take it as is.

LHC: He doesn't know the Middle East.

RD: There was a disconnect between the Americans and the Syrians on that issue. That was the problem. Mr. Assad went in saying, "Do I get my land back? Do I get my land back?" Three times. And

Mr. Clinton couldn't say, "Yes, I give you your land back." He couldn't promise him.

LHC: This is the second time that happened to Clinton. I was with President Clinton in Syria, and I blame the State Department for not briefing Clinton correctly.

RD: What year was that?

LHC: Must be five years ago, because DeeDee Meyers was press secretary. His visit was a disaster, a total disaster. Evidently he wasn't briefed well enough. Because you can't make the president move to a situation and not have something come out of it. You lose the prestige of the presidency.

RD: It was a disconnect that was really dangerous. I think the team made mistakes, and there was a misunderstanding thereafter, because some people were saying that he promised that he would only want to speak about the shore, not the waters of the lake, but then when he couldn't get his point, then he said probably, "You know, I don't want to speak about the shore at this point. I want to speak about the water, too." So he was upping the ante. And even now, there are ways to rescue it, but I think they went too far in presenting the position of Mr. Barak, rather than guide. The very important role of coordinator or mediator, or—what is the official word for the United States in the peace process?

LHC: Facilitator.

RD: Facilitator. And they lost that edge. I still don't think it's over. I still think that there is a possibility that somebody will do something magical and some vehicle will be used to resume the negotiations.

LHC: Because necessity makes it so. Communications are opening up all over the world. It's a global world, Syria has to join a global economy, and you have to feed your people and house them. If they're not making a living you've got unemployment and you've got to do something. This is what moved [Egyptian President Anwar] Saddat. You know that very well, what moves the King of Jordan.

RD: They have to need it enough. I think it was "needed enough" for the Israelis to pull out of Lebanon and they went and left. It was "needed enough" for the Syrians to accept such a pull out, so they didn't make any trouble. In fact they are really not complicating the withdrawal and thereafter. The Lebanese, of course, needed that above all. Now the Syrians and the Israelis must feel that they need it enough to arrive at a peace treaty. Mr. Assad and Mr. Barak.

LHC: Let's move to the West Bank a little bit. What do you hear about the PLO and the Israeli negotiations?

RD: You know that they were having parallel negotiations in Oslo and so you have a great argument in the media and amongst commentators: Is this a good thing or a bad thing to have these parallel, secret negotiations? I think the jury is still out about where Oslo will lead us. I really don't know. It's the approach that we go step by step, and it lends itself to the politics, to the equations of politics, and to the influence of politicians from different groups. I'm worried more about the Palestinian track.

LHC: It's a tougher deal.

RD: I think so. If I were an Israeli, I wouldn't want to be greedy. I would give the Palestinians the best deal possible, so that I could really start to coexist in peace. Because they are there, they are amongst each other. There is no wall to separate them.

LHC: Shimon Peres had a concept that you do everything and then you leave Jerusalem to the final aim. I think you may have to reverse that. I think you should tackle Jerusalem, because if you figure out Jerusalem then everything falls by the side.

RD: Neither party can just say, "I want it all my way." There has to be a compromise.

LHC: I can't give you the resolution, because I'm not Israeli and I don't tell the Israelis what to do. But it seems to me that if they could find a resolution to this problem, I think the whole thing would start to move much easier. I think they have to attack that problem, whether it's Abu Dis or not Abu Dis, but I know that if they resolve that issue, they'll be able to make peace with the Palestinians.

RD: And the issue of the refugees?

LHC: That can be solved.

RD: Eventually, Leon, I also am optimistic on that one.

LHC: So what will you do for a living when this ends?

RD: I shall write books.

LHC: How is the bilateral relationship between Jordan and Israel?

RD: Quite fine. Except, of course, all of these relationships are not going to go the full distance, as long as there isn't that aspired peace in the region. Because they will be affected by certain parties within a certain country, by what a certain country does towards another. I think there is a sense that a comprehensive peace in the Middle East is the one that will liberate the frozen peace, or the cold peace, or that sort of thing, between countries who have relations with Israel. I think the most important thing is that it's comprehensive.

LHC: I think reasonable people believe that. I don't know how people who are on the right or very strong fanatics, I don't know how that works out. I'm sure that you don't either. That's the tough problem. The fundamentalists.

Both these guests were pretty optimistic. Let us pray that they are correct.

Raghida Dergham was confident that the Israeli withdrawal would eliminate Syria's control of Lebanon. It hasn't happened. Dergham denied rumors that ill health was dogging President Assad. Obviously she was wrong. Assad's son, Bashar, a former ophthalmologist, was named as president of Syria. The Western World was hopeful that Bashar Assad would change Syria's attitude politically to a more peaceful direction. As of this publication that has not happened. Moreover, in the presence of Pope John Paul in Damascus he delivered a virulent anti-Israel and anti-Semetic diatribe before a world audience.

NASSER AL**KIDWA**

Nasser Al Kidwa, the Ambassador to the Palestinian Mission to the United Nations, is the nephew of Yasser Arafat . This interview barely preceded Clinton's Camp David Summit II. Anticipated that a new summit might result in the formation of a Palestinian state by the Fall of 1999, he was in favor of swapping West Bank land for a treaty.

LHC: Is this a big event for the Palestinians? [Camp David II]

NAK: Of course. I think it's a big event for the whole Middle East. And let's hope that it will succeed.

LHC: Now you returned recently?

NAK: Yes, from Palestine. We had just finished the meeting of the Central Council.

LHC: Was that the meeting that says that you'd like to declare a state by September?

NAK: That was among the decisions taken by the Central Council, yes. With the end of the one year extension period of the transitional five years agreed upon by the two sides, we have to take measures to actualize the declaration of independence from 1988.

LHC: You people analyze Israel all the time, as Israel analyzes you people. Do you believe that Barak is going to Washington with a directive from his government or do you think he is weakened by what has transpired over the last few days, where Natan Sharansky is threatening to, or will pull out his party and also the National Religious Party will desert the governing coalition?

NAK: Yes, indeed, he definitely has some troubles within the government, but I think he is not that weak. I also think that no Israeli prime minister would have an absolute power within the Knesset. So maybe Mr. Barak's plan is to go directly to the people. So if you can combine both, his relative strength, not absolute strength, plus his plan to go directly to the people, you would conclude that he is not in that bad of shape.

LHC: So you believe that he could bypass the Knesset and go directly to the people if he brings back a deal. President Clinton said yesterday that he lowered expectations, saying that if he got a framework, or an agreement to agree and then an agreement not to agree, as we had sometimes in Camp David I, he would be in a sense satisfied. Would that satisfy the Palestinians?

NAK: Well I think that we will have some serious efforts in Camp David. We also probably have kind of a process or a whole procedure. I don't think there will be only a few days meeting followed by an agreement. Probably we will see more than that, maybe a continuous meeting with some interruptions, maybe two or three meetings. I'm not sure as yet. But we have been hearing about process, which will lead to an agreement. The most important thing is to meet the critical deadline, which is the 13th of September of this year.

LHC: That's very important, what you said now. Because when we did Camp David I, the idea was to wrap up an agreement. What we got was an agreement in principle in September and then we did the treaty in March. And you're saying to me, is that this might be a process, and then stop and then go into a process again. Some people contend that President Clinton organized the Camp David II meeting in July to give him some more time in case he has to convene again.

NAK: That's probably correct. What we are talking about here are terms to reach a framework agreement and then maybe some kind of referendum in Israel, then another attempt to reach final agreement. And maybe at a later stage, after some kind of implementation, we will talk about a treaty. So there are several steps ahead of us.

LHC: The deadline is for a treaty, or for what, in September? What does the deadline call for?

NAK: Well, we might try to reach a treaty by the 13th of September. I personally think that this might prove too much for the parties. If we succeed in reaching a framework agreement, followed by a referendum, and then an agreement itself, a final agreement—

LHC: A referendum for the Israelis? And then what about the Palestinians? Do you need a referendum also?

NAK: We have our constitution and institutions. We have the PNC [Palestinian National Council, legislative body of the Palestinian National Authority], we have the Central Council, we have the Legislative Council also of the Palestinian Authority. And that for us I think will be enough.

LHC: So you don't think you have to go directly to the people. You go through the process that's called for in your constitution?

NAK: I think so. That would be enough. But in any case, after the agreement, after the establishment of the state, of course there should be some new elections for both the president and the Parliament—in Palestine.

LHC: When did you see your uncle last?

NAK: Just two days ago.

LHC: I'll assume he's tired. That's for sure. But is he excited about going to Camp David?

NAK: He is tired, as you said. I think his life pattern is too hard. I think it's hard for even young ones to take. Continuous work, continuous travel, continuous flying, continuous tension. And of course, that's tiring. You add to that of course, the responsibilities, especially during this period where we are probably very close, to

achieving something big for the first time for the Palestinian people. I'm sure that he feels the burden of the responsibilities while
coming here to Washington for the summit.

LHC: How big a team will he bring?

NAK: I think there will be some limitations imposed by the host, given
the limitations of the place itself. I heard about twelve persons
from each side, plus some additional delegates staying in a place
maybe ten or fifteen miles from Camp David.

LHC: They do this, by the way, to have a news blackout. This thing seems
to have happened so quickly. I'm not sure President Clinton knows
where he wants to drive this. Do you have a feeling about it?

NAK: Of course I don't have information, but I doubt that the President
doesn't have a fair idea about the direction. Let's not forget that
the administration has been engaged in this thing for the last seven
years. If that administration, after seven years, does not have an
initial idea—

LHC: I know there are ideas, but I don't know if they can solve the real
big issues. As I understand it, Jerusalem is a big issue, refugees are
a big issue—

NAK: Indeed.

LHC: Indeed, those are the two big issues, right? Is there a third big
issue?

NAK: Well, probably all the issues are big. The one that becomes the
biggest is the one that's being negotiated at that point. But I think
all of them are big. The territorial dimension is important.

LHC: Do you really expect that the refugees who left Israel in '48 can
go back and physically live in Israel? Or are they looking for compensation there?

NAK: On all the issues we have two aspects that are most urgent. One
is the principles involved, international law, on which the parties
have to agree. The parties have to accept the provisions of international law. The other issue is the practicalities of the matter;
what kind of mechanisms we can agree upon to implement a kind
of solution. I think if we apply those two aspects to all issues,

including the refugees, we can find a reasonable solution.

LHC: Really? That's good to know. What about the big issue of Jerusalem?

NAK: Same thing. International law is clear when it comes to Jerusalem. Israeli occupation of the Eastern part of the city is not acceptable. Also, the international community agrees that the city must remain united, must not be closed to anyone. Freedom of access to all, not only inhabitants, but to all people of the world should be guaranteed. And on the basis of this, I think we can find a solution that would respond to the rights of the two peoples, and also the rights of the three religions of the world: Judaism, Christianity, and Islam.

Jerusalem does not accept exclusive ownership, and I think that the Israeli side understands that. Now, as an opening position, one could say it's not subject to negotiations, but in fact, if Jerusalem, as the capital of Israel is to be recognized by the international community, if this is to be accepted by the Palestinians, the Arabs, and the Muslims, all Israeli officials know that a reasonable solution should be found, one which responds to the rights of the Palestinian people and the rights of the Muslim—

LHC: So you're saying that it's a possibility that you could accept Jerusalem as the capital of Israel provided that the three religions have access to the city?

NAK: No, no. I was talking about principles, but we can accept Jerusalem as the capital of Israel if East Jerusalem is accepted as the capital of Palestine.

LCH: What about Abu Dis? It's a suburb of Jerusalem. Aren't you building a building there for Parliament?

NAK: Yes, yes. Of course, we will have to expand the original East Jerusalem into new suburbs, including Abu Dis. The issue remains, of course, the Arab neighborhoods in Jerusalem itself.

Let's try to record certain facts. One, the overwhelming majority of Israelis have never set foot in the Arab neighborhoods of East Jerusalem. Two, the East including the Old City, remains overwhelmingly Arab, in spite of all the settlement activities and things of that sort. Three, the city, if not formally divided, is distinguishable.

The moment you cross from West Jerusalem to East Jerusalem, you immediately notice the new situation you are seeing. So the differences are there. The actual distinction is there. What we need to do is formally recognize the existing differences and the distinction that is there, and to try to find the best political and legal formulas to accommodate both sides.

LHC: The negotiators, have they been working on these problems continuously?

NAK: Negotiators have been working on these issues.

LHC: So you're pretty hopeful.

NAK: I am hopeful as long as the two sides are willing to make the necessary decisions. I think from our side, the Palestinian side, the will to make those decisions is there.

LHC: There's a lot of rumor around that your uncle has a tough time convincing his population to make any compromise. Is that true?

NAK: I think that the situation is basically the following: the Palestinian side correctly believes that they have already made the compromise. The Palestinian people believe that all Palestine is theirs. Just as many Israelis believe that all mandated Palestine, this territory, Israel, whatever you want to call it, is theirs.

The Palestinian side now accepts the compromise of establishing their own state on a mere 23 percent of the size of the whole territory. That's less than a quarter of Mandated Palestine. So, as such, the Palestinian people believe that they have made their share of the necessary compromise.

Nevertheless, I'm not saying that that will be it. We will be also ready to show some flexibility, but certainly a very limited one, given the fact, as I was trying to explain, that we have done our share, we believe.

LHC: When you teach your children in your schools about 1948, or 1947, when there was a partition of Palestine, what happened? What do you teach in your schools?

NAK: We don't have our own curriculum. The schools now follow the Jordanian and Egyptian curriculum. We are still in the process of establishing a new one for all schools in the West Bank and Gaza. But I think, regardless of such changes or such development, we will have to explain to them some objective facts.

That until the late '40s the Palestinian population was the majority. They owned most of the land in Mandated Palestine. And then things developed in a different way. The General Assembly partitioned Palestine, then the Arab–Israeli war started, and the whole conflict entered into a new stage, I would say.

At this stage in history, we cannot ignore our rights and our history. But at the same time, I think we have to be decisive, as the other side has to be, in accepting the historic compromise we are getting into.

LHC: If you look back in history, and you can't always do that, don't you think it was a mistake not to accept the partition?

NAK: In retrospect, of course, everything is easy. In retrospect one could say, of course it was a mistake, because had we accepted the partition resolution, the agony and the suffering of the Palestinian people would have been reduced and we would have had a state.

LHC: Has Barak said officially that he would recognize a Palestinian state?

NAK: I don't think that he said that in that clear terms. But I also think it's a given now, that there will be a Palestinian state. I think the Israeli side understands that this might be even beneficial to them, to have an agreement between two states is something different than having an agreement between a state and an authority. So to achieve all the benefits of a final agreement I think that agreement has to be concluded between two states.

LHC: So you think it works well for both sides?

NAK: Absolutely. Of course, it's much more important for us. This is the cornerstone of our national struggle for years, now. To achieve a Palestinian state for the Palestinian people, not only for those who live there now, but for other Palestinians around the world as well.

LHC: How old were you when you said, "Maybe one day there'll be a

Palestinian state?" When did you get involved in this?

NAK: I have always been convinced that there will be a Palestinian state. You have people here, a proud people with history and determination to find a place under the sun, as we say. I have never had any doubt that this is going to happen. Now at some point, maybe we thought of a democratic state for everybody, Muslims, Christians, Jews, living together.

LHC: You mean one state? Under one flag?

NAK: In the '60s this was our political program, which was totally misunderstood by the other side. It was understood as an attempt to destroy Israel more than anything else. And then we came up with another political program, with an additional concession, I might say, that was the political program of establishing a Palestinian state alongside Israel, which we are trying to do now.

LHC: Do you have any trade with Israel now?

NAK: We have lots of trade, but very unbalanced trade. We import from Israel and we barely export anything. Until now we have to recognize that the whole Palestinian market is taken hostage, I would say, into the hands of the Israeli economy. We are, of course, in favor of economic relationship between Israel and Palestine, but I think that this economic relationship should be based on the usual fair internationally accepted norms between the two sides.

LHC: Do you have a banking system?

NAK: We have a banking authority, a centralized one.

LHC: Would this authority raise rates, like the Federal Reserve here?

NAK: Yes, largely like any central bank anywhere. And this authority also has plans for new Palestinian currency.

LHC: And you have passports now?

NAK: We do have passports.

LHC: And you have a customs authority in Gaza?

NAK: We have customs authority, yes, but the international crossing points are not totally under the Palestinian control. It's under shared control between Israeli and Palestinian control. And frankly, the Israeli side is not making our life easier. There's still lots of difficulties and problems which make any serious development efforts extremely difficult.

LHC: If you look at the Israeli side, there's been a lot of terrorism against the Israelis, so they're trying to protect their people, obviously.

NAK: Yes. You know something? The other day I was thinking about some U.S. positions and about some statements made by the Secretary [Madelaine Albright] herself in the wake of some bombings which took place in Israel. The Secretary spoke about the impossibility of morally equating the bombs with bulldozers. She was referring to settlement activities. In other words, she was calling for the need of complete cessation of such terrorist activities for the bulldozers to stop.

LHC: I don't think that'd be a great statement with the Israeli people, who lost a lot of lives. You can't compare a bulldozer to a terrorist.

NAK: That's what I was saying, so these things stopped for the last two years. But the bulldozers did not stop.

LHC: Are you working actively with the Israelis to stop terrorism?

NAK: I think there is enough security cooperation between the two sides; of course, I don't have concrete information, but this is my understanding.

LHC: A state. What does it mean?

NAK: It means everything.

LHC: You want to have an army, a foreign minister, a defense minister?

NAK: An army, which is really very big and expensive, I don't think so. Maybe we want to have an army which is more of a symbolic one.

LHC: So just a symbolic army?

NAK: We are a small country and I don't think it would be a very smart thing to have a—

LHC: —big defense budget.

NAK: The United States will not be ready to finance that, and we don't need it.

LHC: And how about a foreign ministry?

NAK: Of course, of course. We will have all the trappings of a state. But on top of that, the state will mean dignity for every single Palestinian.

It will mean, of course, identity, nation, and a new beginning for Palestinian institutions. And hopefully also a new beginning in our relationship with our neighbors, including the Israelis.

LHC: You know, the press has reported that Barak has offered you 94 percent of the West Bank already. Do you know anything about that?

NAK: I heard something like that. Of course, I don't like the concept of "giving us," and then figures. What we want to see, frankly, is the correct logic. We need to be talking about the implementation of Security Council Resolution 242, which means total Israeli withdrawal. So we are taking back what belongs to us.

Now, we will also be ready to hear the Israeli needs and to try to accommodate those needs on the basis of this position. Including possible adjustments of the border line to at least absorb part of the problem created by settlements building in occupied territory. So this is the logic which we will try to apply.

LHC: Did you hear anything about the possibility taking land in a different region and swapping it for land in the West Bank?

NAK: I think it's a must. Because, as I said, the principle is the withdrawal, complete withdrawal from the occupied territory in accordance with the principles of the inadmissibility of the acquisition of territory by war. Now, if the Israeli side needs some adjustments, if they need to maintain part of this land, as I said, to try to reduce the problem created by the settlement activities in the occupied territory, probably then, we will have to swap this land with other lands, maybe adjacent to the Gaza Strip or maybe the North of the West Bank.

LHC: In order for a Palestinian to travel between Gaza and the West Bank, he needs to pass through Israeli territories all the times, which could be intrusive—problems with terrorism, etc. So they have to find a combination which allows the Gaza people to connect with the West Bank people without being obstreperous to the Israeli population.

NAK: And I think this is an extremely important element, by the way.

LHC: So that's the way you think the state will look. You hope that you'll have Jerusalem and then the West Bank, and then a bridge over to Gaza or something else that connects it.

NAK: A connection between Gaza and the West Bank. When it comes to Jerusalem, we hope to have the eastern part of the capital of our state, while the west part is the capital of Israel. Special arrangements would have to be made for the religious sites, including those holy to the Jewish people and those holy to the Muslims and then the Christians. And some additional arrangements to ensure freedom of access to all believers in the world would also be needed. The city will have to remain open, will have to remain undivided. We don't disagree with that. This is a position which is strongly advocated by the Israeli side and we accept it.

LHC: A year from now, where will things be?

NAK: Well, I think that a year from now we will have two Embassies, a Palestinian one in Israel and an Israeli one in Palestine.

Nasser Al Kidwa, a dentist by profession, prophesied that there would be two embassies representing both Israel and the PLO but it did not take place. On the eve of Camp David II, the Palestinians were conciliatory. Though Barak met 95% of their demands, there was no agreement. Of course, Al Kidwa believes in the return of the refugees, but that has become a deadlocked issue and it has backfired against Chairman Arafat. He continues to favor the validity of land swapping between Israelis and Palestinians. Even the leftist parties of Israel know this proposition is self-defeating. Al Kidwa believes the parties can find a "reasonable solution." This is a minority view today.

COLETTE**AVITAL**
& ERIC**FETTMAN**

Colette Avital, currently a Knesset member, believes that control of Jerusalem is the sticking point. She believes in the possibility of Arabs rejecting the conception of their own state and becoming integrated with Israel.

LHC: What brings you to the United States?

CA: I am here on behalf of the prime minister to try to explain to the Jewish community what is going on in Camp David, what the odds are, what the possibilities and chances are, what would happen if we get an agreement, what kind of agreement we would like to get, and what happens if there is no agreement. So I am part of the team who tries to convey not only to the Jewish community, but to all the Americans.

LHC: When's the last time you talked to the prime minister?

CA: I spoke with him about a week ago in Israel.

LHC: Have you talked to any of the senior people?

CA: Yes, I'm in contact with them every day. You probably know that Barak is totally incommunicado. He doesn't speak to most of the people most of the time.

LHC: He's used to that, though. When he headed the commandos he didn't talk too much either.

CA: Well, some of the things we do are better done quietly.

LHC: Last night the Israeli press was told to pack up and be ready to go, and then Bill Clinton announced that he was going to Okinawa, but that Madeline Albright, the Secretary of State, was going to take over and the two teams, both Palestinian and Israeli were going to continue to negotiate under the auspices of Ms. Albright. Is it a vacation until he returns, or are they really negotiating, Colette?

CA: Actually they have been working very hard around the clock for ten days now. The crisis was a real crisis. The prime minister thought that he had come forward with many good proposals, and has gone as far as he can go. But there was no equal response on the other side. So it was not only the press that was packing, the whole entourage was already on the plane.

At the request of the president, however, the prime minister decided to give it another try. There will be some negotiations while the president is gone, and there probably will be renewed negotiations when the president comes back. The question is, differences are so great—can we really bridge the gap? What measure of good will, of flexibility can there be on the other side? I think we have reached the point where we cannot go any further. But we expect a similar gesture and a similar attitude on the part of the Palestinians.

LHC: Do we know exactly what's on the table. We know that the subjects are Jerusalem, refugees, and land swapping. But let's talk Jerusalem.

CA: Borders, settlers.

LHC: I think those things I heard from some of the back door characters that most of those issues can be resolved. The key issue is Jerusalem.

CA: No doubt.

LHC: Where are you personally? What do you think about Jerusalem?

CA: I think that Jerusalem right now is such an important issue, so highly emotional on both sides, but certainly on our side, that I don't see a way that it can be resolved now. My own feeling is that since the other side is not going to compromise, I don't think we can reach a solution. What the other side wants is two capitals in one city, Jerusalem, an open city. They say that they don't want to divide the city and what do we care if there are two capitals in that city. This is a solution that we cannot accept.

Falling short of that kind of solution, there are many other possibilities in which we believe that we can live in peace and harmony with the Palestinian population. We can take into account some of their interests, give satisfaction to some of their political aspirations or claims, but certainly neither in the framework of a divided city nor in the frame of two capitals inside of one city.

LHC: Years ago, when I worked on Camp David I, not II, Ezer Weizman, your former president and defense minister, said to me, "Leon, the one subject that all Israelis are wall-to-wall on is Jerusalem."

CA: Absolutely. Absolutely.

LHC: And we told that to Mr. Sadat at that time and he sort of let it go, and he said you know, if we put a flag on a mosque maybe that would work or something. Two or three weeks ago I had the ambassador from the Palestinian organization to the United Nations—

CA: Mr. Al Kidwa—

LHC: He, in a very calm way, said that unless we get East Jerusalem there will be no deal. You know, we need to have East Jerusalem as our capital. And that came from his uncle's mouth, and that seemed to be the real tough point. On refugees, he said, compensation— as long as Israel confirms that they are refugees and that they're returning refugees, then we can work this deal out. They wanted some confirmation to go back to all the UN resolutions, etc. But I got the impression that the thing that was really busting every-thing one way or another was, as you say, Jerusalem. I don't know if, politically, Arafat can withstand going back to the Arab world and not have Jerusalem as his shared capital.

CA: Depending on how much he has tied his own hands. Because I know that before coming to Camp David he's not only made the rounds of the European capitals, he's also gone to see Mubarak, the president of Egypt, and it's very possible that the position that he represents is also backed by some of the Arab leaders and therefore he finds that it may be more difficult for him. But I cannot speak on his behalf, and I think that you have represented their point of view. I can only speak for our point of view.

You are right, there is consensus on Jerusalem, there is no way that we can divide the city. I think that if there's going to be, and probably there's going to be, a Palestinian state, and we're talking about this very calmly, but when I was here three years ago I think, the last time, the mere idea of a Palestinian state would get everybody up the wall. So I think we have made a lot of progress. And it's not very easy. You take this almost for granted.

If and when the Palestinians have a state, they can have a capital, they don't necessarily have to have it in East Jerusalem proper. They can have it in one of the suburbs of Jerusalem. One of the possibilities that was being considered was to have their capital in a suburb which at the time was part of Jerusalem and it's Abu Dis. It's considered part of Jerusalem by the Palestinians.

It's a proposal that has been on the table for at least one year. And I think that in a way for many of us who have visited Abu Dis, and have seen that there is almost a full structure of a parliament in Abu Dis, by the way, built under the nose of Benjamin Netanyahu, who accepted it; those who see that, must understand that somehow, among the Palestinians too, this is a possibility that they have envisaged and probably adopted. So I think where there is a will, there's a way.

My message, if it counts at all, and if it is seen by Palestinians at all, and not only by people who are on our side, my message is that I don't think that Yasser Arafat will be able to get a better deal. I think we're running out of time. I don't see any other leader coming and negotiating and making a generous offer like Ehud Barak. And if we don't succeed this time, I really don't know when the next opportunity will come.

The Palestinians lost one opportunity, 1948, perhaps it was not their fault, at that time. They lost a second opportunity in 1978; let us hope that they understand not only that this is really the hour of truth, but if we postpone it, I'm not sure that we will have the same circumstances.

LHC: So it's a deal-breaker.

CA: I think so.

LHC: And probably Barak can't go any further than he did. I understand that he has gone further than anybody in the history of Israel.

CA: There's no way we can do it. Absolutely. Even the doves in Israel are astonished. Interestingly enough, even though the doves are astonished, I think that many people on the right side of the map can be happy and satisfied that he is taking care of the very vital interests of the whole population of Israel, including the settlers. I think that if we came to an agreement where 90 percent of the settlers will remain in their homes, I think this would be a real achievement.

LHC: Why did [Natan] Sharansky and Shas [ultra-orthodox religious right party] leave your voting block?

CA: Well they each left for different reasons. And I do not wish to use this interview to criticize them.

LHC: I don't want to be critical, I want to illuminate the public.

CA: I really don't know. Sharansky was afraid of the Camp David II Summit. Sharansky did not want even the prime minister to go and talk and I found this attitude rather surprising, coming from a man like Sharansky. An enlightened man, a man who came out after suffering in the Soviet Union because of human rights. I found this attitude outright strange and, I would say, limited in thinking. I think that Shas did not leave because of that reason. I think the reason why Shas left the government is compounded by many frustrations dealing more with internal issues.

LHC: Ok. Mr. Deri's [the leader of the Shas party] going to jail for three years. Is that going to affect the political landscape in Israel?

CA: I think so, to a certain extent.

LHC: Should I call him Rabbi Deri? I'm not sure.

CA: We don't call him Rabbi Deri anymore, he's back into politics, and he's shown his old instinct for politics and for leadership. And there has been one long festival around him as if the man was a holy man or a fabulous leader, and not a man who has been convicted to prison. But that's part of the Israeli scene, and I think that what we're about to see is a real competition for leadership in the next two years.

Is it going to be Mr. Deri who will continue to conduct the Shas party from jail? Will Mr. [Eli] Ishai, who is currently the head of the party, will he be able to control the party, use that time that Deri is in jail to really take over the party and make his own appointments?

As you probably know, that party, it has been said, is not exactly a democratic party. People are not elected by the process we all go through, primaries; they are appointed. And the word comes out from the rabbi's mouth. But the person who will appoint the next members on the list for the Knesset will be the leader of the party, so we will see a big fight for leadership.

LHC: If Camp David fails, what happens?

CA: If Camp David fails, paradoxically, there is quiet at home. There is much more interior domestic political support of political parties for Ehud Barak. He can actually make any coalition that he wishes, and he can devote his time to the problems that have been besetting Israel society, which badly need his attention.

LHC: The internal problems.

CA: The internal problems, economic problems, social problems. The unemployed, the hospitals, the various strikes, and the salaries, and we have plenty of those problems.

LHC: Is there a government functioning today, truly?

CA: To a certain extent I think there is a government, but since many of the cabinet ministers must be replaced, it is not functioning full speed, and even before, because of all the bickering, I would say that it did not function the way it should have functioned. Now if we fail, however, I would say that, not withstanding the fact that he may have less domestic problems, we will all be beset with the possibility of having a new wave of violence from the Palestinians.

We're talking of a population that by and large is frustrated. It needs to see some type of progress. Arafat may not necessarily control all of the street. If he comes back without an agreement, he may be weakened. We may see Hamas growing in its presence on the street, but not only its presence, but in its influence, in its impact. We've already seen part of these things when the prime minister of France was in Israel and, if you recall, he went to one of the Universities and he received plenty of stones. I mean the Intifada. We may see waves of violence against our own population. We may see renewed terrorism. So this is something which may happen. And it is this type of bloodshed that we should all try to avoid.

LHC: By the way, when we spoke with Al Kidwa, the Ambassador, it wasn't a big deal to him, declaring a state. It didn't seem that important to him. It's amazing, you know. And I don't know what it would do for them. I think that Arafat is using this as a bargaining chip. I don't think he cares that much. I mean, it's my own feeling.

CA: I think he cares very much. I think he sees himself as the Moses of the Palestinian people who is going through the desert and who wants to lead them to independence. I think it is extremely important for them, for most of the Palestinians. They want their independence, for their independence means—

LHC: But I don't think the date is that important, Colette.

CA: Maybe the date is not that important, the symbolism is. He's committed himself, and it's very difficult now for him to go back on that commitment. But I think it's very interesting, what you said about Al Kidwa, because it echoes what I've heard among many

Palestinians. Mainly Palestinian intellectuals, some members of Parliament, even some members of the cabinet whom I've met not long ago, about two weeks ago. The trend now among some of the Palestinians is to say, "You know what? If it's so difficult to get a state, if we have to sacrifice this, that and the other, let's forgo that state. Let's forget about it. Let's wait patiently. Slowly but surely, we will become part of Israel. Let's ask the Israelis to annex the territories. Let us become citizens of what will become a bi-national state. And let us see then what the Jews will say." Obviously, this is not just a threat. This is a thought that's going around. I personally, will do everything in my power to avoid that kind of a situation.

LHC: Ok. You know, I interviewed one of your colleagues, Azmi Bashara—

CA: Oh, nice colleague.

LHC: He's a Minister of the Knesset, he's an Arab, an Israeli-Arab. Ph.D. in philosophy from Berlin, I think. Fairly bright guy, but he looks at Israel as a nationalistic state that has nothing to do with Judaism.

CA: Yes, but he also represents a very extreme brand of Arab nationalism within Israel, as an Israeli citizen. But still, I would say that he's probably very much to the left-left-left of the Israeli political scene. And he does not accept Zionism and he would like Israel not to be a Zionist or Jewish state, but to be a State of all its citizens. And obviously we disagree on these issues.

LHC: Have you had tea with him in the Knesset sometimes?

CA: Actually, I have not had tea yet, but I think that's a good idea.

LHC: Colette, if they come back from Camp David with a half-baked agreement, what happens then?

CA: I think the general perception is that we cannot make the amount of sacrifice and give up a lot of land for a half-baked agreement. It's worth really going all the way if we know that we have an agreement that spells out that this is the end of the conflict. Otherwise, for a half-baked agreement, we may make half-baked concessions. And I don't know where that's going to lead us, but it can go, it can fly, it can be accepted. In the Knesset it can be progress, but we will not get to the moment of truth when we have to cut.

LHC: If we were to say that at the end of the day, "Let's do a final resolution"—

CA: It would be preferable for anyone.

LHC: The moment is right.

CA: Well, look. Supposing that we don't do it, and supposing that we await more time, and in the interval there is more violence and people get killed, at the end of the day, after all the victims will come back to the negotiating table, and we will have exactly the same issues on the table, and we will have resolved nothing, only lost human lives. And it may even be worse, because some of the trust that we have been able to build between ourselves will have vanished. There is no vacuum in politics. Situations may only deteriorate.

LHC: Are you worried about some of the right-wing elements in Israel, if there is an agreement? There are the evil Amir types [Yigal Amir, Yitzhak Rabin's assassin], you know.

CA: Yes I am worried. There is violence. The attacks continue. Maybe there is less violence, but there is, and I've seen many people and heard many people saying things and accepting statements that we would have not accepted twenty years ago. But on the other hand, I think the Israeli security forces are much more alert.

If I may blow my own horn, about a week ago as I was leafing through the Internet, I found a site which was incredibly disgusting. With images of Hitler and Ehud Barak interchanged and Ehud Barak saying, "I will end the job, Hitler, that you have not finished." And you get to the next place—by the way, coming from America—we're seeing now, this is going to be a game. You can hit the prime minister, click your mouse and you can actually kill him. If you click fast enough, which many of us did, all of a sudden you see blood spilling over your screen.

So what I did was I complained that same day to the police

and I asked them to look into it. The Israeli police probably working very quickly and in close cooperation with the FBI, managed to get to the bottom of the matter and that site disappeared. But we have to be very vigilant and not allow such incitement.

There is, obviously, freedom of speech and you can criticize as long as you want. But the moment you start using expressions like "Hitler" and "Nazi" and "traitor" and so on, this becomes very dangerous. And I think that most of us are alert today, and I sincerely hope that we will not get into that kind of a situation again.

LHC: Well, we all hope that. Hopefully they can track these characters. Tell me, David Levy, your foreign minister, didn't go to Camp David. He said they thought it wouldn't work out. And he's, you know, a member of the Israeli One party. What's the story behind the story there?

CA: I really don't know. I'm sorry about it. I think that if he thought that it would not work, that's not enough reason not to go to Washington. On the contrary, I think he could have contributed. I think it would have been his business to be there, to be around and to help. He is an old hand in politics and he is a good negotiator. And I personally think that that decision was not the right decision.

LHC: Do you find that, many people say that Ehud Barak is a loner and that he doesn't spread his ideas amongst his ministers enough. Do you find that?

CA: Barak has his own style. He speaks a lot to a lot of people around him. But at the end of the day, like many political leaders, he makes up his mind alone. I think that most big leaders are lonely up there. It is, I think, our task to try to help them. I think that he is an extraordinary bright talented person with qualities that we haven't seen on the Israeli scene for a long time. And maybe sometimes wasted because of all the little petty political scandals. In many ways, by coming to Washington, notwithstanding the kind of difficulties that he has in the Knesset, I think he's shown that he's a statesman, and not only a politician. So I trust him very much. I think he's the right man in the right place, and I sincerely hope that Arafat understands that too.

LHC: You said something interesting. You said that Arafat should go to Brooks Brothers, maybe change his garments, and get out of the military.

CA: Yes, yes. I think it's time now to change the uniform and to become a civilian. And that is not only a change in garb, but a mental switch.

LHC: Colette, Bashar Assad became the President of Syria. Very fast. Elected very quickly and made a really tough speech the other day. Your feeling? Can you do something collaterally? In other words, can you do a very quick agreement with the Palestinians at the same time with Syria?

CA: No I don't think so. I think Bashar is a new leader. We're getting new leadership in the Arab world, young leaders. It's very interesting to watch. Hopefully a change of mind, hopefully a change of mentality, more openness to the West, more openness to the Internet, to CNN. Maybe they will allow cellular phones soon in Syria.

LHC: The Internet could be a big thing there.

CA: Well he has started allowing it. But I don't think he can afford to do it now. I don't think it will come quickly. I think he's got to consolidate his position and his leadership. After all, this is a minority government. Even though he's been elected massively, he must prove first that he can take care of their problems at home, domestic problems, the economy. Only then will he be able to come to terms with our negotiations. If and when he does, I have a feeling that he may go further than his father did. That he will not be trapped in the old concepts that his father could not free himself from.

LHC: Is it more fun being a diplomat or a politician?

CA: I have been able to tell you so many things and to speak out my mind in such manner that I would not have been able to do if I were a diplomat. So it's great fun. And sometimes I also hope that at the end of the day, we can do useful things.

LHC: Last question. If Barak comes back, would he have to run for a new election? Would there be a new election, or will he get the parties together?

CA: He may decide to do that. He may decide to do a referendum. He may decide to go to elections.

LHC: He's obligated to do a referendum, isn't he?

CA: A referendum, he's not obligated. He wants to. He might be obligated to in the case of the Golan Heights, but not in the case of the West Bank because this is not sovereign Israeli territory. But he wants to do it, and if the Knesset doesn't allow it the way we should do it, the normal way, meaning a normal majority, then maybe he will choose to go to elections. If he chooses to go to elections, whichever way, referendum or elections, I assure you, he's going to win.

LHC: First he has to bring it to the Knesset if he brings back an agreement, and then they have to agree on a referendum? Or they set the rules up for a referendum, is that it?

CA: Exactly. We do not have any laws. We need a law, and that law has to be enacted by the Knesset. There are various proposals of the right-wing that are totally undemocratic, I must say, because they require a majority of all the registered voters. A thing that doesn't exist in any other country, save for maybe one little country in Africa.

But we will table the government, that is, we will table its own resolution or its own law proposal which will mean a regular majority of the people who will vote. The people will receive the agreement, will be able to look at it, will be able to consider it, will be able to analyze it. Nothing will be secret, there will be no secret clauses. And after reading, considering, studying, the people will say "yes" or "no." And I hope it will be "yes."

LHC: All right. Maybe we'll see Yasser Arafat in a homberg and a Brooks Brothers suit after he reads this.

Colette Avital, former consul general in New York City, has been a Labor Party mem-

ber of Knesset for many years. She confirmed a general opinion that Prime Minister Barak was a loner, not conferring with his cabinet on most issues. Before Barak departed for the Clinton Camp David Summit, the Shas party left his government along with Natan Sharansky who resigned as Minister of Trade and Industry.

Avital remains a left-wing pro-peace advocate but she is adamant about no division of Jerusalem. She suggested that Arafat doff his military fatigues and opt for Brooks Brothers clothing.*

Eric Fettman, is currently a columnist for the New York Post. *He compares the presidencies of Carter and Clinton, how they conducted their summits. He also examines comparisons between Ariel Sharon and Benjamin Netanyahu.*

LHC: You heard Colette Avital, and you were at one time a citizen of Israel—

EF: I still am.

LHC: Still a citizen of Israel. You were the managing editor of the *Jerusalem Post*, which is high profile. Is everybody on the right track here, trying to put the Camp David thing together? Or Is It so implausible that maybe Clinton will be deemed to have had a failure and should never have done it?

EF: Well, I think she's right. I found myself agreeing with Colette Avital more than I have in the past.

LHC; It's not a usual occurrence for you.

EF: No, it's not. I think she's right in analyzing the situation. Where we disagree is in terms of whether an agreement should be reached, whether Barak has gone too far. But certainly, it's true, he's gone further than any prime minister has ever done, or probably would ever have thought of doing, including Yitzhak Rabin. And he's gone further than he indicated he would have, in terms of the red lines he set for himself beforehand. It's also true that if Arafat won't accept an offer like this, he's not going to accept anything. It tells you a lot about his willingness or his ability to be a real partner

---

* When the author met with Arafat in Tunis he had similar thoughts.

for peace. If he can't take this offer, then what's the point?

LHC: It's a deal-breaker, that's for sure.

EF: There's another thing that wasn't mentioned before. The two things he needs—of course, Jerusalem has, since your days of Camp David [i.e., Camp David I with Jimmy Carter], has always been the issue that everybody wanted to put off, because they knew that she's right—there is no real solution for this. There's nothing that's going to be found that's going to be mutually accept-able. Maybe to the leaders but certainly not on the street [in Jerusalem], whether it's in HarNof on the Israeli side or Abu Dis on the Arab side.

But the other thing that Barak needs that he apparently has not been hearing so far, is the need to get an explicit guaranteed commitment that this is the end of the conflict. This is the end of any and all Palestinian claims against Israel. These are the max-imum concessions that he's offering, and what if they come up with a whole new set of demands?

LHC: Well I think what you're saying is true, but it's like getting a gen-eral release in business. You know, that you need to be released from everything. I think one mistake has occurred here, and a big one. I think that President Clinton should not have left, and should have stayed with these guys.

I think that there is a certain momentum in negotiations that carries on. Maybe you take a break, maybe for a day, but it's going to slope, it's going to go down. Madeline Albright is no President Clinton. And I can tell you from my experience with President Carter, that he would have never left. He was so obsessed with his commitment to find the Middle East peace, and it was the cra-dle of civilization for him. I'm not critical of Clinton, I just think it's a mistake.

EF: Well I think Clinton should have taken a lesson from Camp David. How many days was that, thirteen? I mean, he knew the G-8 [summit of top seven Western industrialized nations plus Russia] was coming up, I mean he should have realized that this thing was not going to get solved overnight, and what he was going to run into—unless, however, he tried to use that as—

LHC: As leverage.

EF: Exactly. "I need something before I leave." But now he's blinked.

LHC: He couldn't solve the problem of Jerusalem in eight days, and it's Clinton's fault. It's the preparation of guys like [Dennis B.] Ross and [Aaron D.] Miller and these guys [i.e., U.S. mediators]. When President Carter did Camp David, we had a blueprint form: exactly where it would go and how it should go. He didn't know if he would get it, but he knew exactly where it was going to wind up. I saw this happen with Clinton in Syria. He went to Syria to visit Assad. It's the first time a president has visited Assad, or Syria, in twenty years, since Nixon. And he came away with nothing. And I saw Dennis Ross, and I said to him, in a sort of a question, "Why did they let the president come if he wasn't going to come back with something?" I mean, it's embarrassing to the presidency.

And the same thing here. You know, Clinton's a very busy guy. You make a very important point, his aides should have seen that there are only eight days here, and you can't stop and go. You know, he took a day off to go to the NAACP, he made a speech there, he left for eight days

There's a certain commitment that you miss when you have the absence of a leader. I guarantee you the drop is going to be phenomenal today and tomorrow. I don't believe much can be done without the President.

EF: Especially because the issues were so much more difficult. These were final status issues. You know, to go back to the analogy of Camp David [I], in certain respects it was a bit easier for Carter. Because you had one side, Sadat, who was really interested in one thing: getting back Sinai. And getting something on paper that would show that he hadn't abandoned the Palestinians. Begin, on the other hand, was the lawyer who was dotting every "i" and crossing every "t" and was interested in every single acre of land. But when you had one side that was very accessible and only one that was being difficult from an American point of view, it was a bit easier for Carter. Clinton didn't have that.

LHC: Not only that. Carter had the strength to say to Begin, "Look, you do this, or else I'm going to do something else." And the same to Sadat. He had leverage. Clinton doesn't have any leverage today.

EF: He was prepared to publicly blame Israel, which Israel was not—

LHC: When, yesterday?

EF: No, I'm talking about Carter.

LHC: He was prepared to force the issue to make sure that an agreement was had. Begin was packing up, we heard it all the time, Sadat was leaving, I mean, it's the same stuff. But Carter had leverage, and he had backbone. Clinton is more of a political personality than Carter. I don't think that Clinton wants to push anybody.

Maybe the only way to solve this thing is that you do push. If you say to Arafat, "Look, we're not going to fund you. We're not going to give you any recognition, you're going to be out there like a nomad in no-man's land. Take it or leave it. Barak is giving you a great deal. You've got a Palestinian state. So, you don't have a capital in—"

EF: But you said something very important before that illustrates the difference. Clinton is a political animal. Carter had a very strong sense about what he felt was a just agreement for both sides, and he knew what he was aiming at. Clinton wants an agreement that is going to ensure his legacy, possibly win him a Nobel Peace Prize, and help elect Al Gore and Hillary Clinton. That's what he's aiming at, his short-term political goals. He doesn't particularly care about the long-term ramifications which, whatever criticisms we have of Carter, and I have a lot, he at least was looking toward what the long-term implications were going to be.

LHC: And by the way, this does not detract from Clinton's energy and the amount of time and energy that he's spending on this. He's really trying to do it, he's trying to get this out. His reasons, at the end, may be totally different than Carter's. Carter may have been religious and messianic in a way, because he thought it was the cradle of civilization.

Clinton is a political person. You're not going to change him because he's in a negotiation about Jerusalem. That's his personality, that's where he's going. I'm sure, knowing Clinton, that he looks at the billiards on the table and says, "Well, Hillary's got this going on, and Gore's got this going on...." I'm sure.

Carter was pure on that. Maybe from his background as a Christian or whatever it was, but it was something that he really wanted to pull. He was great at it. He did a great job.

EF: His approach was a bit more simplistic. He really didn't want to know the history that—

LHC: Well he knew, but the pivotal point of Camp David, was when he went in and he talked to Begin. He had a deep talk with Begin about his grandchildren and Begin's grandchildren, and this was the moment when the whole Camp David changed. I mean, these guys were packing also. So, I hope I'm wrong. I hope that Clinton comes back and maybe he can wrap up something that works. But I don't know.

EF: I think what you and Colette were saying was right. They may come back. They will come back with some sort of a piece of paper, even if it's only an interim thing that pushes the issues off again. I think Arafat has been successful in using the statehood and the implied violence that Albright foolishly warned against. What they call the warning of violence, which has really been a threat of violence.

They want to avoid a unilateral declaration because that will have to provoke a response from Barak and that will involve confrontation. So Barak has indicated that he's even prepared to recognize a state without a declaration. But he wants some sort of a piece of paper that shows that he's not doing it out of fear.

LHC: What do you think Arak [Ariel] Sharon is thinking now?

EF: Arak Sharon is thinking that Barak is endangering the country. I know what he's thinking; he said it.

LHC: But you don't believe that Sharon would join a unity government tomorrow?

EF: He's resisted it. There are others in the Likud who have felt it's a good idea. He was in favor of a unity government early on, but he felt that a unity government, for its own sake, is wrong. There has to be an agreement about certain basic principles.

LHC: Obviously. They do.

EF: Well that's what they were never able to reach. He and Barak had discussions on it.

LHC: Let's play politics a little bit. Assuming Barak comes back and he gets a referendum, or he's able to get a referendum through the Knesset. I don't know if he can do it! Because the Knesset is wild right now. Colette says unless they pass it at the Knesset and they set up the rules, there's no referendum. So then you have to go to new elections. Who leads the Likud today?

EF: That's part of the Likud's problem. The Likud is weak.

LHC: You want to try?

EF: Sharon is the leader, and certainly, he's a recognized strong figure. But there are a lot of people who are looking to knife him in the back and who feel that they want to lead the party to glory.

LHC: [Silvan] Shalom?

EF: Shalom, there's Meir Sheetrit—

LHC: And Bibi [Netanyahu]!

EF: And Bibi! Bibi made his first foray back into politics a few weeks ago.

LHC: I saw Bibi about four weeks ago in his office, and he was non-committal about that. The first thing he wanted to do was to get his criminal investigation over with.

EF: Well they're holding that over his head. At this point, until Barak comes back, they're not going to officially—

LHC: Do you believe that was a political move in Israel?

EF: Everything in Israel is a political move, Leon.

LHC: I think Bibi would be a very strong contender against Barak, and maybe the best hope of the right wing.

EF: No, I don't think so.

LHC: Really?

EF: I think he disappointed a lot of people, myself included, in his term as prime minister. Who realized the guy is heavy on style but short on substance? He's doing fairly well in the polls right now, but I think that's reflecting, not so much strength for him as he seems to believe, but weakness in Barak. It's like Ted Kennedy, when he was running for president in the '80s—

LHC: Don't remind me.

EF: Well, he always used to score well in the polls before the election, but once the campaign actually started and it looked like he might be a candidate, and in 1980 when he was, zoom—back down. Because people started thinking about—

LHC: They found Jack Daniels in his suitcase all the time. He wasn't for real.

EF: The thing is, Bibi acquired a lot of negatives. And he was a weak prime minister and he was a disappointment.

LHC: He told me that he made a lot of mistakes.

EF: And people aren't going to let him forget it. The two problems with the Likud is that nobody has really seized control of the party, and Arak [Ariel Sharon] hasn't done that. To be honest, he's been distracted—

LHC: Isn't he acting chairman?

EF: Yes, he's the acting chairman, that's been confirmed. He's been distracted in the last few months, with the death of his wife.

LHC: Would you personally like to see him as the prime minister?

EF: Yes. I understand the concerns that some people have, but Arak's success has always been that he has been underestimated and that people consider him a danger when he really isn't. There have been a lot of misconceptions about him, and a lot of underestimation of him. The man has a strong sense of what's needed. He's not the type who's going to run off half-cocked. You can't do that anymore in Israel.

The problem with the Likud though, and Arak is included, is that they know what they're against, but they have not yet come out with a positive message as "What kind of an agreement, what kind of understanding are we prepared to meet with the PLO? We can't just be against what Barak or Rabin or Peres wanted, and no one has been able to articulate what kind—"

LHC: One Palestinian personality told me, he says we were kneeling in the same place with Bibi as we are with Barak. Bibi was ready to go with a lot of things.

EF: There were a lot of likenesses between Bibi and Arak when Arak was foreign minister as well.

LHC: Next week we'll analyze what has happened at Camp David. Hopefully they'll have something to report. Let's hope that they do something that keeps the peace in the Middle East.

Eric Fettman, an Israeli cltlzen and former editor of The Jerusalem Post, *is currently an editor on the* New York Post. *He has consistently favored the right-wing of Israeli politics and correctly assumed that Sharon would win the election and become a popular leader.*

At present, Sharon has a 75% approval rating. Benjamin Netanyahu had been a popular choice on the eve of the Likud primary but declined the run. Sharon became the candidate and went on to win. The general opinion regarding Netanyahu's future indicates that he will try again when Sharon retires in a few years.

In an editorial Fettman compared the spirit of Camp David I with the failure of Camp David II. Arafat had not been prepared properly and was unable to satisfy Clinton's hope or Barak's ego.

AFTERWORD

You've just read the reflections of prominent political figures, diplomats and journalists over an eleven year period.

As this book goes to press there is a faint hope that negotiations are resuming. The range of solutions is wide. Recently elected Prime Minister Ariel Sharon, the former hawklike general, seems to be moving carefully. Some believed, especially those who had known him over his fifty-two years in politics, that he would continue his hawkish ways. This has not been the case. Foreign Minister Shimon Peres is credited with influencing Sharon to a more moderate stance. Despite numerous terrorist attacks and great pressure from the right side of his unity government Sharon has instituted a policy of "restraint." The Israeli government policy is to retaliate against attacks, not to initiate. Moreover, the retaliation would be aimed exclusively at military targets, unlike the Palestinians who target civilians on a daily basis.

Yasser Arafat has been intractable as Chairman and chief spokesman. Most Israelis doubt that he has the courage and capacity to sign a peace treaty. Moreover, Arafat is not the sole force in Palestinian politics. There are many groups committed to the destruction of Israel. Very recently President Bashar Assad of Syria, in the presence of the Pope, spoke in virulently anti-semitic tones calling for Israel's elimination.

Egypt and Jordan, who have signed peace treaties with Israel, are slowly moving towards fulfilling the promise of meaningful reciprocal relationships. However, both countries are dogged by sections of their population which are fundamentally anti-Israel. As of this writing Egypt has recalled its Ambassador to Israel and Jordan has not replaced its outgoing ambassador.

Will there be an exchange of land for a treaty? Will there be a Palestinian state? Israel is a tiny country, perhaps too small to house two separate nations. And the city of Jerusalem? Left-wing leaders think a solution might be the creation of a legally ironclad open city. This is a minority view.

Leon H. Charney with former U.S. President Jimmy Carter at the publication of Mr. Charney's first book Special Counsel

The bulk of the Israeli population believes firmly in maintaining Jerusalem as the Jewish capital. The city's fate remains an emotional issue.

The alternative to an abiding treaty will be the continuation of assaults and killings. In addition the extreme wings of the Palestinians have brainwashed and produced a number of suicide bombers or "kamikaze" terrorists willing to sacrifice their lives to dramatize the conflict. It is certain that this Israeli goverment's first task is the implementing of a long-term truce, a compact to cease hostilities or at least a state of non-belligerence.

While the Israeli economy remains strong, the cost of maintaining the military remains a heavy burden. And tourism, a major factor in the country's financial welfare, has been damaged by these attacks.

Negotiations over the years have been a mixed bag. A treaty will, inevitably, be achieved but perhaps not in this generation.

The Peres' solution of making a European union type of fiscal arrangement will not transform regional hostilities. The world has many fundamentalist groups attacking liberal and centrist positions. Unfortunately the Middle East is a hive of religious fanaticism controlled by unstable clerics. Zealots abhor the true meaning of religion, which I consider the highest form of humane and human experience.

Until the fundamentalist approach is altered, true peace is doubtful. However, I have been involved in the "peace business" for more than twenty years. As these pages indicate there has been an increase in understanding in resolving some of the conflicts. I refer to the Camp David agreement, the Jordanian-Israeli peace, and steady if stumbling talks with the PLO.

I vividly recall visiting with Prime Minister Golda Meir with a U.S. Senate delegation. We informed her that we had the ability to facilitate a secret meeting with senior Egyptian officials. She totally rebuffed the idea, saying that Israel was powerful and had no need to talk with enemies. Approximately a year later Israel was involved in the Yom Kippur War which it won at great cost, collapsing Mrs. Meir's government and disgracing her defense minister, Moshe Dayan, who resigned. Five years later the Camp David Peace Agreement was signed by Egypt and Israel.

In 1995 I invited the Jordanian ambassador to an interview. He condemned Israel and said it was in Jordan's interest to see Israel destroyed. Seven weeks later I was filming Rabin executing a treaty with King Hussein of Jordan. And back in 1990 I was sent to meet with Arafat in Tunis. I was the emissary because it was then a crime for Israelis to meet with PLO members. My task was to understand the PLO's agenda.

Once again the world has changed. There are constant meetings and exchanges of ideas between Israelis and Palestinians. As observed by the examples shown, there has been incremental improvement in their relationship although with the rash of recent terrorist attacks and suicide bombings, it is highly doubtful, at the present time, that these meetings have much value.

The Middle East is the genesis of all religions and the cradle of civilization. It also has been a consistent source of conflict. Is there hope? Is the conflict eternal?

One must never forget that the Holy Land is a place of miracles. And it has been said that in order to live in the Middle East, one must believe that miracles are reality.

— Leon H. Charney
August, 2001

INDEX

Abdullah (king), 7, 210

Abraham (biblical), 132

Al Kidwa, Nasser,   212, 261-271,275,279

Albright, Madeline, 17, 189, 191, 269, 274, 286, 289

Allon, Yigal, 160

Amir, Yigal, 16, 281

Annan, Kofi, 245,246

Arafat, Yasser, 9, 12, 13, 17, 23, 25, 27, 30, 35, 75, 107, 111,
        112, 112, 113, 115, 119, 121, 123, 124, 125, 126, 130,
        131, 132, 133, 138, 143, 149, 156, 158, 159, 172, 177,
        181, 190, 199, 201, 212, 216, 227, 237, 249, 261, 271,
        275, 276, 279, 283, 284, 285, 288, 289, 292, 293, 295

Assad, al-Hafiz, 88, 116, 227, 239, 253, 254, 255, 257, 259,
        260, 287

Assad, Bashar, 254, 255, 260, 283, 293

Avital, Colette, 273-285, 289, 290

Avitan, Adi, 251

Avraham, Benny, 251

Baalyia, Yisrael, 240

Baker, James, 13, 26, 67, 83, 150, 153, 154

Barak, General, 123, 144, 146

Barak, Aharon, 166

Barak, Ehud, 17, 18, 50, 75, 156, 195-203, 196, 207, 217, 219,
        220-228, 231, 232, 235, 237, 239, 240, 242, 244, 246,
        248, 254, 257, 258, 259, 261, 262, 267, 270, 271,

Barak, Ehud (cont.) 273, 277, 278, 281, 282, 284, 285, 285, 286, 288, 289, 290, 291, 292

Barak, Nava, 226

Baram, Uzi, 69

Bashara, Azmi, 227, 231, 280

Begin, Benny, 20, 123-129, 163, 178, 198, 207, 231

Begin, Menachem, 11, 20, 39, 66, 78, 81, 88, 89, 92, 117, 148, 151, 160, 171, 174, 176, 201, 248, 287, 288, 289

Beislin, Yossi, 69

Ben Gurion, David, 4, 44, 100, 159, 166, 167, 206

Blumenthal, Naomi, 235-242, 236

Braudel, Ferdinand, 164

Brezhnev, Leonid, 162

Bronfman, Roman, 240

Burg, Avrum, 176

Burg, Joseph, 169-176

Bush, George, 14, 26, 72, 82, 150-151, 153, 154

Butler, Richard, 213

Carter, Jimmy, 11, 65, 73, 93, 151, 285, 286, 287, 288, 289

Carville, James, 226, 238

Castro, Fidel, 81

Chamberlain, Neville, 171

Christopher, Warren, 130

Churchill, Winston, 43

Cleopatra (queen), 165

Clinton, Bill, 17, 35, 116, 117, 199, 208, 222, 223, 237, 246, 251, 257-258, 261, 262, 264, 274, 285, 286, 287, 288, 289, 292

Clinton, Hillary, 223, 288, 289

David (king), 1, 96

Dayan, Moishe, 65, 66, 68, 93, 96, 295

Dayan, Yael, 65-75

Dergham, Raghida, 251-260

Deri, Arye, 219-220, 229, 230, 278

Eagelberger, Richard, 154
Eben, Abba, 169, 181, 190
Ehrlich, Paul, 43
Einstein, Albert, 45
Fettman, Eric, 285-292
Finkelstein, Arthur, 225-226, 238
Ghandi, Mr. *See* Ze'evi, Rehavan
Gold, Dore, 205-217, 206*p*
Gorbachev, Mikhail, 31, 60, 61, 63
Gore, Al, 288, 289
Graham, Katherine, 229
Greenberg, Stan, 226, 238
Gur, Mordechai, 51-64, 52*p*
Gur, Rita, 62
Hartman, David, 176
Hassan, Prince, 209
Hatami, Muhammed, 215
Hatch, Orin, 160
Herzl, Theodor, 230
Herzog, Chaim, 39
Hitler, Adolf, 281, 282
Hugo, Victor, 232
Hussein, Saddam, 13, 14, 51, 55, 56-57, 58, 117, 151, 217
Hussein (king), 13, 26, 129, 130, 131, 132, 134, 135, 196, 295
Husseini, Faisal, 223, 227
Ishai, Eli, 278
Ivan the Terrible, 162
Jabotinsky, Vladimir, 3, 178, 241
Jacobson, Harry, 43
John Paul II (pope), 260, 293
Kahalani, Avigdor, 21, 137-146, 207, 225
Kahane, Meir, 20, 175
Kamal, Hussein, 209
Kaseck, John, 160

Katzan, Moishe, 167
Katzer, Ephraim, 37-50, 38
Katzir, Aaron, 42
Kennedy, Ted, 291
Kissinger, Henry, 24, 54, 149
Kollek, Teddy, 91-100
Kosygin, Aleksei, 161
Kreiskey, Bruno, 161
Lahad, Antoine, 244
Lancry, Yehuda, 243-251
Landau, Uzi, 163, 198
Lapid, Yosef "Tommy", 229-233, 230
Levy, David, 224, 282
Lieberman, Avigdor, 20, 223-224, 240
Majali, Abdul Salam, 130
Meir, Golda, 38, 295
Meridor, Dan, 21, 224
Meyers, DeeDee, 258
Miller, Aaron, 287
Mitterand, Francois, 249
Mordechai, Yitzhak, 21, 207, 224, 225, 228
Moscowitz, 179
Moyne, Lord, 5
Moynihan, Daniel P., 93
Mubarak, Hosni, 67, 90, 116, 200, 201, 276
Nasser, Gamal Abdel, 8
Navon, Yitzhak, 39
Netanyahu, Benjamin "Bibi", 16-17, 18, 50, 75, 123, 124, 129,
        145, 146, 156, 157, 160, 163, 176, 177, 181, 191, 195,
        196-198, 199, 200, 201, 202, 203, 206, 207, 214, 217,
        219, 220, 221-229, 231, 232, 235, 236, 237, 238, 239,
        240, 242, 249, 250, 276, 285, 290-291, 292
Nixon, Richard, 287
Olmert, Ehud, 235

Orr, Ori, 111-121

Paz, General, 6

Peres, Shimon, 12, 16, 29, 35, 52, 69, 75, 108, 127, 130, 132,
     136, 141, 150, 155-167, 176, 177, 195, 196, 223, 259,
     292, 293, 294

Primakov, Yevgeny, 217

Rabin, Leah, 35

Rabin, Yitzhak, 14, 16, 23-35, 24p, 39, 50, 69, 74, 75, 105,
     109, 111, 114, 115, 124, 125, 126, 128, 129, 131, 132,
     133, 134, 138, 139, 140, 141, 142, 143, 144, 145, 146,
     149, 150, 157, 158, 159, 172, 175, 177, 181, 192, 198,
     213, 220, 223, 238, 281, 285, 292, 295

Ramon, Chaim, 69, 115

Ravitz, Rabbi Avraham, 185-193, 186p

Reagan, Ronald, 25, 26, 63, 152

Rivlin, Reuven "Ruby", 176-183, 177, 198, 239

Ross, Dennis, 181, 287

Sadat, Anwar, 11, 96, 81, 88, 89, 116, 135, 161, 258, 275, 287,
     288

Savir, Uri, 225

Schifrin, Dov, 129-136

Schultz, George, 25, 26, 30, 152

Shalom, Silvan, 290

Shamir, Yitzhak, 12, 13, 58, 59, 66, 67, 73, 94, 114, 126, 129,
     147-154, 148p, 158, 162, 163, 171, 192, 200

Sharansky, Avital, 161

Sharansky, Natan, 20, 223-224, 240, 242, 262, 277, 285

Sharett, Moshe, 206

Sharon, Ariel "Arak", 12, 18, 167, 171, 183, 206, 220p, 228,
     235, 242, 247, 285, 289, 290, 291, 292, 293

Sheetrit, Meir, 227, 235, 290

Shrum, Bob, 226, 238

Stalin, Joseph, 162

Suwid, Omar, 251

Thatcher, Margaret, 63
Truman, Harry, 43
Tsinker, Alexander, 240
Walesa, Lech, 60
Weizman, Chaim, 41-43, 77, 79, 175
Weizman, Ezer, 47, 65, 66, 74, 77-90, 78, 93, 158, 161, 275
Weymouth, Lally, 219-229
Wiezel, Eli, 64
Yacobi, Gad, 101-109, 102
Yeltsin, Boris, 60, 162
Yosef, Rabbi Ovadiah, 220
Ze'evi, Rehavan "Ghandi", 57, 59